Colossians, Ephesians,
First and Second Timothy,
and Titus

Westminster Bible Companion

Series Editors

Patrick D. Miller
David L. Bartlett

Colossians, Ephesians, First and Second Timothy, and Titus

LEWIS R. DONELSON

Westminster John Knox Press
Louisville, Kentucky

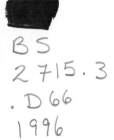

© 1996 Lewis R. Donelson

Book design by Publishers' WorkGroup
Cover design by Drew Stevens

First edition

Published by Westminster John Knox Press
Louisville, Kentucky

This book is printed on acid-free paper that meets the American National Standards Institute Z39.48 standard. ∞

PRINTED IN THE UNITED STATES OF AMERICA

96 97 98 99 00 01 02 04 05 — 10 9 8 7 6 5 4 3 2 1

Library of Congress Cataloging-in-Publication Data

Donelson, Lewis R., 1949–
    Colossians, Ephesians, First and Second Timothy, and Titus / Lewis R. Donelson. — 1st ed.
        p.   cm. — (Westminster Bible Companion)
    ISBN 0-664-25264-8 (alk. paper)
    1. Bible. N.T. Colossians—Commentaries.   2. Bible. N.T. Ephesians—Commentaries.   3. Bible. N.T. Pastoral Epistles—Commentaries.   I. Title. II. Series.
BS2715.3.D66   1996
227'.07—dc20

95-46676

Contents

Series Foreword

This series of study guides to the Bible is offered to the church and more specifically to the laity. In daily devotions, in church school classes, and in listening to the preached word, individual Christians turn to the Bible for a sustaining word, a challenging word, and a sense of direction. The word that scripture brings may be highly personal as one deals with the demands and surprises, the joys and sorrows, of daily life. It also may have broader dimensions as people wrestle with moral and theological issues that involve us all. In every congregation and denomination, controversies arise that send ministry and laity alike back to the Word of God to find direction for dealing with difficult matters that confront us.

A significant number of lay women and men in the church also find themselves called to the service of teaching. Most of the time they will be teaching the Bible. In many churches, the primary sustained attention to the Bible and the discovery of its riches for our lives have come from the ongoing teaching of the Bible by persons who have not engaged in formal theological education. They have been willing, and often eager, to study the Bible in order to help others drink from its living water.

This volume is part of a series of books, the Westminster Bible Companion, intended to help the laity of the church read the Bible more clearly and intelligently. Whether such reading is for personal direction or for the teaching of others, the reader cannot avoid the difficulties of trying to understand these words from long ago. The scriptures are clear and clearly available to everyone as they call us to faith in the God who is revealed in Jesus Christ and as they offer to every human being the word of salvation. No companion volumes are necessary in order to hear such words truly. Yet every reader of scripture who pauses to ponder and think further about any text has questions that are not immediately answerable simply by reading the text of scripture. Such questions may be about historical and geographical details or about words that are obscure or so loaded with meaning that one cannot tell at a glance what is at stake. They may be about the fundamental meaning of a passage or about what connection a particular text might have to our contemporary world. Or a teacher preparing for a church school class may simply want to know: What should I say about this biblical passage when I have to teach it next Sunday? It is our hope that these volumes, written by teachers and pastors with long experience studying and teaching the Bible in the church, will help members of the church who want and need to study the Bible with their questions.

The New Revised Standard Version of the Bible is the basis for the interpretive comments that each author provides. The NRSV text is presented at the beginning of the discussion so that the reader may have at hand in a single volume both the scripture passage and the exposition of its meaning. In some instances, where inclusion of the entire passage is not necessary for understanding either the text or the interpreter's discussion, the presentation of the NRSV text may be abbreviated. Usually, the whole of the biblical text is given.

We hope this series will serve the community of faith, opening the Word of God to all the people, so that they may be sustained and guided by it.

Introduction

All Christian theology must be both conservative and creative; it must be both old and new. It must be old because it must be faithful to the ancient truths of the gospel. It must be new because the gospel requires new formulations in new moments. To conserve this living gospel we must say new things.

The five letters discussed in this book—Colossians, Ephesians, 1 and 2 Timothy, Titus—illustrate how this conservative and creative task might be done. They reach back into the letters of Paul, and there they find insights into their own day. They attempt to see their churches through the eyes of Paul. And yet, when they formulate this Pauline gospel for their churches, they say many things Paul did not say.

Paul's influence on Christian thought has been powerful and formative. To some degree, it is impossible to engage in any Christian theology without addressing Paul. Overstating the case somewhat, we might say that all modern theology must be Pauline. We cannot recognize ourselves apart from our indebtedness to Paul. We are all his theological children.

These five letters, all of which have Paul's name as author, are viewed by many modern scholars, including me, as later works not written by Paul. Consequently, they are often called the "deutero-Pauline epistles." Even though it is the view of this book that these letters are not written by Paul, I acknowledge that this is a debatable conclusion. I will examine the case for Pauline authorship for each of these letters in the section titled "The Question of Authorship." It must be admitted at the outset that the evidence can be read in a variety of ways. Nevertheless, it is my opinion that there are in all of these letters shifts from classic Pauline theology that cannot be explained by the normal deviations of a person's thought. These letters are not by Paul.

Furthermore, these shifts are profound and important reorientations of Pauline thought. The fact that these letters deviate from Paul says

1

nothing about their profundity, importance, or status within the canon. In fact, these shifts represent what Christian theology throughout the centuries has typically done with Paul. We apply Pauline insights to our own day and combine those insights with other theological ideas. The results are unpredictable: The gospel will be both old and new.

In some ways, we are more the brothers and sisters of the writers of these deutero-Pauline letters than we are of Paul himself. Like them, we live in postapostolic times. Like them, we face an incomprehensible variety of theologies, truths, and communities that seek our allegiance. And like them, we want our churches and ourselves to believe and practice a Christianity that is apostolic in its shape.

It is my opinion that no task is more important to the church's life than the search for its apostolic roots. The early church was convinced that no church was really a church unless it had apostolic foundations. Jesus, they believed, had sent apostles to establish and order churches. A church derived connection to the risen Lord through allegiance to the Lord's apostles. Furthermore, the traditions of the apostles gave the postapostolic communities a standard for deciding what is true and what is not, what is Christian and what is not.

We too need this. We need standards in order to evaluate the competing ideas that come our way. And, more important, we need real connections to the risen Lord. These letters say to us that the road to all of this is found in rearticulating Paul. We must look back to those people and traditions that we know to be reliable, namely, to Paul and his gospel; and we must look at the needs of our day. In doing this, we must in our allegiance to Paul develop new formulations that Paul could not have foreseen.

As we will see, Colossians, Ephesians, and the Pastoral Epistles—1 and 2 Timothy and Titus—provide three different readings of Paul. I believe that all three have value for us. Of equal importance to the particular results in these letters is the fact that they show us how to proceed, for they succeeded magnificently in what we want to do.

This book should be understood as part of a conversation. As Christians we must be in constant conversation with biblical texts. That conversation involves hearing the voice of the text and speaking our own voices and concerns. A book of this kind wants first of all to assist the hearing of the text. We must raise up the voice of the text, letting it speak in its own terms of its own visions. That is the primary task of this study—to raise up the historical perspective of the biblical text. But I have also tried to point to some possibilities of how we in our day might participate in this conversation. Nevertheless, these remarks about our situation and what the text says to us can be no more than initial and incomplete pointers, for the meaning of these texts for each reader is too complex and too personal to be anticipated adequately here. Thus I must invite each reader to continue the conversation of which this study is but a beginning.

Colossians

Introduction

The letter to the Colossians is a delightful and inspiring reminder of the amazing hope of the gospel. It contains an inviting series of theological images that have inspired many readers to further theological work (of which Ephesians may be the first). It also contains gentle yet persistent imperatives to love another. And behind all of this, the letter has a pressing concern: It wants to strengthen the faith of wavering and wandering Christians at Colossae. Through the centuries the letter has reminded Christian readers of the certainty of our salvation, of the power of Christ over all other powers, and of the need to love one another. It is a delicate yet powerful letter.

The letter moves on a cosmic scale, giving a vision of God's eternal plan, of the role of Jesus in creation and redemption, and of the cosmic function of the church. It then insists that the truths of this cosmic theology must be lived out in the ongoing loves and hates, agreements and disagreements, of our daily lives. Thus the letter takes us from the heart of God, where we learn of God's eternal intentions for creation, to the mundaneness of human relationships. The whole journey is articulated with brilliance and gentleness. The gentle passion of the letter derives not only from the author's confidence in the truth and hope of the gospel but also from a concern over the weakening faith of Christians in Colossae. As we will see, the problems with faith that were of concern in Colossae still haunt us today.

The promises of the gospel do not always match up with what happens in life. On the one hand, we proclaim to each other in the gospel that God in Jesus Christ has conquered evil; but, on the other hand, we see evil still flourishing. This paradox raises these questions: Is faith in Jesus sufficient? Do we need outside help against the evils of the world? Apparently, in Colossae some Christians thought they did.

In the ancient world most people were polytheistic—believing in the existence and potency of many cosmic beings. Thus, when the Christian life became difficult, when it became apparent that faith in Jesus did not banish all evil from human life, these Christians remembered the cosmic powers that had once ruled their lives. They turned back to these gods and looked for ways to pacify them. They did not think they were denying Jesus in doing this, for Jesus was still the ultimate Lord for them. However, in order to deal adequately with the realities of life, they felt they must hold hands with many powers. Jesus alone was not enough. We Christians today may not believe in multiple gods, but we do share this doubt and we also rely on many other powers. The question still remains, What kind of power does Jesus really have?

The task confronting the author of Colossians is to call these wandering Christians back to the truth of the gospel. He wants to remind them of the amazing hope that the gospel contains. He wants to recall them from their fascination with other gods and other powers. He wants to calm their fears that these powers can still harm them. He wants to focus their ethical lives upon the simple ethics of the Christian life: love, submission, and forgiveness.

Even though the author has hard theological work to do, he brings a delicate touch to his task. Readers throughout the centuries have been struck by the poetic quality of this letter. It weaves its theological arguments into delicate exhortations that evoke and prod. There is little sense of hard argument, of proof, or of theological system. We find here gentle exhortation and an almost fragile theology.

We are uncertain who the author was. It is my conviction that Paul did not write Colossians (see "The Question of Authorship"). But saying that the letter is not by Paul is not the same thing as saying who the author was. Whoever he was, he was deeply rooted in Paul's letters, taking Pauline insights and Pauline terms and weaving them into a new theological vision.

A major task of Colossians is to detail this theological vision; thus we will not attempt that here. We note only the most striking shift from Paul, the shift that has led many readers to doubt Pauline authorship. Paul clearly expected Jesus to return soon. Not only did he expect this great day of the Lord; he built his theology on that expectation. Readers of Paul have long noted the great tension in Paul between the present time and the future time of the kingdom. That tension drives most of Paul's theology. In Colossians this tension is greatly relaxed. Colossians looks less to the future and more to the heavens above. The primary tension in Colossians is between above and below. Colossians has moved from Paul's temporal theology to a spatial one. This is not to say that all thoughts of the future have disappeared in Colossians; that would be nearly impossible for a Christian theology. But the focus has shifted, and this shift will produce intriguing deviations from Paul's own thought.

This means that the author is someone dedicated to Paul's thought, someone who has struggled with Paul and learned from him. But this person also has his own unique view. Thus he is probably writing after Paul's death and is calling upon Paul's thought and authority for his new situation. He is trying to be Pauline.

Precise information about the author or the Christians in Colossae is beyond our reach. Colossae was a small city in the Lycus valley, which is a tributary of the Maeander River. The Maeander and the Lycus river systems formed the major east to west thoroughfare in ancient Phrygia. Apparently Colossae was originally the leading city of the area. But during the centuries immediately preceding the Christian era, it had competition from Laodicea and Hierapolis. Colossians indicates that there were Christian communities in all three and that there were cordial working relationships among them (Col. 1:2; 2:1; 4:13–16; Rev. 1:11).

There is no indication that Paul ever visited the city or even the immediate area, although during his stay in Ephesus such a visit would have been easy enough. In any case, Colossians assumes that Paul has never been there and that the community does not know him personally (1:4, 9; 2:1). This means that Paul's apostleship is conceived differently in the letter. In Paul's own mind apostles are founders of churches; they lay the foundation. This gives them unique authority over the churches, for they are responsible for ensuring the orthodoxy of the churches' beliefs and practices. We see Paul attempting to exercise this unique authority in all his letters, excepting Romans. But in Colossians Paul as apostle becomes the guarantor of tradition (as it is explained in the letter) and the embodiment of the Christian life. Paul thus acquires in Colossians apostolic authority over any and all churches, even churches he has not founded. He is beginning to attain canonical status.

There are curious notes by two authors in antiquity who mention an earthquake in the Lycus valley in the first century. Tacitus reports that Laodicea was destroyed by an earthquake in A.D. 60–61, and Eusebius claims that Laodicea, Hierapolis, and Colossae were destroyed by an earthquake in A.D. 63–64. However, coins referring to an inhabited Colossae date from the second and third centuries A.D. Thus, whether Colossae was destroyed or whether it was uninhabited for a time is not known. No sufficient archaeological excavations have been done on the site. The city was abandoned in the eighth century.

It has been suggested that Colossae was picked as the destination for the letter specifically because it had recently been destroyed. This means it would have existed during Paul's life but did not at the time the letter was written. The letter thus becomes a general exhortation to communities who do not know Paul face-to-face. This coheres nicely with the instructions to read the letter in Laodicea (4:17).

The date and place of origin are not easy to determine. If the letter is by Paul, then it comes from a period of his imprisonment. Pauline imprisonments occur in Ephesus (ca. A.D. 53–55), Caesarea (ca. A.D. 56), and Rome (late 50s and perhaps early 60s). But if the letter cannot be anchored in the lifetime of Paul, it becomes much more difficult to locate. The author of Ephesians knows the letter, and the author of 1 Peter probably does as well. But neither of those letters can be dated with much certainty. Our first reasonably secure date is an apparent quote in the letter of Clement of Rome to the Corinthians (1 Clem. 49:2). This letter can be dated with some certainty around A.D. 96. In an attempt to be more precise, we can imagine that some time has passed since Paul's death and that some more time will pass before Ephesians begins to rework Colossians. This would suggest sometime between 70–75. It would most likely have come from a center of Pauline activity, suggesting Rome or Ephesus. But almost anywhere from Caesarea and Antioch in the east, to Rome in the west, including Asia Minor in between, is possible.

Whatever the facts of its origin, the theological purpose of the letter is clear—to address the question of power. Given that we confess Jesus as Lord, what does this say about the way the world actually works? What kind of power does Jesus have? What is the relationship between Jesus and all the other powers, both good and bad, in the world around us? When we order our lives, how do we calculate the real presence of Jesus? The question is a believer's question: How powerful and how effective is this Lord of ours?

The answer we give will be shown in how we choose to live. Do we gamble our lives on Christian love or not? Therein, in our decision to take on the weakness and suffering of Christian love, we demonstrate what we really think of Jesus' power. For Colossians, to believe and to love are intertwined.

Commentary

SALUTATION
Colossians 1:1–2

> 1:1 **Paul, an apostle of Christ Jesus by the will of God, and Timothy our brother,**
> 2 **To the saints and faithful brothers and sisters in Christ in Colossae: Grace to you and peace from God our Father.**

Paul and Christians in Colossae

The letter begins with a Pauline-style greeting. Paul's greetings are a modification of normal Greek and Roman forms. Most ancient letters began with the name or names of the senders, frequently with identification given. They then gave the name of the recipient and concluded with the greeting itself. In comparison with most personal letters, Paul typically expands all three parts with careful theological comments. Here, Paul's identification as "an apostle of Christ Jesus by the will of God" agrees precisely with 2 Corinthians and is nearly identical with 1 Corinthians. This greeting is much briefer than that found in both Galatians and Romans, where the larger theological concerns of the letters emerge within the respective greetings. On the other hand, Philippians and 1 and 2 Thessalonians all show shorter forms than Colossians.

It is difficult to know how much importance to give these brief theological notes in the salutation. Certainly, it would be the assumption of most readers that Paul is an apostle of Christ Jesus and that his apostleship was done through God's will. An apostle of Jesus Christ must be sent by Jesus to do Jesus' own ministry. In fact, the letter will detail Paul's role in God's plan of salvation in 1:24–2:5, which is to reveal the mystery about Jesus. Thus Paul is an apostle "of" Christ Jesus both in the sense that he is sent by him and he tells the truth about him. As we will discover, the revelation of the truth is necessary for God to effect salvation.

Timothy is designated as co-sender of the letter, as he is in 2 Corinthians, Philippians, 1 and 2 Thessalonians, and Philemon. According to Acts 16:1, Timothy's mother was Jewish and his father was Greek. Furthermore, Acts reports that Paul circumcised Timothy in order not to offend Jews. This account of Paul's behavior stands in curious contrast to what Paul himself declares in Galatians 2:1–3 regarding Titus. Apparently, Paul took Titus, an uncircumcised Greek, to Jerusalem to confront the Judaizers. He notes with evident pride that Titus was not forced to be circumcised.

In any case, Timothy is regarded in the Pauline letters and in the Pastoral Epistles as a key member of the Pauline entourage. He is mentioned as performing important apostolic work for Paul in both Thessalonica (1 Thess. 3:2–6) and Corinth (1 Cor. 4:17; 16:10). And his frequent designation as co-sender of Pauline letters indicates his crucial role in Paul's work.

We should be reminded by this that the image of Paul as a loner, doing God's work by himself, is misleading. Although Paul does stand outside of normal apostolic channels in some respects, he works very much in community. Paul enlisted a number of co-workers who participated somehow in his apostolic authority and who did his apostolic work when Paul himself could not be present. In fact, Paul's sending of one his co-workers to one of his churches often seems as important, if not more important, than the sending of the letter. A person is able to answer direct questions and to make on-site spiritual judgments that a letter sent from afar cannot. Not only are we subject to the voice of the Bible; we are subject to one another. Faithful people should have authority over one another.

The designation of the recipients as "saints and faithful brothers and sisters in Christ in Colossae," although using typical Pauline theological terms, has a somewhat more general cast than most Pauline greetings, which typically begin like that in 1 Corinthians: 1:2: "To the church of God that is in Corinth, to those who are sanctified . . ." It is often suggested that the more general tone of the greeting in Colossians alludes to the fact that this letter is really a general epistle without a specific designation—a letter, not by Paul but by a later admirer, which is intended for inclusion in a Pauline corpus that already enjoys general readership. The designation "saints," although important to Paul, plays no noticeable role in the later argument of Colossians. However, the idea of faithful brothers and sisters does. The letter repeatedly calls the readers to renewed faithfulness to the truth of the gospel—a faithfulness that Paul and Epaphras will model.

The NRSV decision to attempt to render the inclusive intentions of the Greek with more inclusive sounding translations surfaces here. As the note in the NRSV text indicates, the Greek says "brothers." However, the NRSV translators decided that the Greek did not intend any gender exclusiveness. As the letter proceeds, it is clear that both male and female readers are assumed. Thus, in modern English, with our gender sensitivities, the Greek "brothers" is best translated "brothers and sisters."

The Greeting Becomes a Blessing

As we noted above, the typical salutation in ancient letters ended with "Greetings." We can see this form in Acts 15:23 and James 1:1. Paul altered the Greek *chairein* (greetings) into the theological term *charis* (grace). Thus he transformed a greeting into a blessing. Colossians follows this model.

The salutation in Colossians of "grace to you and peace from God our Father" is typical of Paul except that the Father is usually coupled with "our Lord Jesus Christ." Given the pivotal role that Christology plays in the letter, there is clearly no attempt here to emphasize the Father over the Son.

We must wonder whether such blessings of grace and peace ought to initiate all conversations between Christians (or even between any two persons). This does not mean there is no controversy here. There are serious theological disagreements that the letter will address. But first and finally (see Col. 4:18), we must bless each other with God's grace.

We should note here and throughout the letter the subtle transformation in language that occurs from normal Greek letter forms. In order for Christians to speak the gospel to one another, we must transform the language and ideas of our culture into a new key, the Christian key. On the one hand, Christians possess no special language; nothing is lost in the power of the gospel when we move from Greek to English to Spanish. On the other hand, no language possesses perfect terminology for the gospel. In fact, the gospel defies perfect and final articulation. Speaking the gospel puts strain on any language.

Thus modern Christians must not flee new images or new ways of speaking for the gospel. The gospel itself demands such creativity. Of course, all such new formulations should emerge from old formulations. Colossians recasts the language of Paul and the language of Greek philosophy into a new formulation. Grace and peace are central Pauline themes. In particular, peace is a major theme of Colossians, although it will be emphasized even more in Ephesians.

THANKSGIVING FOR THE COLOSSIANS
Colossians 1:3–8

1:3   **In our prayers for you we always thank God, the Father of our Lord Jesus Christ, ⁴ for we have heard of your faith in Christ Jesus and of the love that you have for all the saints, ⁵ because of the hope laid up for you in heaven. You have heard of this hope before in the word of the truth, the gospel ⁶ that has come to you. Just as it is bearing fruit and growing in the whole world, so it has been bearing fruit among yourselves from the day you heard it and truly comprehended the grace of God. ⁷ This you learned from Epaphras, our beloved fellow servant. He is a faithful minister of Christ on your behalf, ⁸ and he has made known to us your love in the Spirit.**

Paul Prays for the Colossians

Paul's letters normally begin with a prayer, blessing, or literary remembrance of Paul's prayers. Colossians begins with this last, where Paul recalls how the Colossians are included in his prayers. Furthermore, the opening prayers typically lay out the theological themes of the letter. Such is the case here, where hope, truth, and love, the main theological motifs of the letter, are mentioned for the first time. As we noted in the "Introduction to Colossians," this letter pleads for the truth of the gospel, detailing its precise content, noting that this truth contains secure hope for those who believe and are faithful to it, and insisting that belief must show itself in love. This theological program is outlined here in the opening verses.

According to verses 7 and 8, Epaphras has brought a report to Paul of the faithfulness and love of the Colossians. Epaphras is designated in 4:12 as "one of you," suggesting that he is part of the church at Colossae. His role as intermediary has some precise limits, for he seems to bring messages from Colossae to Paul, but not from Paul to Colossae. Tychicus and Onesimus (4:7–9) seem to be the designated emissaries from Paul to the Colossians. The image given through all this is one of continuous communication between Paul and a church he did not establish. Paul's concern for this community extends beyond his normal duties as an apostle to nurture *his* communities and includes this non-Pauline church. He not only prays for this non-Pauline church, but attempts to establish the truth, the apostolicity, of the gospel in which they believe. Paul can, hereby, become an apostle for communities he did not establish. Thus Paul's role in this letter mirrors his role throughout Christian history.

Churches of all times have tried to confirm the truth of what they believe by comparing it to what Paul said to his own churches. This enterprise has always required a careful restatement of Paul's thought. Colossians, I believe, represents the first attempt to do this—to rearticulate Paul's thought in a new key while being faithful to the apostle.

It may be that the mention of specific persons who carry the Pauline message to Colossae represents an attempt to locate persons contemporary to the author who can embody the Pauline tradition to the next generation. If this is true, the Colossian community would enjoy the presence of real persons in their midst with the apostolic seal of approval. We will see this assertion stated forcefully in the Pastoral Epistles. However, the author of Colossians devotes minimal attention to any notion of personal descent from Paul and focuses instead upon theology. The way to anchor one's own gospel in Paul is by studying and restating Paul's own gospel. Consequently, classic Pauline themes and motifs are taken up, comprehended anew, and reconfigured into a distinct theological framework. What we find throughout the letter is not so much new terms (it all sounds like Paul) but a new attitude toward the cosmos and new applications of traditional terms.

Hope is the Heart of the Gospel

Immediately, one striking shift from Paul emerges. Paul often links faith, hope, and love (see, e.g., 1 Thess. 1:3; 1 Cor. 13:13) in order to give a brief summary of the Christian life. But in Colossians, this triad is organized in a way we have not seen in Paul. In Colossians, hope is described as the anchor for faith and love. Notice the precise way the author portrays the relationship among faith, hope, and love: "we have heard of your faith in Christ Jesus and of the love that you have for all the saints, because of the hope laid up for you in heaven" (1:4–5). Hope provides the ground for love and faith. For the author, this is so because the gospel itself is primarily a message of hope. He will emphasize throughout the letter the absolute surety of this hope and will call for corresponding trust and confidence in the future. God has established salvation for those who are faithful, and nothing but faithlessness can undo it.

Churches who stand in Martin Luther's shadow find this configuration inadequate. Faith must be the ground for love and hope. In some ways, Luther and the author of Colossians are doing the same thing; they are both trying to state what they understand Paul to have said. The fact that they light on different places in Paul's thought upon which to anchor their own theology does not undo the power of both readings. As I have noted above, Colossians is providing us with our first Pauline commentary.

The author has potent reasons for focusing upon hope. As we will discover later in the letter, it is exactly this question of hope, of the surety of our salvation, of the adequacy of the power of Christ to overcome *all* other powers, that is being attacked. The exact nature of this attack and the precise defense of the gospel given by the author should become clear in what follows. For now, the author is placing on the table the terms he will need to make his case, and he has already begun to configure the terms in the way he will want to use them.

Hope, however, manifests itself in love. The love that the Colossians show to one another evidences the truth of their gospel and the certainty of their salvation. The formulations in 1:6 are precise about this: "Just as it [the gospel] is bearing fruit and growing in the whole world, so it has been bearing fruit among yourselves from the day you heard it and truly comprehended the grace of God." Several things must be noted here. The gospel must be correct, and it must be comprehended properly. Colossians devotes much of its energy to detailing the precise content of this gospel. Paul's authority is crucial, for his apostolic credentials give him the capacity to validate and invalidate versions of the gospel. He will do both in this letter. He will refute the false gospel of the opponents and articulate the true gospel of Paul. Thus, first a correct and sanctioned version of the gospel must be proclaimed and believed.

Second, the gospel must bear fruit. Bearing fruit may mean producing converts. However, given the focus on ethics, here and elsewhere in the letter, it more likely has its more common meaning of producing the good Christian life, the life of love. Thus Epaphras' report of the Colossians' love for one another in 1:8 demonstrates both the authenticity of the gospel held by those in Colossae and the strength of their hope. If truth and hope are the theological anchors, love is the proof. The necessity for this life of love will be emphasized throughout the letter. Here in the opening prayer, the core theological argument of the letter receives its initial outline.

We Christians today in our church debates often separate truth and love. "I shall hold to the truth of the gospel, and I do not care who gets hurt." Or "I shall love you and accept you, no matter what you think or do." Such exclusive stands have no place here. There is no seam between truth and love. The truth leads to love, and there is no love apart from the truths of the gospel.

PRAYER FOR THE COLOSSIANS
Colossians 1:9–14

1:9 For this reason, since the day we heard it, we have not ceased praying for you and asking that you may be filled with the knowledge of God's will

in all spiritual wisdom and understanding, [10] so that you may lead lives worthy of the Lord, fully pleasing to him, as you bear fruit in every good work and as you grow in the knowledge of God. [11] May you be made strong with all the strength that comes from his glorious power, and may you be prepared to endure everything with patience, while joyfully [12] giving thanks to the Father, who has enabled you to share in the inheritance of the saints in the light. [13] He has rescued us from the power of darkness and transferred us into the kingdom of his beloved Son, [14] in whom we have redemption, the forgiveness of sins.

Joyfully Giving Thanks

The literary form of thanksgiving, which was indirectly employed in 1:3–8, is continued in these verses, again in indirect form. Paul recalls his former prayers: "We have not ceased praying . . ." Then he exhorts the Colossians to pray for the same things for which he has been praying, namely, for knowledge, good works, and the power of God. Note the combined form in verses 11–12. Paul prays for them to pray that they be "made strong . . . , while joyfully giving thanks." This indirect form of prayer fits nicely with the social function of an early Christian letter, which might be read in worship but would not be prayer itself.

The care with which the author has anchored his letter in prayer, specifically in thanksgiving, must be recognized. The spirit of thanksgiving to God for God's acts of salvation, which pervades the letter and which provides the initial and fundamental mood of the letter, connects to the theological theme of hope. The author will be contesting a theology that he believes reduces the surety of salvation. He will, in turn, emphasize the absolute dependability of the salvation that is our hope. Prayers of thanksgiving are the proper and normal prayers of persons secure in their salvation.

Knowledge and Good Works

The linkage among the gospel, knowledge, and works, established in 1:3–8, is continued in verses 9–14 with several new twists. Readers of this letter have often noted that the theology is not laid out in precise, formal patterns, but rather is built up by continuing comment and elaboration. Themes are introduced and then repeated, but with slight modification. This procedure results in a rather fragile and imprecise theological structure. We should be careful to avoid trying to oversystematize the poetic and delicate theological formulations in the letter.

In any case, into the mix of hope, knowledge, good works, and gospel are added notions of the Spirit, the power of God, the kingdom of the beloved Son, and redemption. The author begins with Paul's prayer that the Colossians be filled with "knowledge of God's will" (1:9). The letter itself will go far to supply that knowledge, for it will rehearse the proper content of the gospel as the author understands it.

Again, notice the immediate linkage in 1:9–10 between knowledge and works. The order of this linkage is significant, for it emphasizes that knowledge of the true version of the gospel leads to the capacity to lead lives worthy of the Lord (see 2:2). "May [you] be filled with the knowledge of God's will . . . *so that* you may lead lives worthy of the Lord." Obviously, knowledge alone is regarded as insufficient, for much of the letter will be devoted to exhortation to live that life and to further description of the content of that life. Thus one needs to know the truth about Jesus; one needs to feel secure in one's hope; and one needs to strive for the virtuous life.

The long history of Christianity is filled with the struggle to "lead lives worthy of the Lord." Despair over the attempt to please God is a major reason that the Protestant doctrine of grace is formulated as it is. The letter to the Colossians does not evidence the theological care we normally find in Paul over the distinction between faith and works. There is no evident hesitation to insist upon the necessity of good works for salvation. The author clearly would not want to say that anyone is saved through works. (We might acknowledge as well that Judaism does not claim this either.) However, the author of Colossians obviously assumes that works are a necessary part of salvation, for knowledge of the truth must produce the life pleasing to God.

In Paul's undisputed letters, the gospel itself is power—the power of God for salvation (Rom. 1:16). The real presence of God's power is what distinguishes gospel from human words. Thus we read in 1 Thessalonians 1:5 that Paul acknowledges the chosenness of the Thessalonians "because our message of the gospel came to you not in word only, but also in power and in the Holy Spirit and with full conviction." The spirit of God rides the words of the gospel, transforming human proclamation into the gospel of God. However, none of this is explicitly recited here. Rather, Paul prays directly for the Spirit. "May you be made strong with all the strength that comes from his glorious power" (1:11). A direct echo of the closing phrase in 1:8 occurs here (the NRSV follows the Greek word order in this case). The capacity to love is based upon the power of the Spirit. Without the Spirit there is no possibility of realizing a life pleasing to God.

We cannot discover exactly how the author envisions the connection between the gospel and the Spirit, for he does not directly enumerate the relationship. But we can be confident that good works owe their ultimate cause to God, even if we must be exhorted to accomplish them. Som . kind of divine act must occur. It is not simply the case that we are told the truth, that we muster up the nerve to believe it, and that then, realizing the possibilities of judgment and salvation, we attempt to please God with good works. Such a sparse and Spartan religious life cannot be harmonized with the author's pressing insistence upon hope and his intense confidence in our salvation. Such a life cannot be characterized as a life of hope. Instead, *God* must act to accomplish our salvation. Thus the author may insist upon good works, but he does so in the context of joyfully praising God, "who has enabled you to share in the inheritance of the saints in the light" (1:12). The final judgment, the heaven imagery, is crucial to the mood the author wants to create. God has established us for eternal salvation. We, who must now please God with our lives, feel no trepidation about judgment but only joy and gratitude for what God has done. Thus Colossians agrees with Paul on this much: Good works are fruits of the Spirit. The Christian life is a life lived out of the power and guidance of the Spirit.

This divine act can be understood only on a cosmic scale. The author begins to move us to that level with his concluding remark: "He [God] has rescued us from the power of darkness and transferred us into the kingdom of his beloved Son" (1:13). Cosmic powers are in conflict here. In fact, this conflict among the cosmic powers is one of the driving issues of the letter. We will move to the cosmic scale in the great christological hymn that follows. In that hymn, the very structure of the cosmos will be detailed. We will learn what is the real design and intent of creation. And of course, Christ will be the key.

Before concluding this section, we should note a curious but important pattern of argumentation that surfaces here for the first time. The larger structure of the letter itself evidences a careful shift from great cosmic christological arguments to down-to-earth entreaties to bear fruit in good works. The great cosmic battle shows itself in the capacity and practice of Christians loving each other. Thus here we are admonished, so to speak, to live as if we have been transferred to the kingdom of the beloved Son. We, of course, do not see into the heavens where this victory over the powers has occurred; rather, we know it has, because the spirit of God, God's own power, enables us to love. A great cosmic event has taken place—the redemption of the cosmos (1:14, 20). And it exists here as we love each other.

THE HYMN
Colossians 1:15–20

> 1:15 **He is the image of the invisible God, the firstborn of all creation;** [16] **for in him all things in heaven and on earth were created, things visible and invisible, whether thrones or dominions or rulers or powers—all things have been created through him and for him.** [17] **He himself is before all things, and in him all things hold together.** [18] **He is the head of the body, the church; he is the beginning, the firstborn from the dead, so that he might come to have first place in everything.** [19] **For in him all the fullness of God was pleased to dwell,** [20] **and through him God was pleased to reconcile to himself all things, whether on earth or in heaven, by making peace through the blood of his cross.**

These verses are both the most studied and the most influential verses in Colossians. Here we find the first Christian attempt to describe the cosmic Christ. This is the first literary evidence we possess that connects Christ and the entire creation in a systematic way. This brief hymn has inspired a long series of further meditations upon this theme, providing to such meditations both the basic configuration of the relationship and much of the vocabulary. Moreover, as so many readers have insisted throughout the generations, this is a magnificent and powerful little hymn.

A Christian Hymn

It is common these days to refer to these verses as a hymn. However, the term *hymn* must be understood in a rather loose way, for the exact liturgical function of these verses is not clear. We know little detail about the liturgical practices of the early Christian communities. We suspect, of course, that they varied considerably from one group to the next. We know that they sang hymns, but we possess no secure knowledge of what the hymns were like. In any case, these verses evidence quite careful formulation. There is a fairly consistent rhythmic pattern to the verses, which is more noticeable in the Greek than in English. Most readers of the Greek believe they detect hymnlike structures. However, even in the Greek, the verses are not laid out in precise parallels like a modern hymn. It is the case that ancient music did not follow consistent meters as music does in the modern era; thus this imprecision does not exclude all hymnic possibilities. Nevertheless, we cannot be certain that this hymn was ever sung. Other liturgical settings have been proposed; this might be a baptismal confession, for instance. In any case, the rhythmic patterns and the occasional parallelism indicate to most readers that these verses are a community product, worked out and rounded off through the persistent liturgical practices of the community.

Having said all of that, it is possible that the author of Colossians, using liturgical style, formulated the verses himself as the christological heart of the letter. Whether he did or not is in some ways irrelevant, for he concurs with the hymn. It represents his own thought, whether it originated with him or not. And here, in these verses, we come upon the key theological moment in the letter.

Is the World Good or Evil?

It is also the case, as historians persist in pointing out, that this hymn did not emerge in a vacuum. Even if this is the first-known Christian attempt to interrelate Christ and cosmos, it does so in a world that had meditated long and hard over the structure of the universe. And much of that meditation is echoed here. We can detect, for instance, the influence of both Stoic and Platonic thought in the Colossians hymn. But this hymn is especially reminiscent of earlier Jewish wisdom hymns. Many of these pre-Christian speculations share the concerns of Colossians: Does the cosmos have benevolent order or not? Is the divine core of the universe accessible to humans or not? Can we live in accordance with God's intentions or not? The most common answer to these questions in ancient texts is affirmation of the goodness and order of creation. And although Colossians has some stunning deviations from its non-Christian and Jewish predecessors in its answers, it agrees with the majority in affirming goodness and order in the universe.

The closest parallels to the formulations in Colossians are found in Stoicism and Jewish wisdom. Stoicism was the most influential of the Greek philosophies in the time of Colossians. Jewish wisdom grew out of Jewish interaction with this Stoicism and with other Greek philosophies. The Wisdom of Solomon and Sirach, which are both in the Roman Catholic Bible (Protestants place these books in the Apocrypha), are good examples of this Jewish wisdom. In any case, both Stoicism and Jewish wisdom affirmed goodness and order through the cosmic role of an intermediary. God creates through the divine word or wisdom, and it is word or wisdom that provides order, coherence, and purpose to the world. Furthermore, as proper parts of this creation, human beings possess within themselves this divine word or wisdom. By locating this divine order within themselves and by living according to its prodding, people can live the best life, the life God intended for them. In Jewish theology, the revealed law supplements, manifests, and articulates this cosmic order. Thus the cosmos is benevolently ordered, and humans have access to this goodness and order.

On the other hand, it is clear that not everyone in antiquity would admit to this vision of life. In fact, some early Christian theology, especially that which we now call Christian Gnosticism, states exactly the opposite. For the Gnostics, creation is evil, and the creator is either ignorant or malevolent. Many readers of Colossians detect Gnostic thinking in the author's opponents. However, that is not necessarily the case. As we will see, it is very difficult to determine in any detail what the author's opponents were thinking.

If the author of Colossians concurs with many of his predecessors in affirming order, he will diverge from them in two significant ways. First, in Colossians, word and wisdom—the divine principles of creation—take on the form of a person. Jesus Christ functions in the cosmos as word and wisdom, for he is the agent, the purpose, and the bond of creation. Furthermore, this person is the personal Lord of the Christian community. Thus the divine word of creation now converges upon a particular community. The tensions inherent in this claim emerge in several ways in what follows.

Second, this creation must be redeemed. There is no account of the fall in Colossians, although one might assume safely enough that the Genesis narratives are presupposed here. Moreover, Paul in Romans 8:22–23 assumed the fallenness of creation itself and its longing for redemption. Jewish theology in general shared this understanding of a need for redemption, or re-creation, of the cosmos. Unfortunately, we cannot ascertain exactly what the author of Colossians is thinking about the fallenness of creation, except that, as he notes in Colossians 1:13, there are powers of darkness from which one needs to be rescued. Furthermore, he seems to assume some kind of guilt, and thus liability to God's wrath, in his brief reference to atonement in 1:20 and sin in 1:14.

Therefore, although the author of Colossians concurs with many of his predecessors that creation has benevolent order, he diverges in significant ways. Perhaps the real uniqueness of the hymn lies in the particulars of the Jesus story. One's understanding of the universe is governed by one's understanding of Jesus Christ, whom one confesses as Lord. Thus it is Christology and its particular capacities that drive the formulations in the hymn.

In all of this we discover what are persistent questions today: Is creation ordered by a benevolent, merciful God or by indifferent, cold, cosmic laws? Or, perhaps, is it not ordered at all? Is there something here to be trusted? Is there a plan? Are there reasons for all this? Do we find ourselves living in an alien, unconcerned world in which we must create meaning out of nothing? Or, if we believe there is a God, how does this God relate to creation? Did God create this world as a good place, a home for us, or as a testing ground, destined for oblivion, a place from which to escape? Our questions about the created order are nearly innumerable, and our judgments about it determine the basic character of our lives. In Colossians, we have one fundamental Christian proposal for how creation is ordered and what this means for us. It is a potent proposal, but it is not the only Christian option and is not the only proposal made in the New Testament.

The Structure of the Hymn

The hymn itself, although evidencing careful formulation, is difficult to diagram. There are many proposals for how it is structured, but the most common, and, I believe, the most successful, is that it is composed of two parallel strophes, or stanzas. The first stanza deals with Christ and the creation of the world, the second with Christ and the redemption of the world. The first stanza would begin with verse 15: "He is the image of the invisible God." The second stanza would begin with either verse 18a, "He is the head of the body, the church," or verse 18b, "He is the beginning, the firstborn from the dead." In the Greek, the hymn begins with a relative pronoun, linking the entire piece to the beloved Son in 1:14. A second relative pronoun occurs at 1:18b, which the NRSV renders as "he is the beginning." This suggests to many readers that the hymn should be divided into two strophes at this precise point.

However, some readers wonder whether the "He is the head of the body, the church" does not belong thematically with what follows it, rather than what precedes it, for it deals with redemption not creation. The uncertainty over this point and the multiplicity of interesting proposals for how to divide the hymn suggest that we should be restrained in our attempts at dissection. In spite of repetitive, rhythmic structures, it may not contain a precise strophic pattern. We should be careful not to pound a delicate and elusive hymn into a shape it does not properly hold. The NRSV seems to prefer this more circumspect reading of the hymn. Note that it is not laid out in metrical form and that no attempt was made to impose a literary structure upon it. In the NRSV the hymn reads as a delightful, energetic, and fragile accumulation of and interaction among many theological images.

In this same vein, readers have noticed numerous theological tensions within the hymn. For instance, the presence of two different notions of redemption—one based on the resurrection and one based on the blood of Jesus—is seen as a theological problem by many. Others detect a tension between images of Christ as head of the cosmos and head of the church. This has led to numerous speculations over whether we have an older hymn that the author had taken over and modified. In this view, the theology of this earlier hymn, although useful to the author, is perceived as not being identical to the author's own theology. Thus the author's editing has produced both the theological inconsistencies and the irregularities in the parallelism.

All this speculation is unnecessary, even if it is interesting and not entirely implausible. In fact, it is arbitrary to insist that the author maintain only one clear theological system or that the "hymn" must be precisely parallel in structure. There are no compelling reasons to insist on either. Neither theology nor poetry is normally so precise. Inconsistency, ambiguity, and paradox befit them both. Thus we should conclude that, whether the author wrote the hymn or not, its theology represents the theology of the letter. It says what he wants it to say.

Christ and the Cosmos

The hymn tells us, using ancient philosophical language, the story of Jesus and the cosmos, beginning with creation and ending with redemption. Grammatically, the entire hymn is a definition of Jesus. In Greek the hymn is composed as two relative clauses with Jesus as the antecedent. This is the story of Jesus.

The creation part of the story begins with classic philosophical language: "He is the image of the invisible God." The term *image* is being used in a precise way. First, the ultimate transcendence of God is maintained; there is a distinction between God and creation, which the term *image* preserves. Second, the term *image* is not intended to denote a lifeless copy, like a photograph. Rather, in this context image denotes the power, the activity, the manifestation of the true being of God. The reference to the "fullness of God" in 1:19 assures us that the author is not intending the word *image* to denote a lack of connection between the real being of God and the real being of Jesus, the agent of creation. Third, image refers to manifestation in the sense that something of God is now knowable. What we can know about God is confined to the person of Jesus. He is full manifestation of the being of God. There is no other avenue of knowledge of the divine. All we can know of God must be known through Christology. This is a persistent theme of the letter.

The second phrase in the hymn, "the firstborn of all creation" (1:15), has proven to be an awkward one. Apparently, during the Arian controversy in the fourth century, this phrase was used as evidence that Christ was not preexistent, that there was a time, before time, when Christ was not. However, the following verses make such a reading highly improbable, for the hymn clearly wants to assert the primacy of Christ and the full dependence of all of creation upon him. Thus the phrase "firstborn of all creation" is trying to walk that difficult line all Christology must walk, namely, to assert the unity and distinction between Father and Son. Furthermore, the fine trinitarian language of Father and Son and the precision implied in such language are not present in Colossians. This letter precedes the great christological controversies of the third and fourth centuries. Note that the author feels free to refer to God and God's image, as though Jesus is not God. We should not expect the linguistic precision of later times to be present in the initial christological formulations of the church.

In any case, the firstborn of creation refers to Jesus' priority and superiority. He is then "before all things" (1:17), not simply the first of many. And he is superior in the sense of being both agent of creation (1:16) and the bond and Lord of the universe (1:17, 18). Thus we must understand verse 15 in the context of the entire hymn. Its purpose is not to address classic trinitarian problems but to establish the relationship of Christ to the cosmos. Of course, this cannot be done without being precise about how Christ and God connect.

The role of Christ in creation is carefully explained in verse 16: "In him all things in heaven and on earth were created." Note the care taken to insist that "all things" indeed means all things—"things visible and invisible, whether thrones or dominions or rulers or powers." It is unlikely that the author is giving here a precise list of known cosmic entities; rather, he is simply attempting to ensure that "all" includes all. Nothing can be conceived that is not part of the creation in Christ. The NRSV notes a translation uncertainty at the beginning of the verse: "in him" can also be rendered as "by him." "By him" points to Christ as the agent of creation, "in him" as the ongoing locus. The ambiguity in the Greek might well be intentional—Christ is both the agent and locus of creation. Certainly, as the hymn proceeds, both thoughts are included.

Not only have all things been created "through him" but they are also created "for him." The Jewish concern for last days, the final denouement of human history and the created world itself, surfaces here. The great end-time visions of the kingdom of God that frequent the teachings of Jesus and Paul's genuine letters do not seem to have had much influence on the theology of Colossians. This is one factor that separates Colossians from other Pauline letters. Nevertheless, the author takes care here to include all of time. Creation is intended "for Christ." He will always be its head. Past, present, and future belong to Christ. This idea will be elaborated in interesting ways in Ephesians.

The shift from Paul's end-time, future-driven understanding of the cosmos to this created, present-driven understanding of the cosmos constitutes one of the author's major contributions to Pauline thought. This shift has often been described as the transition from a temporal view of the world to a spatial. The author's theology is driven less by notions of how time is organized and more by how the powers of the universe are currently ordered. Who is above and who is below and what does this mean? This change in focus from temporal to spatial probably does not derive from any careful theological rethinking of Paul on the author's part. It is more likely that we have simply moved from Jewish end-time presuppositions to more typical Gentile ones. He thinks of the world as a typical Greek or Roman, in present order terms, not final-day scenarios. He is not driven primarily by notions of the end of the world. Christ is above, "seated at the right hand of God" (Col. 3:1).

We can now see part of what the first two verses accomplish. We see a creation story, told through the lens of Jesus. Before creation Jesus was the image, and he is the image now. He has primacy and ascendancy above all created things. Further, he is the agent and goal of created reality. To use ancient terms, he is the word and the eternal torah. The classic images of created order and primacy are located in the divine person Jesus. The beginning of Christianity's great argument with Greek philosophy is etched in these brief verses.

Colossians 1:17 takes us further into the creation story. Here another classic Stoic and Jewish wisdom idea is transformed by Christology. The questions of what holds the cosmos together, what provides for its security and longevity, and what gives it order were recurrent in Greek philosophy. And many answers were given. In Stoicism and Jewish wisdom the divine agent of creation was the very agent that provided ongoing coherence to the world. The author of Colossians will agree; of course, his agent of creation is the person Jesus Christ: "in him [Jesus] all things hold together." This means that Jesus was not only the creating agent at the beginning of time, but is so now as well. We are to imagine that if Jesus withdrew, if God's power was removed from Jesus, then the world would revert to chaos. Therefore, we can see that, in these delicate and pious verses, the author is proposing that Jesus is the entire and single key to cosmic and human existence. The striking exclusiveness of Christianity is emerging here. Jesus, and Jesus alone, possesses divine power. There is no religious or philosophical truth outside of Christ. In fact, the only knowledge we have of God comes through Jesus, who is God's very image.

In verse 18 the hymn modifies yet another classic Stoic idea. The image of the cosmos as a body and the divine word as the head are traditional images. Its inclusion here adds to the cosmic powers that Jesus accumulates in this hymn: agent of creation, goal of creation, bond that holds creation together, and now the highest currently operating power. Jesus as "head of the body" fills out nicely the theological agenda of the first part of the hymn—Jesus is above all other powers.

But then a puzzling thing happens. The hymn defines the body as the church. It is not the cosmos that relates to Jesus as a body to its head, but only the church. The cosmos may be subject to Jesus, may have emerged from Jesus, and may be destined for him, but the cosmos still needs redemption. It and Jesus are not yet one. It will be united with him, but it is not now. The church, on the other hand, is already redeemed. In this little clarification that the body of Jesus is the church, we should hear echoes of 1:13: "He has rescued us from the power of darkness and transferred us into the kingdom of his beloved Son." We are already united with our Lord. In fact, the redemption of the cosmos is prefigured in us. As explicitly stated in Ephesians, at some point church and cosmos will be the same thing, and Jesus will become head of the body, which has become the cosmos. Furthermore, this note sets the tone for the second half of the hymn, wherein the story of redemption is rehearsed; and it provides for the cosmic role of the church and for the purpose of Christian ministry. Paul himself will be the perfect example of all this in what follows (1:24–2:5).

At this point, the story of redemption begins. "He is the beginning, the firstborn from the dead" (1:18). The great redemption anticipated in Jewish literature on the last day has, according to Colossians (and most of the New Testament), already begun. The resurrection of Jesus is the beginning of the end. Fallen and rebellious creation, needing re-creation, is destined for redemption in Christ. But just as the first creation begins with

Jesus, so does the second as well. Thus, in both the old order and the new, Jesus is preeminent. As the hymn insists, he is the firstborn from the dead, "so that he might come to have first place in everything" (1:18).

All of this places the church and the readers carefully within the story of salvation. Redemption has begun, and the church is the locus for God's redeeming activity. Furthermore then, it must be through the church that God, in Jesus, will redeem creation itself.

"For in him all the fullness of God was pleased to dwell" (1:19). The notion of God's fullness will become famous in Christian Gnostic circles. But the peculiar problems involved in Gnostic speculations probably have not yet emerged. Instead, the author is addressing again the whole question of the sufficiency of Jesus. Does Christ possess in himself adequate power against all the forces in the world? Should we add other allegiances to our allegiance to Christ? How do we deal with all the cosmic powers that influence and even dominate our lives?

Note the peculiarity of the syntax wherein the fullness of God rather than God is the subject of the sentence. We are treading at this point once again on the problem of God's transcendence and God's presence. The circumlocution "the fullness of God" provides effective middle ground, allowing the author to assert God's real presence while maintaining God's transcendence.

Although, as we noted above, the term "fullness of God" will acquire technical and precise theological meaning in the debate with Gnosticism, no such theological precision is likely here. Rather, fullness must simply note the complete presence of God's power in the person of Jesus. No divine power is held back or allocated elsewhere. Jesus possesses it all.

The notion of God dwelling among Israel is a classic Old Testament image. God or God's presence dwells upon Sinai, upon Zion, in the temple. The rabbis were equally careful in all this to insist upon the ultimate transcendence of God. In Colossians this classic Jewish notion is modified by Christology. God no longer dwells in a place but in a person. In fact, *all* the fullness of God dwells in Jesus. Thus no temples, no mountains, no texts are sacred. Only the person Jesus partakes of the divine. If this is so, not only is there no room for Greek and Roman religions, but Judaism itself must be seen through the lens of Jesus, for only Jesus can manifest God. God is present to us only by way of Christ. This has been so from the beginning, is so now, and shall be so in the end. Pushing this image into modern discussions, we must note that the focus on the person of Christ contradicts any attempt to regard the Bible itself as sacred. No text is holy, only the person Jesus can be.

The conclusion of the hymn returns to the theme of redemption that was alluded to in 1:14. In 1:13–14 the author refers to the powers of darkness and our sin. In those verses we find brief reference to traditional reasons that redemption is necessary. We need to be saved from the powers of evil, and our sins have placed us under the wrath of God. However, none of the details of all this is explained in Colossians. We can only assume that normal Jewish, early Christian, and Pauline ideas about cosmic evil and personal sin were shared by our author. Furthermore, this assumption works well with both the hymn and the larger theology of the letter, for in the hymn we learn that all the cosmos is reconciled, and in the rest of the letter we learn that we have already been reconciled.

The language here is typical of early Christian statements: "Through him God was pleased to reconcile to himself all things . . . by making peace through the blood of his cross" (1:20). Although the author does not detail what notion of atonement he might have in mind or how the blood of the cross reconciles the cosmos and not simply human sin, it is probably acceptable to employ the Pauline discussions in Romans as the best guess for what the author had in mind. In Romans 3:21–26, Paul details the traditional notion of atonement, and, in Romans 8:18–25, he connects the fate of the whole cosmos to human redemption. These connections seem to be assumed in Colossians.

In all this, the hymn produces a marvelous vision of the cosmos. Christ is the agent of creation, the bond that holds the cosmos together; he is the present head of the church, which is already redeemed; he is the destiny of all creation, which will be in turn (in fact, in hymnic exaggeration already is) redeemed. Thus, although this is not explicitly stated, we are to imagine a final victory wherein Christ will be all in all.

The hymn becomes the theological anchor for the letter. It provides the cosmological vision that gives sense and power to the ethics and ecclesiology that follow. In some ways, the rest of the letter is an ethical and ecclesiological commentary on the cosmic hymn detailed here.

Challenges for Today

This hymn has had an enormous impact on Christian thinking. It raises for us a number of questions and challenges.

Perhaps it is the case that modern Christians find nothing particularly provocative in the idea of Christ as the agent and locus of creation, for this is an ancient and perpetual part of Christian theology. But in the first century this was a rather extraordinary thing to say—that the divine agent of creation was a person. Furthermore, the cosmic relativity that concerns the author of Colossians affects us as well. Even though we might confess theologically that the entire cosmos is subject to Christ, we rarely are able to live as though we believe it.

The radical commitment to Christian love that Colossians enjoins can be managed only when we understand that Christ is the ultimate power. Such a commitment to Christian love is just as difficult today as it apparently was in the first century. Colossians insists that Christology provides the only foundation for ethics. We must believe and understand that Christ is indeed the ultimate power before we can give ourselves fully to the Christian life. We typically protect ourselves, hedge our bets. Instead, the author of Colossians dares us to believe that there is no real power in the universe next to Christ, and then enjoins us to live accordingly.

Christians have no one view of the cosmos. Discoveries by modern science into the various possibilities and probabilities for the origin and fate of the universe touch nothing at the heart of the gospel. Worldviews have and will always shift as our best science shifts. It is the task of all Christians to find the gospel in whatever worldview they hold. This is no easy task. Colossians provides us with a magnificent example of how such theological work can be done. The author wants to be Pauline; he perhaps is Pauline; but he does not share Paul's visions of the kingdom. Thus he has theological work to do. His attempts model for us how we might proceed today.

The intellectual and religious wanderings of modern Christians are anticipated in this ancient letter. The author sees his own contemporary audience as becoming lost in the cosmic options. They are giving allegiance to powers that are not real powers. To them he intones the name Jesus and fills the name with all perfect cosmic credentials. The fullness of God dwells in this Jesus who is their Lord (1:19).

In doing this, he calls his readers back to undivided allegiance to Christ. He does not leave them wondering what such allegiance might mean, for he will describe the precise shape of that allegiance in regard to both knowledge and behavior.

For Christians of all times, our classic idolatries come unraveled in this challenge. Our attempts to make our way in the world with a thousand bargains with the powers around us receive in Colossians a potent critique. More to the point, our common despair that there is no power is addressed with the firm affirmation that God has placed full power to redeem us all into the hands of the one who died for us. This is the gospel, which we have heard and which we must continually hear and believe and understand.

Finally, there is more than a general call back to Christian allegiances;

there is a specific proposal for how the cosmos should be conceived. It is created good, through Jesus; it receives its present order through Jesus; it needs redemption; it shall be redeemed, just as the church has been redeemed; and the church has a crucial role in its future. All these concepts, when combined, produce a peculiar attitude toward life. Even though the world has fallen and even though Christians have been separated from the darkness of the world, the world cannot be abandoned. There is a strong denial here of end-of-the-world despair about the world and notions of escape to heaven. The world is from and for Jesus. The gospel story is a story about the redemption of this world of which humans are but one part. And we, the already redeemed, are proof of the world's redemption. We cannot, of course, expect modern environmental sensitivities in a first-century text, but the basic orientation in this hymn coheres with the modern Christian environmental movement. The world is precious; it is being redeemed; God shall never abandon it; and we, ultimately, cannot be disconnected from it.

APPLICATION OF THE HYMN
Colossians 1:21–23

> 1:21 **And you who were once estranged and hostile in mind, doing evil deeds,** [22] **he has now reconciled in his fleshly body through death, so as to present you holy and blameless and irreproachable before him—** [23] **provided that you continue securely established and steadfast in the faith, without shifting from the hope promised by the gospel that you heard, which has been proclaimed to every creature under heaven. I, Paul, became a servant of this gospel.**

The great cosmic christological hymn of 1:15–20 is immediately grounded in the life of the individual Christians and in the ministry of the church. This kind of rhythm is fundamental to Colossians; what occurs at the cosmic level must find actuality in the mundane of human life. Our acknowledgment of the truth of the hymn is less a case of saying something than doing something. We must live out this truth.

The power of Jesus, articulated in the hymn as the agent of creation and redemption of the cosmos, is known through our own personal redemption. The proof of the gospel is this—we are indeed now reconciled to God.

A Call to Steadfastness

Again in 1:21 we see an unexplained reference to human estrangement from God: "And you who were once estranged and hostile in mind, doing evil deeds . . ." We should note that in this compressed language the two classic notions of human estrangement from God are included. First, as Paul himself notes, it is not merely our individual transgressions that alienate us from God but the entire orientation of our being. Humans possess deep hostility against a God who wants us to be righteous when we want to be sinful. Second, this hostility lives in evil deeds. Rather than live the righteousness that God envisions, and even demands from us, we express our alienation from God with our evil lives. Both of these must be overcome in any act of redemption.

You who were estranged "he has now reconciled in his fleshly body through death" (1:22). There is an obvious echo here of 1:20. But once again it is not clear what notion of atonement is in force. Perhaps we must simply assume that the details of how atonement works were not a concern of the author. In any case, he regards the need for reconciliation and the actuality of it in Christ as fundamental to the gospel. The references to death and "his fleshly body" (or the body of his flesh) suggest that traditional ideas of substitution are the most likely. Thus he is probably recalling Romans 3:21–26. Jesus paid for our sins. On the other hand, in 1:13 the author states that God rescued us from the powers of darkness, which may recall ideas of Jesus' great victory over the powers of evil on the cross. In one, we are dealing with sacrificial ideas such as in the Jewish temple; in the other, with images of great end-time battles. Both of those contexts were crucial to early Christian theology; thus it would be no surprise to see them here. The author's confidence that such brief allusions are sufficient shows the great range and popularity of these ideas in early Christianity. He feels no need to explain them.

As already noted, Colossians typically links theological statements to an ethical result. Thus God's act in Christ must manifest itself in our behavior "so as to present you holy and blameless and irreproachable before him" (1:22). The language here becomes traditional to Christianity; it indicates the ongoing danger of God's wrath, the necessity for our good behavior, and God's intent to make us blameless. The Christian pattern of believing both that God is working in us to produce righteousness and that we are responsible for our own deeds surfaces here. This paradox is fundamental to the gospel; both God and humans, working together, produce salvation. Thus the great acts of God enumerated in the hymn must be coupled with exhortations to believers to live accordingly.

Thus the warnings in 1:23 are appropriate. The language in 1:23 echoes that of 1:4–6. In both we hear the complex of terms *faith*, *hope*, and *gospel* combined with an exhortation to steadfastness. The gospel provides us with the cosmological story that gives us reason to hope. This story of hope must be received with faith and faithfulness. The letter of Colossians itself is perhaps the author's prime example of how we should respond; we must proclaim the true gospel and exhort each other to the righteous life, as his letter does. Furthermore, within the letter itself Paul and his ministry will illustrate for us the proper Christian behavior. Thus the concluding remark in 1:23, "I, Paul, became a servant of this gospel," sets the stage for the Pauline example in 1:24 –2:5 and further connects the christological hymn to a particular form of Christian behavior.

PAUL AS A MODEL
Colossians 1:24–2:5

1:24 **I am now rejoicing in my sufferings for your sake, and in my flesh I am completing what is lacking in Christ's afflictions for the sake of his body, that is, the church. [25] I became its servant according to God's commission that was given to me for you, to make the word of God fully known, [26] the mystery that has been hidden throughout the ages and generations but has now been revealed to his saints. [27] To them God chose to make known how great among the Gentiles are the riches of the glory of this mystery, which is Christ in you, the hope of glory. [28] It is he whom we proclaim, warning everyone and teaching everyone in all wisdom, so that we may present everyone mature in Christ. [29] For this I toil and struggle with all the energy that he powerfully inspires within me.**

2:1 **For I want you to know how much I am struggling for you, and for those in Laodicea, and for all who have not seen me face to face. [2] I want their hearts to be encouraged and united in love, so that they may have all the riches of assured understanding and have the knowledge of God's mystery, that is, Christ himself, [3] in whom are hidden all the treasures of wisdom and knowledge. [4] I am saying this so that no one may deceive you with plausible arguments. [5] For though I am absent in body, yet I am with you in spirit, and I rejoice to see your morale and the firmness of your faith in Christ.**

Paul is presented here as the model for Christian behavior. The assumption is that the commitments and responses of Paul should be ours as well. Paul is the faithful apostle, whose name gives weight to the theology of the letter and whose behavior is our guide.

Suffering and Mission

Because the author is a student of Paul, it is no surprise that he begins his account of Paul's ministry by pointing to Paul's suffering. Paul himself constantly points to it as a sign of his unity with Christ. However, the exact formulations in Colossians are something new. "I am now rejoicing in my sufferings for your sake, and in my flesh I am completing what is lacking in Christ's afflictions for the sake of his body, that is, the church" (1:24). To speak of Paul's suffering for the body and of completing what is lacking in Christ's afflictions is not the way Paul himself normally talks. These are curious phrases that have caused much puzzlement to readers. What in the world could this mean?

As is always the case, there are many proposals for how to understand this verse, and we cannot rehearse them all here. However, a few things should be pointed out. It is probably significant that the author refers to Christ's afflictions and not to his sufferings. The sufferings of Christ had technical meaning in Paul's letters and designated the atoning sufferings of the passions. It would be quite difficult to comprehend how one could have any doctrine of atonement and still maintain that something was lacking in that atonement. Thus the author is probably not imagining that Paul's suffering completes the passion and atoning work of Christ.

We must imagine something else. Paul's own letters give a certain mystical quality to suffering. Christ suffered; thus, if Christ is in us, we will suffer too. Our suffering becomes a sign of our unity with Christ and thus a cause for our rejoicing. We rejoice because we know that suffering, when endured in Christ, leads to the glory that Christ himself enjoys. As a reader of Paul, the author may well be echoing Paul's rather complex ideas.

However, it is much more likely that we are dealing here with the sufferings attendant to the mission of the church. The cosmic hymn in 1:15–20 established the entire cosmos as the recipient of Christ's redemptive work. And of course, it is incumbent upon the church to accomplish key moments in this process of redemption. Paul is modeling here how the church's mission must be done. He is the prototype of the Christian believer, for he is taking on the tasks of the Christian mission in spite of its costs. The notion of suffering as an inescapable companion to mission probably arises from early Christianity's end-time worldview. The great cosmic victory of the powers of God over the powers of evil includes suffering for those involved. If the world is to be redeemed, and it shall indeed be, then it will be a painful process. This suffering required in the mission for the ongoing redemption of the world is "what is lacking in Christ's afflictions." This fits perfectly with the context of this verse in Colossians. Paul's suffering is for the sake of the church; it is Paul's mission work and the purposes and trials of that mission that are the focus of the following verses.

Thus the implications of Paul's behavior for us are not what they at first seem. He does not finish off the suffering of Christ, leaving us to suffering-free lives. It is rather the opposite: Paul models the suffering required of all people dedicated to the gospel. We must all be about the task of "completing what is lacking in Christ's afflictions for the sake of his body, that is, the church."

This gospel-suffering, according to Colossians, is cause for rejoicing. Joy in the midst of suffering is, of course, a classic Pauline theme. Suffering that derives from obedience to the gospel makes us rejoice, for it is a sign both of our connectedness to Jesus and of the gospel's victory over the powers of evil.

Paul's function as model is crucial here. Note how the themes laid out in the previous verses are echoed in this description of Paul: (1) we must have knowledge; (2) the content of this knowledge is Christ himself; (3) this knowledge of Christ gives us hope; and (4) this knowledge is inevitably and necessarily accompanied by the life of love.

Proclaiming the Mystery

Of course, certain nuances to these persistent themes are added. The gospel is here termed the *mystery*. Mystery is a religious technical term in antiquity that refers to a secret divine story that has saving impact upon those who learn it. In one sense, the content of this mystery is contained in the hymn in 1:15–20. In another sense, the entire letter details this mystery. Thus the mystery is not hidden anymore; it "has now been revealed to his saints" (1:26). This mystery, this gospel, is capable of being learned and taught. It submits to language. However, it is also true that the content of the mystery is Christ himself, the living Lord, who transcends all human accounts of him. This Lord brings not only knowledge, but real transformation. Those who learn this Christ are saved from the powers of darkness and are enabled to love.

Our modern sense that knowledge is objective content is inadequate here. Knowledge that comes from the gospel, knowledge of this mystery, is a divine event. These are not human words but divine. We might recall Paul's definition of the gospel in Romans 1:16; it is the power of God for salvation. Paul makes a distinction between regular human words and the gospel, which comes with power (1 Thess. 1:5). Thus this knowledge is not knowledge of things; it is the touching of divine mystery and power. Thus this knowledge must be accompanied by the key theological event; Christ must be in us. The living Lord of the cosmos is the one who gives us understanding.

In 2:2–3, the author returns to the theme of the sufficiency of Christ. He uses "all" language similar to what he used in the hymn. In fact, the entire formulation here echoes the hymn: "so that they may have all the riches of assured understanding and have the knowledge of God's mystery, that is, Christ himself, in whom are hidden all the treasures of wisdom and knowledge." This provides a nice summary of the theology and purpose of the letter. Paul's apostolic behavior, even the writing of this letter, forwards the spreading of this knowledge.

As always in Colossians, knowledge is connected with proper behavior. In 1:28, "Paul" claims that the purpose of his proclamation is to "present everyone mature in Christ." But in 2:2 the sense is that we live in love so that we may have proper understanding. Unraveling the proper order here is probably not the point. We saw in 1:9–10 that the author connects behavior and knowledge without explaining what produces what. Doing and knowing; knowing and doing; these are two sides of the same coin. Here, in 2:3, the author wants to point to knowledge, for this sets up his warning against the heretics in 2:4, which in turn anticipates the full warning against them in 2:8–23. But we must note that both behavior and knowledge steel us against the power of heresy.

FULLNESS OF LIFE IN CHRIST AND WARNINGS AGAINST FALSE TEACHERS
Colossians 2:6–23

2:6 **As you therefore have received Christ Jesus the Lord, continue to live your lives in him, [7] rooted and built up in him and established in the faith, just as you were taught, abounding in thanksgiving.**

[8] See to it that no one takes you captive through philosophy and empty deceit, according to human tradition, according to the elemental spirits of the universe, and not according to Christ. [9] For in him the whole fullness of deity dwells bodily, [10] and you have come to fullness in him, who is the head of every ruler and authority. [11] In him also you were circumcised with a spiritual circumcision, by putting off the body of the flesh in the circumcision of Christ; [12] when you were buried with him in baptism, you were also raised with him through faith in the power of God, who raised him from the dead. [13] And when you were dead in trespasses and the uncircumcision of your flesh, God made you alive together with him, when he forgave us all our trespasses, [14] erasing the record that stood against us with its legal demands. He set this aside, nailing it to the cross. [15] He disarmed the rulers and authorities and made a public example of them, triumphing over them in it.

[16] Therefore do not let anyone condemn you in matters of food and drink or of observing festivals, new moons, or sabbaths. [17] These are only a shadow of what is to come, but the substance belongs to Christ. [18] Do not let anyone disqualify you, insisting on self-abasement and worship of angels,

dwelling on visions, puffed up without cause by a human way of thinking, [19] and not holding fast to the head, from whom the whole body, nourished and held together by its ligaments and sinews, grows with a growth that is from God.

[20] If with Christ you died to the elemental spirits of the universe, why do you live as if you still belonged to the world? Why do you submit to regulations, [21] "Do not handle, Do not taste, Do not touch"? [22] All these regulations refer to things that perish with use; they are simply human commands and teachings. [23] These have indeed an appearance of wisdom in promoting self-imposed piety, humility, and severe treatment of the body, but they are of no value in checking self-indulgence.

The letter now moves to the question of heresy. The refutation of and warning against heretics might have been the immediate cause for the writing of the letter. The author is concerned about incorrect teaching and its related behavior in the church, and he regards these teachings as being opposed to the gospel. However, it is important that he does not move directly to his attack; rather, as we have seen, he first loads his theological arsenal. In 1:1–2:5 he has carefully laid out the content of the gospel. He has exhorted our study of it and fidelity to it. Furthermore, he has articulated the gospel in such as way as to provide refutation of the particular heresy in his church.

A Theological Reminder

Consequently, it is no surprise that this section begins with a theological reminder. The entire letter itself is in some sense a reminder, for it passes on the tradition that its readers need to know. That is not to say that the living Lord submits fully to language, but only that there are incorrect and correct accounts of the great mystery. The author's opponents are preaching the incorrect, whereas the correct can be found right here in the letter.

This brief reminder is anchored by 2:6–7, an imperative clause that exhorts stability and firmness: "continue to live your lives in him [Christ], rooted and built up in him and established in the faith, just as you were taught, abounding in thanksgiving." This language expresses effectively the overall mood of the letter, which is a call to return to solid tradition and to abide unwaveringly in it.

The logic of this argument is a classic Christian one: Correct teaching must live in the correct life. This is often referred to as the linkage between the indicative and the imperative. The indicative statement of salvation in the gospel must be connected to an ongoing imperative to live the gospel life. Colossians expresses this classic Christian connection in both the general structure of the letter, beginning with an account of the gospel and moving to imperatives for the Christian life, and in the constant interaction throughout the letter of theological and ethical statements.

What is striking in this letter is that the exhortation to remain firmly rooted in Christ expresses itself in two ways: first, avoid heresy and hold to orthodoxy, and, second, put off the immoral life and put on the moral one. The logic of 1:5–6 and 1:9–11, wherein proper knowledge of the gospel leads to the proper life, is carried out here as well. The true version of the gospel arms us against heretics and for the moral life. Thus it is appropriate that the initial exhortation is against heresy, for heresy can undo proper understanding and thereby make the ethical life impossible.

The Heretics

There are problems confronting anyone who wants to draw a picture of the heretics in Colossians. First, when the letter refers to incorrect ideas or bad behavior, we cannot always be certain that his opponents would have held exactly these ideas or practiced this behavior. Some of this polemic may be driven more by rhetorical needs than by a desire to characterize with perfect accuracy the thinking of his opponents. Few of us are likely to argue against our opponents with such precision. Second, when we gather the numerous accusations in the letter and then look for parallels in antiquity, we tend to find too many possibilities. Lots of people, with quite different views of the world, could have been described this way. There is simply too little information in the letter for a confident decision to be made.

Nevertheless, the core problem is clear enough. It is a question of cosmic powers; it is a question of the sufficiency and power of Christ. No one appears to be denying that Jesus is Lord and Savior. Rather, people appear to be uncertain whether Christ without the help of other powers can overcome the multitude of cosmic obstacles to our salvation. For the Greek, this puzzle over cosmic powers goes back at least to Empedocles, who envisioned the present world as a battleground among the elemental spirits of the universe. His vision of competing elements fascinated Greek thought. How does one deal with this great cosmic conflict? Through escape? Through ascetic protection? Through worship and propitiation of these powers? The Greek options were many. For the Jew, the solution tended to be more uniform: The law provides protection from and power over these cosmic elements. Of course, having attributed this power to the law, the Jews could go many different directions in deciding how the law did this and what this meant for their personal lives.

All this means, of course, that making a precise identification of the Colossian heretics is impossible, for these ideas are so pervasive that too many possibilities exist. Nevertheless, it is still clear that the author perceives uncertainty and insecurity in the faith of Christians in his community. His great christological hymn and ethical exhortations are intended to resecure the faith and confidence of these wavering believers. He wants to call them back to trust in the perfect sufficiency of Christ.

The Sufficiency of Christ

In 2:8–10, we are warned against wandering after philosophy that is based on analysis of the cosmic spirits and their powers over us. It is true that we need divine assistance, but it is Christ and Christ alone who can provide it. Thus we read that we should adhere to Christ, "for in him the whole fullness of deity dwells bodily, and you have come to fullness in him, who is the head of every ruler and authority." The echoes of the hymn in 1:15–20 are obvious. Christ is all-sufficient Lord of the cosmos. That is our core confession, and it is all we need to know here.

Furthermore, we partake personally of this divine sufficiency. In fact, the question of whether we partake of the full power of Christ may be the real point of contention. We might imagine that the author's opponents confess Jesus as sitting Lord of the universe and have devised ways to be in contact with him. "We need to keep free from the stains of the world," they think, "for the cosmic powers may enslave us. We may even need to manage a journey into the heavens upon our death. For that we will need cosmic assistance." The goal, of course, is Christ; but the methods of accessing Christ are not confined to Christ alone.

To this multiplication of cosmic saviors, the author proposes both the sufficiency of Christ and our immediate and contemporary access to Christ's fullness: "You have come to fullness in him" (2:10). Thus, 2:11–15 should be seen as theological argument for our access to the fullness of Christ, the very fullness that was established in 1:19 and repeated in 2:9.

In 2:11, the classic image of spiritual circumcision, which is found in Judaism and in Paul, is used to denote our escape from the body of flesh. Perhaps the author would admit that these cosmic powers once ruled us, using our flesh as their entry. But now, we have escaped the very body of flesh over which they had access. In 2:12, Paul's image of death in baptism (see Rom. 6:1–14) and the new life that ensues is used to emphasize the fact that we are raised with Christ already. Paul himself normally insisted that our resurrection was in the future (Rom. 6:8). But here, when questions of the adequacy and surety of our salvation are being advanced, it is fitting perhaps to declare that we are already raised with Christ.

In 2:13–15, this sense of salvation is placed into the context of sin and the law. We have been forgiven and the law itself is undone. What is meant by forgiveness, how it might be connected to other theological concepts, is all left unstated. Yet the point is clear: God has released us from all obligations to the law. Furthermore, the cosmic powers that accessed us through the law are thereby "disarmed."

The terminology in 2:14–15 is a little unusual. This is not a common way to talk about the Jewish law. Consequently, many readers have wondered whether this language does not come from those Greek or Roman religions that provided protection from the cosmic elements. If that is the case, the problem comes from some form of Greek philosophy, which the author refutes by using traditional Jewish/Christian imagery. Or the problem could be Jewish legalism, which the author refutes by using both traditional Jewish/Christian imagery and classic arguments from Greek philosophy. Or it is some combination. In any case, we have a fascinating mixture of Jewish, early Christian, and Greek philosophical imagery making a fairly simple point: We have come to fullness in Christ, already and for all time.

Warnings against the Heretics

In 2:16–23, the author appears to take up a direct refutation of specific beliefs and behaviors of his opponents. Colossians 2:16 sounds like a nice summary of the law, although it could refer to Greek or Roman religious regulations as well. Colossians 2:18 is practically untranslatable. The NRSV makes as good a guess as there is. "Worship of angels" could mean worship by angels, but more likely means people worshiping angels. This would accord with the danger of allegiance to non-Christ cosmic powers. People are apparently enlisting the help of angels in the journey to salvation. "Visions" could mean many things, but probably refers either to the vision that is part of the initiation ceremony in many Greek religions or to less formal appearances by divine persons. In any case, neither the reality of angels nor the experience of visions should provide organizing principles for the Christian life. Those principles should come solely from the reality of Christ. This is expressed forcefully in the unusual comparison in 2:17, wherein these old regulations are the shadow and Christ is the substance (literally "the body" in Greek). The proper response to these powers is urged in 2:19: Hold fast to the head. We should note that 2:19 completes the body imagery begun in 2:17 and, of course, echoes the earlier body reference in 1:18. Christ, the head, makes the body healthy when that body holds fast to it.

We should recall that in 1:18 the author uses the word *body*, which normally refers in cosmological accounts to the entire cosmos itself, to designate, not the whole cosmos, but only the redeemed church. This seems to be the case here. Thus it is the church that is exhorted to hold fast to its cosmic head.

Colossians 2:20–23 extends the warning against these heresies with further specifics. Verse 21 sounds again like a proscription against obeying the cultic provisions of the law. And 2:23 is even more difficult to translate than 2:18. Whatever all this might mean, the main point is made clear enough in 2:20: "If with Christ you died to the elemental spirits of the universe, why do you live as if you still belonged to the world?" In fact, this question sums up nicely the whole section. Those real and potent cosmic powers out there no longer have any power over you, for you have been rescued from the powers of darkness and transferred to the kingdom of Christ (1:14). Although the author does not deny the reality of these powers, he insists that Christians are no longer enslaved to them. All the theological images and diverse exhortations make the same point: You belong to Christ, and Christ is sufficient to save you.

No one who surveys modern Christianity or who inspects the hearts of our neighbors or ourselves will doubt that Christians still need to hear this. Jesus is such a quiet Lord, and there are so many noisy powers in our lives. We feel ruled by the world around us and within us. Our personal histories and social histories seem to control us. We are people who feel defined by the things done to us, ruled by time, place, circumstance, and internal biologies. And we, like the ancient Colossians, make constant bargains with these powers.

In response to these bargains and insecurities, Colossians declares that Christ, who is both in you and at the right hand of God, is all you need. It argues that our response to the ongoing power of these dead powers is not to address them directly but simply to trust Christ and, as it insists in what follows, to live the moral life. All those bargains are useless, for you cannot fight those powers and you have no need to. Christ has already defeated them. Your battle now is for the ethical life. The cosmic battle is over; the real battle now is between the immorality and morality of your life.

THE NEW LIFE IN CHRIST
Colossians 3:1–17

3:1 So if you have been raised with Christ, seek the things that are above, where Christ is, seated at the right hand of God. 2 Set your minds on things that are above, not on things that are on earth, 3 for you have died, and your life is hidden with Christ in God. 4 When Christ who is your life is revealed, then you also will be revealed with him in glory.

5 Put to death, therefore, whatever in you is earthly: fornication, impurity, passion, evil desire, and greed (which is idolatry). 6 On account of these the wrath of God is coming on those who are disobedient. 7 These are the ways you also once followed, when you were living that life. 8 But now you must get rid of all such things—anger, wrath, malice, slander, and abusive language from your mouth. 9 Do not lie to one another, seeing that you have stripped off the old self with its practices 10 and have clothed yourselves with the new self, which is being renewed in knowledge according to the image of its creator. 11 In that renewal there is no longer Greek and Jew, circumcised and uncircumcised, barbarian, Scythian, slave and free; but Christ is all and in all!

12 As God's chosen ones, holy and beloved, clothe yourselves with compassion, kindness, humility, meekness, and patience. 13 Bear with one another and, if anyone has a complaint against another, forgive each other; just as the Lord has forgiven you, so you also must forgive. 14 Above all, clothe yourselves with love, which binds everything together in perfect harmony. 15 And let the peace of Christ rule in your hearts, to which indeed you were called in the one body. And be thankful. 16 Let the word of Christ dwell in you richly; teach and admonish one another in all wisdom; and with gratitude in your hearts sing psalms, hymns, and spiritual songs to God. 17 And whatever you do, in word or deed, do everything in the name of the Lord Jesus, giving thanks to God the Father through him.

It can be argued that this section is the heart of the letter, because the purpose of all the theological argument that precedes it is to provide an effective arsenal for the ethical life. Without the actuality of the new life, proper or improper understanding is irrelevant. In our effort to assert the doctrine of salvation by faith alone, we sometimes forget that even Paul connects the indicative of the gospel with an imperative for a new life. We should recall that Colossians began in 1:4–6 by asserting this connection: Faith and love are two sides of the same coin; the gospel, if it is truly the gospel, bears the fruit of good works.

Thus, having laid out the theology and given warning of heresy, it is essential to exhort the ethical life. Colossians provides as fine a summary of Christian ethics as we have in early Christianity. The author of Colossians has a delicate touch; his theological images are fragile and allusive, and his ethical exhortations are evocative and appealing. He sketches a wonderful image of the Christian life.

Seeking the Things Above

The section begins with a brief summary and recollection of the preceding section. We were assured above that we have indeed been raised with Christ; and this means that we should "seek the things that are above, where Christ is" (3:1). Here is an obvious reference to the earlier critique of the relevance of the non-Christ cosmic powers. We should not seek allegiance to the lower powers—whatever they might be—but should align ourselves with the power that is above them all. Thus our real life is not found by wrestling our way through the forces of the world, but by setting our minds on the things that are above, where Christ is.

Again, we should note that there is no denial here of the reality of cosmic powers. The world is still a world of darkness, sin, and evil. What is being asserted instead is that this world of darkness is not our final home. Our life is above with Christ. The sense of homelessness that frequented early Christianity is evoked here. In the classic language of early Christianity, we are sojourners, strangers, aliens, who live in a country in which we are not citizens. We, rather, are citizens of the heavenly realms. But we must be careful here; there is no sense of divine abandonment of creation. We must remember that in 1:20 it is asserted that *all* things on earth and in heaven will be redeemed just as the church already has been. Thus this world, which is not our home, will become our home when it is redeemed. The feeling is less of our escaping to Christ and more of Christ moving in to redeem the entire created order. We will see this idea laid out in more detail in Ephesians.

Although the author emphasized the completed nature of salvation in 2:12, in 3:3–4 he balances that sense of completion with a sense of incompleteness: "Your life is hidden with Christ in God. When Christ who is your life is revealed, then you also will be revealed with him in glory." If Christ is our salvation and if we belong to Christ, it does not mean that the living Lord has become something within the total comprehension of humans. Our life is "hidden." We will not see who we really are until the great day of the Lord. The great mystery of the cosmos has come to expression in the gospel, but that does not mean that humans know all there is to know about God and Jesus.

Modesty about ourselves and our knowledge is a persistent and perhaps even necessary part of the Christian experience. On the one hand, we rejoice in the surety of our salvation; but on the other hand, we know that the kingdom has not fully arrived and that our sanctification is incomplete. Colossians strikes the classic balance in all this. This is sometimes called the already/not yet of the Christian life: We are already saved; we are not yet in our glory.

So if the powers are still there, but Christ, who is hidden at God's right hand, has rescued us from them and transferred us to his kingdom, what do we do now? Do we forget about this life and prepare for the next? Do we abandon our social and moral responsibilities and condition our private souls for heaven? What do we do?

Colossians gives the classic Christian answer: Put off evil deeds and put on love. We do war with the cosmic powers, not by learning how to manipulate them, but by living the Christian ethical life. We are affirming at this point a fundamental Jewish/Christian insight. Jews and Christians have long insisted that morality and immorality are the ultimate categories. This may be the crux of the disagreement in Colossae. The author's opponents may exemplify the modern fascination with physical explanations; we are what the physical forces of nature and human society make us. We are best understood through chemistry, physics, and their like. This means, of course, that we are not to blame. We are what we are. Even our thoughts are determined by powers beyond us. Our sense of free will is simply a certain chemical state in our brain.

In response to this worldview, the Jewish/Christian tradition insists that we are not reducible to physical categories, for we are ultimately moral beings. To know our true selves is to know ourselves as sinners and saints. There is no denial here of the truth of physical categories; religious feelings undoubtedly are mirrored in the physics of our bodies. These forces do have power over us. However, we belong to Christ, through whom all these powers and chemicals and forces were created, and for whom they exist. Because we belong to Christ, our final reality is hidden in him and not in our physical properties. The categories of Christ, the ultimate realities, are moral ones.

Thus the real battle is not over the manipulation of the physics of our bodies or the cosmos, but between the saint and sinner within us. It makes sense then that the cosmic analysis of the first two chapters is completed in an exhortation for Christian ethics. The cosmos will be appraised in the end, not by the energies and masses within it, but by its morality and immorality. The heart of the creator is moral.

Putting Off Evil

The author begins in 3:5 with the negative: "Put to death, therefore, whatever in you is earthly." We recognize here the author's conviction that death occurs in baptism, and that allegiances and even vulnerability to the earthly powers ends in the death of the person who was bound to them. The lists of sins in 3:5 and 3:8 contain the usual early Christian ones. It is normal for fornication to be a leading sin and for the list to contain diverse references to passions and to social sins such as slander and abusive language. However, 3:6 raises an important issue. The danger of sinful deeds lies not in their inherent power to make us miserable or to entrap us by their destructive powers, even though they may do this. Rather, their real danger comes from the theological fact that they place us under God's wrath. It is not simply natural consequences that determine ultimate reality, but rather a moral, creator God who will judge the world. Again, this is the Jewish/Christian and, we might add, Muslim claim. Morality is the ultimate category because God makes it so.

There is here also a certain sense of warning. Putting evil deeds to death requires intentionality and work on our part. It is something we do; it is not an automatic event. And evil deeds are under God's wrath. There is no attempt to address the question of whether a believer can backslide into the realm of death in a final way. Rather, we are simply exhorted to put off the old ways—even our old selves. This becomes classic Christian language: Put off the old self with its evil deeds and clothe yourself with the new self, a self being renewed according to the image of God. Because the image of God is Christ, we are then to put on our Christ-selves. We are to become Christians. This is the definitive theological conclusion in Colossians: We are to put on the cosmic, raised Christ by living the moral Christian life.

Christian language about the experience of salvation has always noted the strange paradox that we perceive salvation as both God's deed and our own. God saves us; we have no power to do so. Yet we do have some sort of essential role. We are not inanimate recipients. Thus the author of Colossians does not exhort us to save ourselves. Rather, we put on salvation. The new self, the one being renewed in knowledge according to the image of its creator, is a self created by God. It is a cosmic event, a reality external to us. We have no capacity to create ourselves as saved persons.

It is always a gift. Salvation comes from God's grace, not from our works. Yet the same author exhorts us to put off and put on. We must act within the event of salvation that is given us. Put on the gift of grace.

The reference to universality in 3:11 sets up the communal tone of the commandments in 3:12–17. The traditional Pauline language of unity in Christ is taken up here into Colossian's emphasis on Christ's universality: "Christ is all and in all." The manner of using Pauline images seen here is typical of the overall theology of the letter. Pauline language and concepts are filtered through the christological hymn in 1:15–20.

Putting On Love

The positive exhortation in 3:12 begins with careful designation of who a Christian is: "As God's chosen ones, holy and beloved, clothe yourselves with compassion." These designations, although traditional Christian ones, coincide with the salvation images in the rest of the letter. When Christ is in us, this places us at the right hand of the holy God, and thus we ourselves must be holy also. God's holiness, or God's fullness, as the letter says elsewhere, is present in us. We have here one example of the persistent Christian notion that the presence of the holy Christ in us makes us holy; we are thereby "saints" (which in Greek is "the holy ones"). We are also the ones who are loved. The gospel, as recounted in the letter, tells us the story of how God loves us, but the point here is that the love we receive from God becomes the ground of our love of others.

"Clothe yourselves with compassion, kindness, humility, meekness, and patience. Bear with one another and, if anyone has a complaint against another, forgive each other; just as the Lord has forgiven you, so you also must forgive. Above all, clothe yourselves with love, which binds everything together in perfect harmony" (3:12–14). It would be hard to find a better description of the peculiar character of Christian love. Christian love is shaped by personal humility, by vulnerability to the community, by forgiveness. This language is found in much of the New Testament, as well as early Christian literature, and it feeds down even into modern Christian literature. And the original theological insight persists: The love of God, displayed for us in Christ Jesus, enables us to love one another.

The priority of the community surfaces in several ways. The virtues themselves are those that refer primarily to loving interaction between and among people: compassion, kindness, bearing with one another, forgiving one another. These are virtues that forward the life of the community. Of course, love is depicted as the great unifier that "binds everything together in perfect harmony." Greek philosophy wanted to identify the virtue that harmonized the other virtues, giving balance and proportion to the soul. Given the communal emphasis in the preceding verses, it is unlikely that love refers here to that which makes the individual soul healthy; rather, love binds the community. Thus peace in 3:15 refers not to personal contentment but to community harmony.

This priority given to the community in our ethical life is important. Paul and the Pauline tradition in Colossians, Ephesians, and the Pastoral Epistles do not imagine the Christian life as primarily a one-on-one interaction between God and the individual soul. The gospel and the spirit of Christ place us in the body of Christ, which is a real, living, and breathing community of believers. We cannot disconnect from this community and still be in the body. The North American fascination with and focus upon the single individual soul misrepresents the Pauline witness. Yes, we are individuals, responsible to God and others, who will probably be saved as individuals; yet, we are bound to the body of Christ in an absolute and unbreakable way. Even if we are each distinct individuals, we are individuals in relationship with others. We can never become noncommunal.

Colossians' recurring themes of knowledge and thanksgiving conclude the section: "Let the word of Christ dwell in you richly; teach and admonish one another in all wisdom; and with gratitude in your hearts sing psalms, hymns, and spiritual songs to God" (3:16). The direct admonition to "be thankful" and to sing songs to God voices in explicit language the general tone of the letter. Most readers note the liturgical sound of the syntax in Colossians. It is a delicate, even worshipful letter, expressing in its own form and mood this admonition to be thankful and to sing songs to God. It is not an overstatement to suggest that the letter itself reads at times like a spiritual song to God.

RULES FOR CHRISTIAN HOUSEHOLDS
Colossians 3:18—4:1

> 3:18 **Wives, be subject to your husbands, as is fitting in the Lord. ¹⁹ Husbands, love your wives and never treat them harshly.**
>
> ²⁰ **Children, obey your parents in everything, for this is your acceptable duty in the Lord. ²¹ Fathers, do not provoke your children, or they may lose heart. ²² Slaves, obey your earthly masters in everything, not only while being watched and in order to please them, but wholeheartedly, fearing the Lord. ²³ Whatever your task, put yourselves into it, as done for the Lord and not for your masters, ²⁴ since you know that from the Lord you will receive**

the inheritance as your reward; you serve the Lord Christ. [25] **For the wrong-doer will be paid back for whatever wrong has been done, and there is no partiality.**

4:1 **Masters, treat your slaves justly and fairly, for you know that you also have a Master in heaven.**

Early Christians and the Ancient Household

The primary social institution for most people in the first-century Roman world was the household. The ancient household was typically quite extensive in character, including far more than the modern, so-called nuclear family. The wealthy households encompassed smaller houses of relatives and clients. The proper function of these household patterns was perceived as essential to the overall health of Roman society. The modern North American complaint about the loss of family values or the devaluation of the family and the devastating impact this has on all of society mirrors the Roman attitude. Thus it is no surprise that early Christianity devoted much attention to the values of the household and the duties of Christians in them.

On the other hand, New Testament ethical norms, especially some of Jesus' sayings, were often seen as dangerous to these household structures. To say that everyone is a brother and sister, that there is no male or female, slave or free, in Christ, does not sound like support for household hierarchies, where some people must have power over other people. In this sense, much of Christian ethics sounded revolutionary—not revolutionary against the emperor, for Christians typically spoke quite positively of imperial power, but against ancient family structures. The church was the new family; you had new brothers and sisters. And it is clearly the case that Roman perception of Christians as antihousehold contributed to early Christian persecution. Apparently, the problem was especially difficult and volatile regarding the proper role of women.

Colossians, Ephesians, and the Pastoral Epistles all devote attention to this problem. Although each will give a somewhat distinct answer, the general assumption of all will be the same: The household pattern with its hierarchies of dominance and submission should be supported by all Christians. There is a strong denial here of any revolutionary tendencies—at least as far as the household is concerned.

In Colossians we find a classic household code where the dominant and submissive pairs of husband/wife, master/slave, and parent/child are addressed in turn. Groupings of this kind are very common in the literature we possess from the Greek and Roman world, and this form of exhortation becomes popular in the New Testament and early Christianity. The Colossians pattern and to some extent the general early Christian pattern of composing household codes differed from the typical Greek and Roman pattern. The general pattern outside the New Testament in these household codes was to address them to the male head-of-household, exhorting him in turn to proper and compassionate behavior toward wife, slaves, and children. More often than not, the submissive partner was not addressed at all. Here in Colossians we see a striking contrast, where the submissive partner is not only addressed but is addressed prior to the dominant partner. In part, this shift probably derives from the simple fact that early churches, including the church at Colossae, were composed more of women and slaves than male heads-of-household. But it also derives from the overall strategy of the exhortation.

That strategy involves the practicing of Christian love in relationships where power is unequal. Christian capacity to submit to evil probably derives from such commands of Jesus as those in Matthew 5:38–48 and from meditations upon the cross (compare Matt. 10:16–25). Whatever its origin, it is clearly in play here. And whenever it surfaces, it has for us a certain embarrassing, illogical, unfair, and imprudent feel to it. These calls to submission, which are repeated throughout the New Testament, have become extremely controversial in modern Christian thought.

Love in the Midst of Injustice

"Wives, be subject to your husbands, as is fitting in the Lord" (3:18). On the one hand, the dominance of the husband is not questioned. The power imbalance is not addressed; in fact, the wife is enjoined to submit to it because it is fitting in the Lord to do so. One's relationship to Jesus Christ does not cancel one's other social obligations, whether those obligations seem just to you or not. Rather, in the name of the Lord, one must submit willingly (perhaps as Jesus himself submitted on the cross). On the other hand, the husband is neither the Lord nor the Lord's vicar. The husband does not stand between the wife and the Lord. This is an important point, because later developments drift in this direction, as we will see in Ephesians 5:22–33.

"Husbands, love your wives and never treat them harshly" (3:19). This is a simple command that would have seemed appropriate to almost everyone in antiquity. The husband's power must be wielded with love and compassion. It was the ancient norm, and Christianity adds little to the mix, except perhaps in terms of emphasis.

The rest of the section proceeds in a quite similar vein. The fact that "fathers" are addressed in 3:21, after children have been enjoined to obey "parents," illustrates the male orientation of the basic form. Many readers have noted the wonderful and insightful warning that children who are provoked can lose heart. That children are addressed in the second person and are treated as moral agents, capable of Christian moral action, is seen by most historians as quite unusual in a world that has so little comment about the moral independence of children. Probably the Christian conviction of the equal worth of all human life is surfacing here in a gentle way.

The admonitions to slaves are by far the most extensive, suggesting perhaps that the author's community was having the greatest problem in this area. There are serious concerns here: How can someone have two masters? Is Jesus the Lord of the slave or not? How can a Christian slave truly obey Jesus when he or she has an earthly Lord? In this passage the NRSV translates the same Greek word two ways: as Lord when referring to Jesus, and as master when referring to humans. But this translation softens the sense of conflict. The response in Colossians to this problem is not to address the question of which Lord has power over what. Rather, the slave is simply imagined under the command of his earthly master and is therein enjoined to obey "wholeheartedly, fearing the Lord" (3:22). This kind of response is typical of early Christianity. There is little attempt to analyze the good and evil in ancient power structures or to propose social alternatives. Instead, Christians are simply placed in those structures and exhorted to practice and display Christlike behavior. Whatever task is before us must be done as if for the Lord. This is not to say an earthly Lord can ever stand between us and our heavenly Lord, but it is to say that in all deeds we do we must show our Christlike selves.

The closing admonition to masters is intriguing. The reminder to the lord that he has his own Lord is straightforward enough: He too must display Christlike behavior and remember his accountability, just as the slave. Thus master and slave come to every deed as equals. This represents classic Christian social leveling that has few implications for social structures. However, the admonition in 4:1 to "treat your slaves justly and fairly" is more provocative. Even though it is standard in Christian and non-Christian lists to exhort kind behavior toward slaves, the language employed here is a bit different. The Greek word translated "fairly" typically means "with equality." It is used that way in 2 Corinthians 8:13, and it occurs frequently in Greek law in that sense.

To enjoin a master to treat a slave with equality is to go way beyond the ancient norm, however. Colossians is moving here toward a social critique or toward the recognition of a need for social reorganization. It may have been that in Christian circles it was difficult to imagine one Christian male being "Lord" over another Christian male. The same problem will surface in Philemon. As we will see in the Pastoral Epistles, women had problems having both Jesus as Lord and a husband as lord, but in Colossians it may be the maleness of the slave that evokes the concern. Whatever the case, the solution is an interesting one. Both master and slave must display Christian behavior. For the slave this means submitting and serving wholeheartedly; for the master it means treating the slave as an equal. Power is released but not seized.

Questions and Problems for Today

The implications and authority of this material for modern Christians has proven to be controversial. The ready acceptance of social patterns wherein power is unequally and unjustly distributed bothers most modern Christians. In fact, we see much of our social task as involving the just distribution of social power. We even perceive kind behavior from the dominant person and gracious submission by the dominated person as not being virtues at all, but rather as perpetuating and authenticating injustice. Moreover, the attempt to redress this imbalance, in the partial surrender of power by the master, is seen by many people as less desirable than the seizing of power by the oppressed. We more often believe that there is a kind of self-esteem and self-knowledge acquired in the act of seizure, making the results more lasting and effective. To be condescended to is not productive of lasting justice.

Furthermore, slavery and the domination of wives by husbands are evils in themselves. We cannot pretend that the only Christian responsibility is to take up wholeheartedly whatever little task is before us, while rampant injustice runs through the systems that want this task accomplished.

So what must we do about this passage? First, we must admit that Colossians, and this passage in particular, does not contain a program for social justice. Furthermore, we should admit that Colossians seems unconcerned about the power imbalance between husbands and wives, and that it shows only minimal concern for the imbalances inherent in slavery. That other Christians were concerned about these things is apparent in the need for them to be enjoined to submit. Why did early Christianity keep pleading with wives and slaves to submit unless some were not submitting?

Thus the ethical program of Colossians does not lie in the desire to restructure the Roman household or the imperial system. The author's concern lies with individuals practicing Christian virtue in every deed and in the creation of a church community, not a Roman community, where there is true Christian love. Thus, when we are involved in relationships that are defined by non-Christian norms, our task is not to engage in social transformation, but to display our Christian virtues. Perhaps the larger Colossian view of the cosmos is determinative here. If one understands the cosmos as not having a future, if one believes that the Christian's true home is in the heavens and that Christ will return and establish the final kingdom, then social programs are not likely to make much sense. Instead, the Christian task becomes one of anticipation: We are to model the future in loving treatment of each other in the church and in the practice of Christian virtue in every corner of our lives. Furthermore, and perhaps this is the determining factor, the author perceives the Christian life as one of submission, humility, and Christlike suffering. The seizing of power would be a non-Christian deed. We are to be like Christ, and Christ submitted even unto death. Justice will come with the great redemption of the cosmos by God through Jesus. It is not within our strength or character to become the new emperors.

The strength of Colossians lies in the conviction that every task can be sacred, no matter where the task originates. Every deed can be done with Christian virtue. That strength lies in its willingness to apply the peculiar logic of Christian virtues, with their emphasis on submission to evil, to even the most awkward of relationships. Its strength lies in its conviction that Christlike behavior, real virtue, is possible for every single Christian, for we are all raised with Christ. After all, suffering mistreatment is a mark of the true Christian. For us this means that whoever you are, wherever you are, whatever time of day it is, whatever person is in the room with you, you must put on Christlike behavior. There is great freedom and hope in all this. And there is a great challenge for power-manipulating modern Christians in this memory of the sacredness of Christian weakness. Finally, it is clear that if we are looking for warrants for programs of social justice, we must go to other texts (of which there are, of course, many).

CONCLUDING INSTRUCTIONS AND GREETINGS
Colossians 4:2–18

4:2 Devote yourselves to prayer, keeping alert in it with thanksgiving. [3] At the same time pray for us as well that God will open to us a door for the word, that we may declare the mystery of Christ, for which I am in prison, ⁴ so that I may reveal it clearly, as I should.

⁵ Conduct yourselves wisely toward outsiders, making the most of the time. ⁶ Let your speech always be gracious, seasoned with salt, so that you may know how you ought to answer everyone.

⁷ Tychicus will tell you all the news about me; he is a beloved brother, a faithful minister, and a fellow servant in the Lord. ⁸ I have sent him to you for this very purpose, so that you may know how we are and that he may encourage your hearts; ⁹ he is coming with Onesimus, the faithful and beloved brother, who is one of you. They will tell you about everything here.

¹⁰ Aristarchus my fellow prisoner greets you, as does Mark the cousin of Barnabas, concerning whom you have received instructions—if he comes to you, welcome him. ¹¹ And Jesus who is called Justus greets you. These are the only ones of the circumcision among my co-workers for the kingdom of God, and they have been a comfort to me. ¹² Epaphras, who is one of you, a servant of Christ Jesus, greets you. He is always wrestling in his prayers on your behalf, so that you may stand mature and fully assured in everything that God wills. ¹³ For I testify for him that he has worked hard for you and for those in Laodicea and in Hierapolis. ¹⁴ Luke, the beloved physician, and Demas greet you. ¹⁵ Give my greetings to the brothers and sisters in Laodicea, and to Nympha and the church in her house. ¹⁶ And when this letter has been read among you, have it read also in the church of the Laodiceans; and see that you read also the letter from Laodicea. ¹⁷ And say to Archippus, "See that you complete the task that you have received in the Lord."

¹⁸ I, Paul, write this greeting with my own hand. Remember my chains. Grace be with you.

Greek and Roman letters that address behavior often have eclectic collections of exhortations at the end. Colossians 4:2–5 seems to be just such a collection. At times these collections serve as formal summaries or rehearsals of the main ideas, but not always, and not here in Colossians. Nevertheless, the exhortation to prayer fits nicely into the larger themes of the letter. The Christian life, when properly understood and lived, culminates in prayer and thanksgiving. Furthermore, the plural form of the imperative reflects the priority of the community for the author. A plea for thanksgiving fits the overall mood and conviction of Colossians, for the letter carefully establishes the grounds for Christian thanksgiving. This is done by rehearsing the true account of the gospel and detailing its implications. Our life is secure with Christ, and no power can prevail against it. For this we must give thanks.

To this general exhortation to prayer, a personal note on Paul's behalf is added. In part this sets the stage for the personal greetings that follow, but it also reiterates major themes of the letter: Pray that "God will open to us a door for the word, that we may declare the mystery of Christ, for which I am in prison" (4:3). The letter's concept of the gospel and Paul's role as apostle find restatement here. The great mystery must be told, taught, learned, and lived correctly. This is a primary function of the letter itself; it articulates the correct gospel.

The brief exhortation to "conduct yourselves wisely toward outsiders" (4:5) seems at first glance to come from nowhere, although it does fit the thought of the letter. However, its placement here probably originates from the language of mystery and the spreading of the gospel in 4:2–4. Spreading the gospel requires conversation with believers and nonbelievers. The letter itself is not a missionary tract; it is directed to insiders who are becoming confused. Nevertheless, the author recognizes that the task of articulating the gospel requires constant contact with outsiders. Here we are enjoined to undertake that task wisely and prudently. We are to wait for the best moment and are to speak gently, with salt.

The final greetings have frequently been seen as proof for the Pauline authorship of Colossians. Unfortunately, there is no basis for taking them that way. Letters we know to be pseudepigraphical, where the real author has given another name, typically a famous one, as the author, often have personal greetings and notations similar to what we find here. In fact, it only makes sense that we should find such in pseudepigraphical letters, for they are styled to look like "real" letters. Real letters have such greetings; consequently, pseudepigraphical ones do as well.

It is my working assumption in this book that Colossians was not written by Paul. Therefore, we must imagine that people are not actually exchanging greetings. Instead, these greetings must have some other literary purpose. Often these greetings have no other purpose than to make a pseudepigraphical letter look like a real letter. But the extensiveness and content of these greetings indicate that more is going on here.

The primary function of these greetings may be to provide positive illustrations of how Christian communities should care and provide for one another. Note the amount of comfort and support that is being provided by these communities for each other. Paul is sending Tychicus, along with Onesimus, to "encourage your hearts" (4:8). The Colossians, probably in concert with the churches in Laodicea and Hierapolis, have sent Epaphras to minister to Paul. It is likely that Epaphras is not presented as the founder of the Colossian church or a member of the Pauline entourage, but rather as a representative of the three churches sent to comfort and support Paul in his imprisonment. Epaphras also models the ideal of proper prayer, which is to be driven by concern for the community: "He is always wrestling in his prayers on your behalf, so that you may stand mature and fully assured in everything that God wills" (4:12). In these instances and more, we have the author providing living examples of proper Christian behavior. They are to be emulated.

The mention of the letter "from" Laodicea, along with the admonition to have both letters read in both places, has inspired much speculation. In fact, one of the pseudepigraphical letters from early Christianity is one pretending to be this lost letter of Paul to the Laodiceans. Frequent attempts by modern scholars to identify this lost letter or even fragments of it have not been persuasive. We cannot tell whether the author actually knew of such a letter or if he is creating a useful fiction. In any case, Pauline letters are depicted here as having audiences larger than their original destination. This is important for a letter like Colossians, which must have a larger audience than a church at Colossae that may not exist anymore. Paul's apostolic credentials make his letters authoritative for all Christians everywhere, no matter when and to whom they were originally written. The letter of Colossians is itself, of course, a meditation on Pauline thought that is intended for a large audience.

In the postapostolic Christian community, the authority of the apostles becomes nearly absolute. In the great debates over the proper shape of Christianity, the appeal to apostolic warrants became almost a necessity. In this instance, Paul is the figure around which the debate gathers. But this can be adequately done only if the community has access to the letters of Paul. Thus the collection begins, along with pseudepigraphical additions to it.

The final benediction is typical of Pauline letters in all respects. Letters were normally dictated to secretaries. And frequently the author would add a concluding note in his or her own hand. The notice that Paul is adding a final greeting in his own hand says nothing one way or another about authenticity. In fact, in the original letter, with its original handwriting, it would make little sense to point out the change in handwriting. Any reader could see the change in hand. Of course, pseudepigraphical letters emerge, not in autograph form, but like the rest of the Pauline collection, as copies. Thus, pointing out the pretended change in hand fits perfectly the situation of a pseudepigraphical letter.

"Grace be with you" (4:18) is, of course, the most common early Christian benediction.

CONCLUSION

A text like Colossians points modern Christians in many intriguing directions. Its theological images are inviting and convicting. And part of what happens to readers of this text is that these theological images begin to work on us, enticing us to think in ways we have not before. For me, the images of hope, the conviction of the goodness of creation, the affirmations of God's benevolent caring for us and for creation, and the promise of the powers of Christ all work into my theology in striking and comforting ways. My reading of Colossians convinces me that the theological imagery in this letter does not answer questions in a final way but instead opens up possibilities. We are invited to think, not simply to accept. We are invited to think about the theological possibilities etched in this letter. And I hope readers of my comments can sense that invitation.

Nevertheless, I would like to point in a different direction in my concluding remarks. Colossians raises for me the question of risk. We are called here to risk the Christian life. As I noted in the study, the real battle, according to Colossians, is not between Jesus and other cosmic forces—that battle is over. The real battle is in us, between our moral and immoral selves. Despite all the emphasis on knowledge in this letter, God and Jesus and the gospel do not finally collapse into human knowledge. They remain, in part, unknown and mysterious. Nevertheless, we must live the Christian life, even though we are short on knowledge. We must risk the possibility that we are wrong, that we do not understand. We must love, submit, follow Christ, even though we cannot think through why such behavior works. We cannot understand love, but we must try to live it.

For me, this is the voice in Colossians that will not turn me loose: "Clothe yourselves with love," even if love looks foolish.

Ephesians

Introduction

Ephesians is a blessing to God for God's blessings to us. In order to enumerate the blessings of God, the author proclaims the truths of the gospel; he tells the story of Christ. The victory of Christ over all the powers of evil and the gifts to humans which flow from that victory compose the heart of God's blessings. God has done wonderful things for us in Jesus Christ, and God must be praised.

The vision of the letter moves from cosmic vistas to the mundane affairs of human life. The letter proclaims a unification of the cosmos that God is accomplishing in Jesus Christ. The letter details God's intentions for the cosmos, moving from the cosmic level to the personal level. The church, Jews and Gentiles, the family, and the individual are all placed carefully into God's plan of salvation.

The letter also exhorts the ethical life. Love and mutual submission are demanded of all Christians. The author takes us into the details of how Christians love each other. The author insists that the great cosmic victory of Christ can never be disconnected from love. Love is not something added on to the gospel, as though there can be good news apart from ethics. The sign, the proof, of God's victory is seen in how Christians love one another. In fact, our capacity for love is one of God's blessings to us. We do not bless God by loving each other; rather, God blesses us by enabling us to love.

Ephesians can be thought of as a commentary on Colossians. More than one third of Colossians is repeated in Ephesians, with some phrases and even sentences repeated verbatim (Col. 4:7–8 in Eph. 6:21–22). More often, however, we find loose paraphrasing and reworking such as Colossians 1:22 in Ephesians 1:4 and Colossians 1:14 in Ephesians 1:7. More important, key theological insights, which are worked out in Colossians, are taken up and reworked in Ephesians. Ephesians is, to a great extent, a meditation on Colossians.

This reworking of Colossians is not done woodenly but creatively. For example, many Pauline themes, lacking for the most part in Colossians, are introduced into the Colossians' christological framework. The relationship between Jews and Gentiles, which is so important in Paul's letters, is addressed here. The great Pauline theme of justification by grace, which so often appears in tandem with the Jew/Gentile theme, is also interjected into the Colossians' cosmology. Beyond that we find careful elaboration of the Pauline themes already present in Colossians. Thus we discover in Ephesians a certain maturation of Colossians' ideas, all of it done in classic Pauline language.

Thus the author of Ephesians must be imagined as a careful student of Paul who uses Colossians as his fundamental literary and theological outline. He cannot be named. Attempts to locate him among the many names in the Pauline letters are little more than wild guesses. And, as with Colossians, it is difficult to determine for Ephesians a precise date or place of origin.

One of the most interesting theories about Ephesians comes from the great American scholar, E. J. Goodspeed. He not only made the initial argument that Ephesians is largely a commentary on Colossians but also proposed that Ephesians was an introductory letter to the Pauline letters and was composed by the initial collector and organizer of those letters. It was not addressed to the church at Ephesus or to any other specific church, but was intentionally general in its approach. Goodspeed speculated even further that this collector and author was Onesimus, Philemon's runaway slave, who had become bishop of Ephesus (thus the eventual Ephesian locale of the letter).

All of this, of course, is speculative and cannot be taken as fact. However, Goodspeed's theories point to important characteristics of the letter: It is general in tone. It reads like a summary of key Pauline ideas. It seems to be unaffected by any specific problem. It is based extensively on Colossians.

With what assumptions can we begin, then? The best we can estimate is that Ephesians must be dated after Colossians and before the Pastoral Epistles, Ignatius, and Polycarp, all of which make references to this letter. Sometime between 80–85 would be a good guess, but it could have been written a little later. Ephesians, like Colossians, must come from a center of Pauline study, perhaps Rome or Ephesus itself. Of course, other locales are possible.

Finally, Ephesians illustrates for us one of the tasks of modern theology, a task I mentioned earlier. Theology must be both conservative and creative. On the one hand, the author reaches back to the apostolic roots of the church, back to Paul, and takes over Pauline insights in order to understand his own time. Christian theology, in order to be Christian, must deal with tradition. We must read the Bible and respond to the Bible in order to be Christian. On the other hand, Pauline tradition undergoes a striking transformation in Ephesians. The author says things that have never been said before.

This means that, in order to be faithful to tradition, we must say things that our tradition does not say. We must use memory and imagination. We must be conservative and creative. The ancient spirit of Christ is always new.

Commentary

SALUTATION
Ephesians 1:1–2

> 1:1 **Paul, an apostle of Christ Jesus by the will of God,**
> **To the saints who are in Ephesus and are faithful in Christ Jesus:**
> **² Grace to you and peace from God our Father and the Lord Jesus Christ.**

This salutation is modeled on the one in Colossians. In fact, it repeats Colossians exactly, omitting only the reference to Timothy and the designation of the recipients as "brothers." Thus the letter starts with a strong indication of its literary origin: Colossians is its primary literary and theological model, although other Pauline letters, especially Romans, will play a part.

As we noted earlier in the discussion on Colossians, this Pauline-style greeting is a modification of the typical Greek or Roman greeting. The usual pattern is "Sender to Recipient, Greetings." Ephesians follows this basic structure but also repeats the elaboration and modification of it that Paul practiced. The self-designation of Paul as "an apostle of Christ Jesus by the will of God" is very important to the authority and theology of the letter. Paul's peculiar and essential role in the plan of salvation is detailed in Ephesians 3:1–11, and Ephesians 2:20 defines apostles as the foundation of the building, which is the church. These delineations of the role of Paul go far in explaining the literary purpose of the letter. Paul is the apostle who details the place of Gentiles in God's plan of salvation. Ephesians itself will rearticulate this Pauline message to the Gentiles. The postapostolic church can be a true church only if it is built upon the foundation of the apostles. Ephesians, of course, provides just such an apostolic foundation.

Other themes that will become important in the rest of the letter are announced in brief form here. Ephesians will emphasize Pauline concepts of grace, which were not the focus of Colossians. The author will borrow language from Romans to redress this perceived imbalance. And the author will designate the peace between Jews and Gentiles and between all people and God as the truth of the divine mystery that has been revealed in the apostolic gospel. We can think of the author as setting, in the very traditional terminology of this salutation, the theological table for what follows.

The NRSV mentions in a footnote that "other ancient texts lack 'in Ephesus.'" This is an understatement, for, in fact, our *best* ancient texts lack the reference to Ephesus. Only Alexandrinus of the major early manuscripts includes "in Ephesus." This suggests that Ephesians was originally a general epistle, lacking a specific origin, which acquired its attachment to Ephesus either because the letter was originally published there or because Ephesus was the first major Pauline center where the letter became well known and frequently read.

SPIRITUAL BLESSINGS IN CHRIST
Ephesians 1:3–14

1:3 **Blessed be the God and Father of our Lord Jesus Christ, who has blessed us in Christ with every spiritual blessing in the heavenly places, 4 just as he chose us in Christ before the foundation of the world to be holy and blameless before him in love. 5 He destined us for adoption as his children through Jesus Christ, according to the good pleasure of his will, 6 to the praise of his glorious grace that he freely bestowed on us in the Beloved. 7 In him we have redemption through his blood, the forgiveness of our trespasses, according to the riches of his grace 8 that he lavished on us. With all wisdom and insight 9 he has made known to us the mystery of his will, according to his good pleasure that he set forth in Christ, 10 as a plan for the fullness of time, to gather up all things in him, things in heaven and things on earth. 11 In Christ we have also obtained an inheritance, having been destined according to the purpose of him who accomplishes all things according to his counsel and will, 12 so that we, who were the first to set our hope on Christ, might live for the praise of his glory. 13 In him you also, when you had heard the word of truth, the gospel of your salvation, and had believed in him, were marked with the seal of the promised Holy Spirit; 14 this is the pledge of our inheritance toward redemption as God's own people, to the praise of his glory.**

The Blessing

This opening section of the letter is a blessing to God for God's blessings to us in Christ. The prayerful, liturgical cast of the language that follows establishes the literary tone for the entire letter. We should, therefore, be careful about reading the theological pronouncements as being precise formulations in an ordered theological system when they are better read as having the imprecision and evocative function of liturgical language. In fact, the entire letter of Ephesians, including the ethical exhortations, can be read as a blessing to God for God's blessings. The ethical life, to which we are exhorted, is a necessary part of the plan of salvation and one of the blessings of God. The great cosmic christological events, the ministry of Paul, the reconciliation of Jew and Gentile and both to God, the moral life of the Christian, are all blessings of God.

Although Colossians also began with an enumeration of God's blessings, it was couched in the more typically Pauline form of a thanksgiving. Ephesians takes up the thanksgiving form in 1:15, but here Ephesians uses the literary form of a blessing. Of the Pauline letters, only 2 Corinthians begins with a blessing of this kind. However, the blessing form is a common one in both Judaism and early Christianity. First Peter duplicates the Ephesians style at this point.

The blessing in Ephesians 1:3 serves as an introduction, not only to the blessing proper in 1:3–14, but also to the letter as a whole. The letter itself is a blessing to God, and its basic content is laid out in 1:3–14.

In the Greek, 1:3–14 is one long sentence, wherein each phrase is either subordinated or loosely connected to the phrases around it. This elaborate syntax reinforces the evocative, liturgical feel of the theological propositions in the blessings. Yet these verses are packed with theology. Nearly every phrase evokes a classic Christian doctrine, and nearly every phrase needs extensive commentary. Furthermore, nearly every term in this passage has extensive parallels in ancient literature. There are echoes here of Paul, the Old Testament, and Greek and Roman philosophy. This is an enormously rich passage, and we can note and comment upon only a few of the most important ideas and themes.

The Revelation of God's Plan

The key insight is that God's eternal plan for the cosmos has been revealed in the gospel. We can all now know the truth, and that truth is "gospel," good news. We are being blessed in what God has done in Jesus Christ. From this comes the first theological task of the letter—to detail the blessings of God for us and the cosmos. The key to the blessings is, of course, Jesus Christ. The good that God has always intended for the world is now being accomplished in Christ. God must be praised for this. Thus the letter begins with a blessing that enumerates the good deeds of God.

We must note that the being of God is not laid out in totality, as though every secret of God and heaven has submitted to human understanding. These propositions are flashes of insight into the being of God. They are true, but God is still transcendent.

Nevertheless, Ephesians 1:8–9, 13 and 3:1–13 declare that the great divine mystery has been made known to us. This theme of revelation of the divine mystery is taken from Colossians but undergoes a transformation in Ephesians. Both Colossians and Ephesians will agree that the divine mystery is revealed in the gospel and that this mystery concerns the exaltation of Christ, our redemption in him, and the ethical life that ensues. Ephesians will add some important ideas, especially the story of the Gentiles and the reminder of the Pauline theme of God's grace.

For the theology of Ephesians an important concept occurs in 1:10. God is accomplishing "a plan for the fullness of time, to gather up *all* things in him, things in heaven and things on earth." God is at work redeeming the entire creation. Two central terms must be noted at this point.

First, in 1:9, the author announces that God "has made known to us the mystery of his will." The term *mystery* comes from Greek and Roman religions, where it refers to a once-hidden story about the gods and humans, knowledge of which effects salvation to the initiated. More immediately, of course, the term comes from Colossians, where it refers to the gospel, which is the true mystery. In Ephesians the term connotes God's secret plan for the universe, which is now revealed in the gospel.

This leads to the second term. God has a "plan" (*oikonomia*) (1:10) for the universe. This plan consists in the workings of the gospel. When coupled with the term *mystery*, the sense of divine providence is highlighted. The world is not an evil place, under the control of evil powers, even though such powers do exist. God has always known how these evil powers were to be conquered. From the beginning, God intended Jesus Christ. And now is the time when the redemption of the world from those evil powers is occurring.

Ephesians is not claiming that evil no longer has any power. Rather, the truths of the divine mystery show that evil is doomed. Jesus Christ has begun their defeat. The placing of Jesus at God's right hand above all other powers (1:20–21) is proof of this victory.

We are being asked here to believe something quite specific about reality. We are being asked to believe that Jesus has conquered evil and that this victory is the ultimate secret of creation.

For proof Ephesians offers the Spirit (1:13–14). The presence of the Holy Spirit is our "seal," God's "pledge" to us that we will inherit eternal rewards. It is also the case that this victory must be demonstrated in the lives of Christians. The capacity of Christians to love each other, to live the Christian virtues, is proof that evil no longer controls us. Ethics, empowered by the spirit of promise, is proof of Jesus' victory over evil. In this way, hope is grounded in ethics. The character of our present lives is a sign of what future awaits us.

The prominence of ethics in Ephesians is hereby explained. We must note that in 1:4 the first thing the author says about God's blessings is that we are chosen "before the foundation of the world to be holy and blameless before him in love." Our freedom from sin, demonstrated in acts of love, is the place of God's victory in our lives.

Of course, the ethical life is not accessed directly, by mere human effort; rather, it emerges from God's cosmic acts in Christ. According to Ephesians it emerges from a combination of grace and knowledge. Thus we have a call to praise "his glorious grace that he freely bestowed on us in the Beloved" (1:6). In 2:1–10 the author elaborates more precisely the nature of this grace.

Colossians, Ephesians, and the Pastoral Epistles all show, though in different ways, an interesting focus on knowledge and understanding. We saw in Colossians that a concern for untrue accounts of the gospel and its resultant incorrect knowledge was overcome by a true (Pauline) account of the gospel and the constant assurance of correct knowledge. Thus we were exhorted to learn the true gospel and avoid the false ones. This concern for heresy is echoed in Ephesians 5:6: "Let no one deceive you with empty words." But combating heresy does not seem to be the dominant concern of the letter. The mood is more that of celebration. We can sense a confessing community enjoying the common affirmation of the truths of the gospel. The amazing truths of the gospel must be proclaimed, learned, and lived; and God is to be blessed for them all.

The word *plan* (*oikonomia*) has a second meaning that will be important in Ephesians. The word might be translated "rules for the household" or "management of the household." The notion of God running the world as if it were God's own house and all people members of that house will surface in two ways in the letter. First, in 2:19 the author declares that we who were once aliens are now "citizens with the saints and also members of the household of God." The image here is one of having fallen under God's parental care. The world is no longer an alien evil place, but a household where God nurtures us and protects us. Second, membership in this household involves certain obligations and duties. These duties are played out in the many ethical imperatives in the letter. The rules for the

Christian household in 5:21–6:9 echo this idea of all Christians being members of God's house.

In conclusion, we discover a theologically rich blessing with echoes of Christian literature, Paul, the Old Testament, Colossians, and Greek and Roman thought. This diverse and complex imagery is woven into an evocative and delightful blessing of God for God's blessings to us. In the gathering of these images the theological table is set for the letter that follows. We can understand some of these images only when we have read what the author does with them in the rest of the letter.

PAUL'S PRAYER
Ephesians 1:15–23

1:15 **I have heard of your faith in the Lord Jesus and your love toward all the saints, and for this reason** [16] **I do not cease to give thanks for you as I remember you in my prayers.** [17] **I pray that the God of our Lord Jesus Christ, the Father of glory, may give you a spirit of wisdom and revelation as you come to know him,** [18] **so that, with the eyes of your heart enlightened, you may know what is the hope to which he has called you, what are the riches of his glorious inheritance among the saints,** [19] **and what is the immeasurable greatness of his power for us who believe, according to the working of his great power.** [20] **God put this power to work in Christ when he raised him from the dead and seated him at his right hand in the heavenly places,** [21] **far above all rule and authority and power and dominion, and above every name that is named, not only in this age but also in the age to come.** [22] **And he has put all things under his feet and has made him the head over all things for the church,** [23] **which is his body, the fullness of him who fills all in all.**

These verses are a poetic reworking of the first chapter of Colossians. The format, the language, and the theological concepts derive mostly from the opening thanksgiving and hymn of Colossians. However, this is not repeated woodenly. The author adapts the material to his own purposes and puts it in his own peculiar syntax. We see his hand, for instance, in the Greek style: verses 15–21 (at least) is one long sentence. But more significantly, the author works these themes and concepts from Colossians into his own literary and theological program.

With this thanksgiving, the account of God's blessings in 1:3–14 receives specific application to the hearers. This prayer places the readers into the great plan of salvation, connecting them as they are connected in Colossians, through knowledge, hope, the Spirit, and God's cosmic power. The heart of the prayer comes in 1:17: "I pray that the God of our Lord Jesus Christ, the Father of glory, may give you a spirit of wisdom and revelation as you come to know him." Each word here is important.

The way God is known is through the revelation in Jesus Christ. This will be emphasized in 1:20–23 where God's power is defined as that power at work in Jesus. It may be true that Ephesians does not show the same intensity of focus on Christology as we saw in Colossians; however, Christ is still the key lens through which both God and the church are perceived.

The statement in verse 17 that God is the Father of glory provides the foundation for hope in 1:18, for hope is directed toward the heavenly glory that only God can give. Of course, the prayer in 1:17–19 for the spirit of wisdom and revelation recalls the content of the gospel in 1:3–14 and the christological account in 1:20–23. The knowledge that comes to Christians is not acquired through normal, rational means; the gospel of Jesus Christ reveals what is to be known. Furthermore, the word *wisdom* here probably refers not only to knowledge of one's hope but also to knowledge of the particulars of the ethical life. Thus, 2:1–10 is anticipated here as well.

Having established the importance of knowledge and hope, the writer points us in 1:19 to God's power as the basis for both. Knowledge and hope are anchored in the power of God, and this power is displayed in Christ. Thus Christology is the key. The story of Jesus, as told in the gospel, is what we know and what gives us hope. In the story of Jesus we see how God's power actually works. Thus, perhaps in an echo of Romans 1:16, the gospel we learn and proclaim is an account of God's power. "God put this power to work in Christ when he raised him from the dead and seated him at his right hand in the heavenly places" (1:20). The gospel is an account of the resurrection and exaltation of Christ. It is a story of amazing divine power, power (repeating the language of Colossians) that puts Christ "above all rule and authority and power and dominion, and above every name that is named" (1:21). What is being named and by whom is not clear, but the theological point is: God's power is complete and perfect.

Christ and the Church

The final theme in this passage is that all this power, manifested in Christ, is present in the church. In the brief phrases of Ephesians 1:22–23, which recall Colossians 1:18–19, the crucial role of the church is established. It is through the church that God's power works. The elevation of the status of the church in the plan of salvation is often seen as the distinctive accomplishment of Ephesians. In contrast to Paul, who always maintains a "low ecclesiology," that is, a modest role and status for the church, Ephesians elevates the church to the center of the gospel story and initiates thereby the high doctrines of the church that early Christianity will develop. This high ecclesiology is often lamented, for it has encouraged both individuals and communities to think more highly of themselves than they ought. We become the saved ones, with special status, and thereby are disconnected from nonbelievers and the world around us. Paul himself, it is argued, would never have allowed that.

It is hard to argue with the dangers of theological arrogance that an overly high ecclesiology might encourage. There is too much evidence for it. However, such arrogance does not seem to be the immediate affliction of North American Christians. Rather, we seem to lack self-definition. Our problem is more that we think the church has no real role and that the faithfulness of our lives matters to no one but God and ourselves. If anything, we need to hear a little of this early Christian "arrogance," for it contains a tremendous challenge. We are key to God's very plan of salvation. Through us, God is at work to save the entire cosmos.

Whatever we conclude about contemporary doctrines of the church, it is clear that Ephesians is working out a new understanding of the church. However, in order to comprehend what the author accomplishes we must wait until other texts in the letter have been examined. Here we find a rather bold and startling beginning. In Colossians 1:19, the fullness of God dwelt in Christ; in Ephesians 1:23 the church *is* the fullness of God. This is a major step.

This is not to say, however, that the gospel as given in Ephesians becomes the story of the church. The gospel is still the Christ story, and the church is a part of the Christ story. It is only in connection with Jesus that the church has any reality. God has placed Christ at the right hand, and we have hope only as we share in this status that Christ has. We must be in Christ. Moreover, this being in Christ determines not only our hope but the shape and character of every moment of our lives. As Christ fills all in all, so shall Christ fill our lives.

FROM DEATH TO LIFE
Ephesians 2:1–10

2:1 **You were dead through the trespasses and sins** [2] **in which you once lived, following the course of this world, following the ruler of the power of** the air, the spirit that is now at work among those who are disobedient. [3] All of us once lived among them in the passions of our flesh, following the desires of flesh and senses, and we were by nature children of wrath, like everyone else. [4] But God, who is rich in mercy, out of the great love with which he loved us [5] even when we were dead through our trespasses, made us alive together with Christ—by grace you have been saved—[6] and raised us up with him and seated us with him in the heavenly places in Christ Jesus, [7] so that in the ages to come he might show the immeasurable riches of his grace in kindness toward us in Christ Jesus. [8] For by grace you have been saved through faith, and this is not your own doing; it is the gift of God—[9] not the result of works, so that no one may boast. [10] For we are what he has made us, created in Christ Jesus for good works, which God prepared beforehand to be our way of life.

This is another passage packed with theological images, but here there is a clear and ordered argument. There is less the sense here of poetic gathering and more the sense of formal argument. Several key theological points are being made.

In the Greek we do not come to the main clause until verses 5–6. This is important for the logic of the passage. The first four verses gather the assumptions and describe the conditions. Then in verses 5–6 the substantive act of God is recounted: "God . . . made us alive together with Christ . . . and raised us up with him." The NRSV heading "From Death to Life" is therefore an accurate description of the main point. The transfer from death to life that was displayed in Christ in 1:20 is now applied in identical language to readers who are in Christ. The christological foundation laid in 1:20–23 is, thus, applied to the individual; and the hope that we might share in the power of God working in Christ is realized.

The result of this power of God is that we too are actually raised up with Christ and are seated with him in the heavenly places. This is an astonishing proposal. To say that we are now seated with Christ goes beyond what Paul has ever said and seems, on the face of it, absurd. After all, we are still right here.

Describing blessings that are normally reserved for our final rewards as being already present is called by scholars "realized eschatology." This means that realities of the last times are already here. Almost all forms of Christian theology have some aspects of this. The end time has begun. The question is more, What is present now and what is yet to come? For Paul, the Spirit is an end-time reality that is present now. In that way it becomes proof of our final blessing. This idea is repeated in Ephesians 1:13–14. But the language of Ephesians 2:5–6 goes beyond what we have seen in Paul.

There is probably more going on here than poetic exaggeration, a careless speaking of heavenly rewards as if present. We saw in Colossians that uncertainties over the adequacy of Jesus' power led to a focus on the completed aspects of salvation. We are already raised up with Christ (Col. 2:12). Ephesians takes up the assurances of Colossians and puts them into the context of Pauline doctrines of grace. Furthermore, we see again a shift from temporal to spatial thinking. Ephesians is driven (as was Colossians) by a concern to establish hierarchies. Who is above whom? How does power descend from God? Christ, the church, the individual, husbands and wives, masters and slaves will all be placed in this hierarchy. Thinking this way, the author places the Christian in the hierarchy; we are above all other powers, seated on the right hand with Christ. He is not talking about the chronological order of events, but who has what power and what status.

Saved by Grace

This careful ordering of powers is balanced by doctrines of grace taken from Paul. Much of the core terminology in this passage comes directly from Colossians. For instance, having been dead in trespasses, having been subject to the cosmic powers, having been children of wrath, being raised and seated with Christ, and being made alive with Christ all come from Colossians. However, the language of grace, taken especially from Romans, is woven into the Colossians language of hierarchy. In doing this the author produces phrases that become classics in Christian thought on grace: "God, who is rich in mercy, out of the great love with which he loved us . . . by grace you have been saved. . . . For by grace you have been saved through faith, and this is not your own doing; it is the gift of God— not the result of works, so that no one may boast" (2:4–9).

One may have enormous status, but one has no grounds for boasting. We are only what God has made us to be (2:10). Our status is God's act, a gift, received in faith. A wonderful theological balance is thereby achieved. Christian arrogance and humility are bound together; each one is in need of the other in order to be true. We are nothing on our own, but God loves us and blesses us and has placed us above all other powers with Christ.

The heavenly status bestowed upon those who are in Christ shows itself not in disconnectedness from the world and the mundane affairs of life but in the Christian life of good works: "For we are what he has made us, created in Christ Jesus for good works, which God prepared beforehand to be our way of life" (2:10). The ethical exhortation in Ephesians 4—6 should not be conceived as nice moral additions to the gospel of Ephesians 1—3. The moral life, the life of love, is part of the gospel itself. Our capacity to love demonstrates our heavenly status.

The reality of evil powers makes the work of Christ necessary. As Ephesians notes, people who are now Christian once followed "the ruler of the power of the air, the spirit that is now at work among those who are disobedient" (2:2). In Colossians, the placing of Christ above those powers was what enabled the individual Christian to escape those powers. The same argument is replayed here. Allegiance to the evil powers showed itself in lives ruled by passions. Just as love shows our connectedness to the raised Christ, the life of passion shows disconnectedness.

The Jewish concept of judgment is also present, although the idea comes more immediately from Paul and Colossians. We, who by nature live according to the passions, being subject to the evil powers, are in truth children of wrath. This is not a contention that an immoral life has, as its natural consequence, bad results for the unrighteous person; rather, the classic Jewish and Pauline notion is in force here. God is righteous and will punish the unrighteous. It is God who makes for wrath. Then, echoing Paul, the same God who makes for wrath undoes the punishment through love and grace. We must remember, however, that the concept of grace given here does not mean that the moral, righteous life is not necessary. To doubt the centrality of the righteous life is to misunderstand the seriousness of the moral exhortations in Ephesians 4—6. Over and over, the author will plead with his readers to live the life for which they are called.

ONE IN CHRIST
Ephesians 2:11–22

> 2:11 So then, remember that at one time you Gentiles by birth, called "the uncircumcision" by those who are called "the circumcision"—a physical circumcision made in the flesh by human hands—[12] remember that you were at that time without Christ, being aliens from the commonwealth of Israel, and strangers to the covenants of promise, having no hope and without God in the world. [13] But now in Christ Jesus you who once were far off have been brought near by the blood of Christ. [14] For he is our peace; in his flesh he has made both groups into one and has broken down the dividing wall, that is, the hostility between us. [15] He has abolished the law with its commandments and ordinances, that he might create in himself one new

humanity in place of the two, thus making peace, [16] and might reconcile both groups to God in one body through the cross, thus putting to death that hostility through it. [17] So he came and proclaimed peace to you who were far off and peace to those who were near; [18] for through him both of us have access in one Spirit to the Father. [19] So then you are no longer strangers and aliens, but you are citizens with the saints and also members of the household of God, [20] built upon the foundation of the apostles and prophets, with Christ Jesus himself as the cornerstone. [21] In him the whole structure is joined together and grows into a holy temple in the Lord; [22] in whom you also are built together spiritually into a dwelling place for God.

The theme of grace that was established in 2:1–10 is developed in an intriguing way in this passage. The sense of gift that pervades 2:1–10 is reinforced here with a message to Gentiles reminding them that they were not the people of the promise. The echoes of Romans 9—11 are strong here; and, in fact, this passage makes sense only as a commentary on Paul's themes of covenant, promise, the abolition of the law, and the ingrafting of the Gentiles.

Furthermore, prior to this passage Ephesians has been moving primarily on a cosmic and individual level. Although there have been allusions to community in references to the church and in the plural form of the address, the main point has been to place the individual believer into the cosmic story of salvation. Here the social, communal, and even political dimensions of the Christian life receive their first real attention. Of course, much more will follow.

New Citizenship

What is curious about the way the passage does this is the apparent primacy that is given to Israel. The pre-Christian condition of Gentiles is described as being "alienated from the commonwealth of Israel." The passage is loaded with citizenship language of this kind. And the Gentile readers are described as various forms of noncitizens. All the terminology used in 2:12 and 2:19 is traditional Greek or Roman political language. Furthermore, the Greek *politeia*, which is translated in the NRSV as "commonwealth," is the normal term for describing the social realities of a given political entity. Fellowship with God is termed citizenship in the political entity of Israel. Gentiles did not possess that; rather, they were strangers and resident aliens to that political system. This means they did not partake of the full benefits that a given system supplies its citizens. Recent experience in the United States with legal and illegal immigrants gives us ready insight into the distinction being made here. The text declares to its Gentile readers: Do not forget that you were once noncitizens in God's commonwealth.

Obviously, this reminder reinforces the call to humility in 2:1–11; however, there is more going on here. The great Jew/Gentile question, which frequents the Pauline letters, receives in this passage a quite distinctive treatment that raises a number of questions. How can the problem be lack of citizenship in Israel, when it is not Israelite citizenship but membership in the body of Christ that effects salvation? As the passage will point out, Jews need reconciliation too. So what is the point?

We can make sense of this only by recalling Paul's theology of covenant and promise. The blessings that come through Christ are the blessings that were promised to Israel. The Messiah is by definition the one sent to Israel; the concept Messiah receives its meaning only from the promises to the people of Israel. Thus, to say that Jesus is the Messiah, the Christ, is to say that he brings the promised blessings to Israel. However, we partake of the now-present promises to Israel, not by becoming Israelites, but by becoming attached to the Messiah who brings the promises. All of this is assumed in this passage.

Thus, to be "aliens from the commonwealth of Israel" is to be "strangers to the covenants of promise" (2:12). In a similar way, we might recall the language of 1:13–14, where the mark of salvation is the "seal of the promised Holy Spirit . . . the pledge of our inheritance." We now have a pledge, a down payment, on the promises in the presence of the Spirit in our lives.

In order to comprehend the rest of the argument here, we need to recall Galatians 3:15–18. There Paul establishes the notion that there is only one offspring of Abraham and thereby only one person who receives the promises, namely, Christ. Christ is the inheritor of the promises to Abraham, and we partake of those promises to the extent that we partake of Christ. In this light, Ephesians 2:13–18 makes sense. First, the political integrity of Israel is destroyed: Christ "has abolished the law with its commandments and ordinances" (2:15). There are obvious echoes here of many Pauline discussions of the law, but the language of Galatians 3:15–18 would suffice. There is no commonwealth of Israel if there is no law. Second, Christ "has broken down the dividing wall, that is, the hostility between us" (2:14). There is much debate over what the author means here. What is the dividing wall? What is the hostility? The law could be the dividing wall that creates the hostility. But we might also have here a reference to the real wall in the Jerusalem temple, which separated Gentiles from the core activity of the temple. If this letter is after the destruction of the Jerusalem temple in A.D. 70, then the author might well be referring to that dividing wall in the temple. Supportive of this reading is the temple language later in the passage at 2:19–22. The old temple is destroyed, and Christ in us is building a new one.

All of this sets the stage for the primary point of the passage. Christ is our peace, and we are all one in him. But note how this peace and unity is accomplished. Gentiles do not become Jews, nor Jews Gentiles; they all become new people—Christians. Christ has created "in himself one new humanity in the place of two, thus making peace" (2:15). The role of the body of Christ is crucial here. It is Jesus who holds the promises, and thus it is only as we are "in" him that we partake of the promises. Being in the body of Christ is the key. The author throughout the letter insists on this point. Our new life is life in Christ. In this passage, this new life is described in terms of citizenship. Thus, 2:19 reads: "So then you are no longer strangers and aliens, but you are citizens with the saints." It is important here that the Gentiles do not become fellow citizens with the Israelites but with the saints, the sanctified Christians. The early Christian awareness of being a new people, a third race after the Jews and Gentiles, is surfacing here. In fact, they will turn this language around and declare themselves aliens and strangers in all earthly political systems, for they themselves are citizens of the heavenly city.

The christological ground for the subsequent ethics is reinforced here. The persistent call to put on the new self emerges from this belief that believers are "in" the body of Christ. In Christ reside the blessings, the promises, and the righteousness of the new life. In Christ, the old patterns, whether they concern personal morality or social enmity, are destroyed. Instead, we have a new life, the particulars of which will be described in what follows. At this point, the initial social point is made: Jews and Gentiles become one in Christ.

There is another reminder here for us that Jews and Christians are eternally connected. Christians cannot tell their story apart from the story of Israel. And, as Paul insists in Romans 9—11 and the author of Ephesians does here, we cannot configure our story in such a way that elevates Christians above Jews. Gentile Christians are the intruders, the noncitizens who now share in the promises and benefits of the people of God. Whatever the unique status of the church might mean, it does not mean that Christians can boast over Jews.

The Temple

The imagery shifts in a fascinating way in 2:19–22. Citizenship with the saints is coupled with being "members of the household of God" (2:19).

Although the household is a primary political category in the ancient world, it also becomes the basis for a second image. We are a new building for God. We are the new temple. We might guess that the notion that the temple was the center, heart, and organizing force of the old commonwealth of Israel suggested the connection here. But other classic notions of the temple are in force here as well. On the one hand, we are members of God's household. This suggests our heavenly abode. We reside with God. On the other hand, right now we constitute a place for God to reside. God resides with us. A temporal distinction must be present; right now we provide a dwelling place for God on earth, just as God will provide a dwelling place in heaven for us.

A curious problem exists around the designation of Christ by the Greek term *akrogōniaios*, which is translated in the NRSV as "cornerstone." In normal usage or with its normal etymology, the word means "highest cornerstone," or "keystone" (as the NRSV indicates in a note). This would mean that Christ is not part of the foundation, as Paul himself insists in 1 Corinthians 3:11, where Christ is the entire foundation. However, in Ephesians the apostles and prophets are the foundation. It is often argued that the image of building up upon a sound foundation requires the translation "cornerstone." Christ is the cornerstone around which the foundation of the apostles and prophets is ordered. Furthermore, Isaiah 28:16 reads in part, "I am laying in Zion a foundation stone, a tested stone, a precious cornerstone." And the Septuagint, the old Greek translation of the Old Testament, renders the Hebrew with the Greek term *akrogōniaios*. Thus Ephesians is assumed to be repeating an awkward Septuagint translation.

The other possibility is that Christ is the "keystone," the highest stone, from which the building hangs. This fits very nicely with the larger theology of Ephesians. Christ is seated on the right hand of God; he is above, and we who are below receive our new life from him. It seems to me that it works either way, and the point is pretty much the same. We are the new temple, and the temple is oriented around the power of God in Christ.

Furthermore, the foundation of this temple is the apostles and prophets. Apostles probably refers here to original bearers of the Jesus story who were sent by Jesus himself. Prophets, on the other hand, probably does not refer to the Old Testament prophets, but to Christian prophets who provided exhortation and guidance to the community out of the revelation of the Spirit. In any case, many commentators see here a striking departure from Paul's own understanding of the role of the apostles and the prophets. For Paul, Jesus is the foundation; apostleship and prophecy are merely two of the spiritual gifts, even if they are the highest ones. This seems to me to be confining Paul a bit too much. It is true, however, that we have a difference here from what we find written in Paul's letters, and it is a development appropriate to postapostolic times.

The second and third centuries of the Christian era were marked by the constant concern for churches to establish their apostolic credentials. When heresy, uncertainty, and innovation increase, the related need for reliable traditions increases as well. How can we tell a real Christian idea from a heretical one? The dominant answer will be that if and only if an idea is apostolic in origin or spirit then is it truly Christian. Given this tendency, Ephesians can be seen as an early attempt to lay an apostolic foundation, by a church looking back at its apostolic traditions. It is significant that this foundation is not laid idiosyncratically or carelessly; it comes through a careful study and reworking of Paul's letters. This is a foundation that certainly wants to be apostolic; it wants to be Pauline.

In all of this, Ephesians serves as a model for us. In order for us to have churches built on the foundation of the apostles and prophets, we must do the kind of work done here. We must immerse ourselves in the language and insights of the Bible, and we must state what we have learned by doing that in language appropriate and relevant for today.

Finally, the reference to apostles and prophets as the foundation of the new temple sets the stage for chapter 3, where Paul's unique role is highlighted.

PAUL'S MINISTRY TO THE GENTILES
Ephesians 3:1–13

3:1 **This is the reason that I Paul am a prisoner for Christ Jesus for the sake of you Gentiles—** 2 **for surely you have already heard of the commission of God's grace that was given me for you,** 3 **and how the mystery was made known to me by revelation, as I wrote above in a few words,** 4 **a reading of which will enable you to perceive my understanding of the mystery of Christ.** 5 **In former generations this mystery was not made known to humankind, as it has now been revealed to his holy apostles and prophets by the Spirit:** 6 **that is, the Gentiles have become fellow heirs, members of the same body, and sharers in the promise in Christ Jesus through the gospel.**

7 **Of this gospel I have become a servant according to the gift of God's grace that was given me by the working of his power.** 8 **Although I am the very least of all the saints, this grace was given to me to bring to the Gentiles the news of the boundless riches of Christ,** 9 **and to make everyone see**

what is the plan of the mystery hidden for ages in God who created all things; [10] so that through the church the wisdom of God in its rich variety might now be made known to the rulers and authorities in the heavenly places. [11] This was in accordance with the eternal purpose that he has carried out in Christ Jesus our Lord, [12] in whom we have access to God in boldness and confidence through faith in him. [13] I pray therefore that you may not lose heart over my sufferings for you; they are your glory.

Paul's Role as Author

It has been argued that this section is a later insertion in Ephesians, because it interrupts the liturgical mood with an autobiographical sketch and could be omitted without damaging the logic of the letter. But this is unlikely. There is no real evidence that Ephesians 3:1–13 is an insertion. More important, this section plays a pivotal role in the letter. Here we find the only real hint why the author chose to write in Paul's name. And we encounter brief theologies of apostleship and proclamation, both of which are essential to the theology of the letter.

The persistent concern of the second- and third-century Christian groups to establish and document their apostolic is important in Ephesians. A church cannot be a real church if it is not built upon apostolic foundations. Having personal connection from a real apostle to other real people in your community is one possible way of providing apostolic credentials. We will see this method in the Pastoral Epistles. For most communities this is not possible, however. Furthermore, Ephesians is not concerned about the credentials of individual communities but of the larger church itself. For this purpose, detailing and authenticating the form of the gospel that one holds as apostolic is more useful. What is needed is a firm apostolic version of the gospel—one that any church can use. Ephesians seeks to provide this.

This is, of course, not a new concern. For example, in Galatians, Paul first establishes a version of the gospel shared and agreed upon by both the Jerusalem pillars and himself, and then uses that shared apostolic gospel to criticize his opponents in Galatia. Second-generation communities cannot make this same sort of appeal. They must look back to people who cannot be brought forth as living witnesses. If you need apostolic witness and all the apostles are dead, what do you do? In Ephesians, we see one response: read, study, learn the apostolic texts, and then rearticulate them for your own community.

The author puts Paul's name on the letter and provides no hint that Paul is not the real author. Many, in fact most, modern commentators argue that writing under someone else's name in antiquity (pseudepigraphy) was a common and perfectly respectable practice. They argue that the author is merely indicating his deep dependence upon Paul and is not intending to deceive. Furthermore, no one minded this kind of pseudepigraphical experiment, as long as it was done out of pious modesty.

However, there is almost no evidence for respectable pseudepigraphy in the early church. Whenever a document was found to carry an apostolic name and not written by that apostle, it was rejected and lost its authority. In the desire to establish apostolic credentials, early Christianity created a multitude of pseudepigraphical documents. We hear of many such documents, and some of them have survived until this day. We have other pseudepigraphical letters from the early church, not only in the name of Paul but also of Jesus, James, Peter, Timothy, and other apostles. Most of these were rejected. And, as far as we know, any and all were rejected whenever it was established that they were non-apostolic.

Having said this, it is possible in the case of Ephesians that we do not have a serious attempt at deception. The authority of this letter rests as much on the coherence of its rendition of Paul as it does upon having Paul's name affixed. If the gospel given here coheres with that of the other Pauline letters, then the apostolicity of the letter is confirmed. However, the lack of any admission of pseudepigraphy, coupled with the presence of details that make the letter look genuine, indicates that some deception is occurring here. The author wants to articulate the Pauline gospel, and he wants to persuade his readers that Paul actually wrote it. This passage is part of that persuasion.

Ephesians 3:1–14 is also a potent account of the role of apostolic proclamation in salvation. Combining the language of the first two chapters of Ephesians with terminology from Paul's letters, especially Colossians, the author makes a case for the absolute necessity of the preaching of the apostles. First, the apostles must receive a genuine revelation. "The mystery" has been revealed to Paul and is being revealed by him. There is curious modesty about the second leg of this. The readers are encouraged to read the first part of the letter, where they can find "my understanding of the mystery of Christ" (3:4). This curious phrase suggests that Paul's understanding might be different from Peter's or that of other Christian leaders. What is given here, perhaps, is the Pauline version of the mystery.

Proclamation of the Mystery

The cosmic tone of the language is instructive: "In former generations this mystery was not made known to humankind, as it has now been revealed to his holy apostles and prophets by the Spirit" (3:5). This grace was given me "to make everyone see what is the plan of the mystery hidden for ages in God who created all things; so that through the church the wisdom of God in its rich variety might now be made known to the rulers and authorities in the heavenly places" (3:9–10). The mystery of God's eternal purpose in creation has now come to human language. It is being spoken in ordinary words by the apostles. It can be written, read, learned, believed, and lived. The theology and ethics of Ephesians are not, in this light, regular theology and ethics; they are reliable accounts of the ultimate truth of creation. The task of the church is to preserve, learn, and proclaim this truth, just as it was the task of Paul to create churches by proclaiming it.

The gospel that gives voice to this mystery is not some shadowy, elusive, unknowable mystery. It can be expressed adequately in human speech. Ephesians itself articulates this mystery. Thus Ephesians, like Colossians, advocates for knowledge. We can know and understand the ultimate mystery. In fact, we must understand, because proper knowledge is a necessary part of our salvation. In the same way, the moral life, based on this true knowledge, is a necessary part of our salvation.

The role of the apostle in proclaiming the mystery is crucial, and churches that hear and understand this apostolic proclamation can truly be said to be built upon the foundation of the apostles (2:20). In fact, given this understanding, Ephesians itself is necessary, for it gives new voice to this apostolic mystery. It does what the church must always do—proclaim the apostolic version of the mystery of salvation. Thus the church, like the letter itself, has both a conservative and innovative task. It must repeat the apostolic truth, and it must do so in its own voice. Ephesians models the proper procedure for all postapostolic theology. We must believe, study, and comprehend the ancient apostolic texts, and we must speak the truth of those texts in our own voice.

The precise content of the Pauline understanding of the mystery centers upon the relationship of Gentiles to salvation. It is certainly the case that "the mystery" refers to all of the first two chapters; however, the explicit reference is the application of that mystery to the Jews and Gentiles in 2:11–22. Of course, this has to do with Paul's special task. He is the apostle to and for the Gentiles. His message is that "the Gentiles have become fellow heirs, members of the same body, and sharers in the promise in Christ Jesus through the gospel" (3:6). The partnership referred to here is not with one another, at least not at this point, but with the Jews. Gentiles are heirs of the promises to Israel. Of course, the Jew/Gentile unification is a species of the grand plan for unification of *all* things in Christ (1:10). And Paul's apostleship is a part of the particular Jew/Gentile moment of the cosmic unification. Thus, once again Ephesians lays out proper theological procedure for its readers. The great truth of the plan can and must be applied to *all* things. Our task is not merely to repeat the Jew/Gentile theme, although that may be important, but to think out the new truths of the old truth for our place and time.

An intriguing play on the Greek term *oikonomia* occurs in this passage. The word appears three times in Ephesians, at 1:10; 3:2; and 3:9. The author probably drew the term from Colossians 1:25. The NRSV translates the term in 3:2 as "commission." This is certainly correct. It is the same meaning the term has in Colossians and is the common meaning for it in the New Testament. Paul has been given a commission, an assignment that he must carry out. However, in 1:10 and 3:9 "commission" would be awkward, and consequently the NRSV translates the same term as "plan," which is a common meaning of the term in non-Christian and Christian literature outside the New Testament. Thus we appear to have a conscious joining of God's plan and Paul's commission in it, by way of the dual meaning of *oikonomia*. Paul has an *oikonomia* in God's *oikonomia*. God's great management of the cosmos includes many commissions given to the church. Paul's is highlighted here, but it will be only one of them.

In a subtle way the powerful cosmic battle that forms the background of the famous exhortation in Ephesians 6:10–20 is anticipated in 3:10. The gospel is being proclaimed to the cosmic powers hostile to God. With the revelation of the great mystery and its proclamation by the church, a great contest begins between the power of God for salvation and the powers of the cosmos for death. As Ephesians 6:12 notes, the enemies of the Christian are not composed of flesh and blood. And it is the proclamation of the gospel that initiates the conflict. The gospel proclaims that Christ is above all and that all things will be unified in him. This is a prediction of the fall and doom of all other powers.

Christian fascination with the power of the spoken word is reflected in these verses. Throughout our history we have often claimed that true gospel speech overthrows all evil powers, even those of sin and death. More than any other major religion, Christianity has emphasized the power of the spoken word. With our voices, at least our gospel voices, we can create truth where there is none. In fact, without our voices the truth remains hidden and even unreal. It is in our speaking the gospel that the gospel exists. Thus our preachers and our preaching have been understood as the very center of our lives. We cannot be Christian unless we speak and hear the gospel. Of course, not any speech qualifies as gospel, no matter what the intentions of the speaker. The gospel must be apostolic.

Furthermore, engaging this gospel puts one at war with the powers of the world. Thus it is fitting that this passage begins by noting that Paul is a prisoner and ends by reminding the readers of the necessity of suffering. This wonderful gospel story, when taken on as one's own, brings warfare, suffering, and prison with it. The cosmic and political powers, all the worldly forces, will attack you. Your defense is, first, to cleave fast to the apostolic gospel. The author of Ephesians says more on this later.

PRAYER FOR THE READERS
Ephesians 3:14–21

> 3:14 **For this reason I bow my knees before the Father, [15] from whom every family in heaven and on earth takes its name. [16] I pray that, according to the riches of his glory, he may grant that you may be strengthened in your inner being with power through his Spirit, [17] and that Christ may dwell in your hearts through faith, as you are being rooted and grounded in love. [18] I pray that you may have the power to comprehend, with all the saints, what is the breadth and length and height and depth, [19] and to know the love of Christ that surpasses knowledge, so that you may be filled with all the fullness of God.**
>
> [20] **Now to him who by the power at work within us is able to accomplish abundantly far more than all we can ask or imagine, [21] to him be glory in the church and in Christ Jesus to all generations, forever and ever. Amen.**

This magnificent little prayer brings the first half of Ephesians to a ringing conclusion and sets the tone for the exhortations that follow. It also looks back on the rest of the letter, calling forth a variety of theological images that have been detailed in earlier passages. It thereby summarizes what has preceded, but does so in terms of a prayer for the complete realization in the readers of the many blessings of God, for which God was blessed in 1:3–14.

The author connects the prayer to what has preceded with the brief phrase "for this reason." He began Paul's autobiographical statement in 3:1 with the same phrase. Many commentators see this repetition as another indication that the Pauline autobiography was an interruption. Thus, here he is taking up the prayer he began above. However, 3:1 connects the phrase "for this reason" with Paul's imprisonment. Thus we probably have a new beginning, and 3:1–13 is part of the "reason" for the prayer. Consequently, "for this reason" means not only "for reason of the wonders of the mystery which have been detailed above," but also "for reason that my commission is for you Gentiles to enjoy the promised blessings of God."

The prayer itself begins with a statement of belonging: "I bow my knees before the Father, from whom every family in heaven and on earth takes its name" (3:14–15). There is a connection in the Greek between father *(patēr)* and family *(patria)* that cannot be rendered in English. We also lack an adequate word in English for *patria*, which means the entire line of relatives descended from a given father. The image is, in any case, clear; we belong to God's family, no matter what our race, clan, or tribe. This sense of belonging was the main point of 2:11–22, where we become "members of God's household." Thus the prayer begins by calling upon one of the great assurances of the gospel: We belong to God; it is as though we were members of God's own household.

Our sense of this belonging comes, first, from the miracle of God's presence. The mystical core of the theology of Ephesians is indicated here. The gospel is not mere words, it is language coupled to a divine act. As noted in 1:13–14, the Holy Spirit is the pledge of our inheritance; it is the proof that we belong to God. Thus the author prays in 3:16 that "you may be strengthened in your inner being with power through his Spirit." Christians partake of the power of God that works in Christ. It is ours through the Spirit. The linkage of the Spirit to Christ, which pervades this letter, emerges again in 3:17. Another way of praying for the power of the Spirit is to pray "that Christ may dwell in your hearts." The power of God for salvation exists only in Christ, and we partake of God's power only as we are connected to this Christ. We must be in Christ, and Christ must live in us.

The idea of strengthening adds something new to what we have seen thus far in Ephesians. So much of Ephesians 1—3 has emphasized the completed nature of salvation. We already sit with Christ in the heavenly places (2:6). But here there is a hint of the necessity of progress. We need strengthening; we grow, increase, and develop. Obviously, this sense of progress and development sets the stage for the focus on ethics that follows. We are now placed on a moral journey that takes effort. The sense of becoming strong in the Christian life will pervade the next three chapters.

Paul also prays for the readers to have knowledge, or, as he says it, "the power to comprehend" (3:18). We have noted many times the need for the acquisition of knowledge of the gospel.

Paul prays that the readers have the power to comprehend and "to know the love of Christ that surpasses knowledge" (3:19). Love, at least love anchored in Christ, exceeds what the mind can grasp. In this brief phrase the author states what becomes a persistent Christian theme: Love is the highest order. The author restates the theme of 1 Corinthians 13: Knowledge is wonderful and necessary, but without love it is nothing. Again, we have a hint here of how deeply embedded some of Paul's ideas are in the mind of this writer. This is someone who is doing his theology out of an immersion in the letters of Paul.

Noting that love surpasses knowledge makes a potent introduction to the exhortation to love that follows. Nevertheless, we must admit that even if love is the highest order, knowledge of the gospel is necessary for salvation. We must hear, learn, and proclaim the gospel, and we must live the moral life that comes from being in Christ.

Finally, the author concludes the first half of his letter with one of the most famous benedictions in all of Christianity. Its role here is, first, to emphasize our security, to assure us of God's capacity to save us. Of course, it adds a fitting liturgical ending to the great liturgical and theological meditations of Ephesians 1—3.

UNITY IN THE BODY OF CHRIST
Ephesians 4:1–16

4:1 I therefore, the prisoner in the Lord, beg you to lead a life worthy of the calling to which you have been called, 2 with all humility and gentleness, with patience, bearing with one another in love, 3 making every effort to maintain the unity of the Spirit in the bond of peace. 4 There is one body and one Spirit, just as you were called to the one hope of your calling, 5 one Lord, one faith, one baptism, 6 one God and Father of all, who is above all and through all and in all.

7 But each of us was given grace according to the measure of Christ's gift. 8 Therefore it is said,

"When he ascended on high he made captivity itself a captive;
he gave gifts to his people."

9 (When it says, "He ascended," what does it mean but that he had also descended into the lower parts of the earth? 10 He who descended is the same one who ascended far above all the heavens, so that he might fill all things.) 11 The gifts he gave were that some would be apostles, some prophets, some evangelists, some pastors and teachers, 12 to equip the saints for the work of ministry, for building up the body of Christ, 13 until all of us come to the unity of the faith and of the knowledge of the Son of God, to

maturity, to the measure of the full stature of Christ. [14] We must no longer be children, tossed to and fro and blown about by every wind of doctrine, by people's trickery, by their craftiness in deceitful scheming. [15] But speaking the truth in love, we must grow up in every way into him who is the head, into Christ, [16] from whom the whole body, joined and knit together by every ligament with which it is equipped, as each part is working properly, promotes the body's growth in building itself up in love.

The cosmic plan to unite all things in Christ receives at this point its first application to the ethical life of the believing community. Whereas 2:11–22 applied the theme of unification to the relationship of Jews and Gentiles, here we encounter an exhortation that could be made to any church community, whether composed of Jews or Gentiles or both. The author takes two basic tacks: first, to emphasize the oneness of Christ, and second, to exhort the kind of moral virtues that promote a harmonious community.

The opening verse in 4:1 echoes the Pauline autobiography in 3:1–13 with the designation of Paul as "the prisoner of the Lord," and it picks up the classic Pauline language of calling: "lead a life worthy of the calling to which you have been called." The early Christian sense of having been called out from their former lives to a new life, with new duties, is suggested here. It is effective language for the beginning of an exhortation. But in 4:2–3 the heart of the exhortation is given.

Love and Unity

Two pleas are given: first, bear with one another in love, and, second, maintain the unity of the Spirit. These are interdependent. The direct entreaty to "make every effort to maintain the unity of the Spirit in the bond of peace" (4:3) reflects the overall purpose of the unification of all things in Christ. We must recall here the many references to peace and unity that have preceded this verse, especially in 2:11–22. Christ makes peace; in fact, "he is our peace" (2:14). Thus the call to maintain the unity of the Spirit in the bond of peace evokes not only personal effort but the christological ground of the effort. Christ is the author of peace. Thus the reference to peace anticipates the christological references that follow in 4:4–6. But the precise meaning of the ambiguous phrase the "unity of the Spirit" is not explained until 4:11–16.

At this point, the key image is love. The unity and harmony of the Christian community depends upon the capacity of Christians to love one another. Thus this unity is not merely theoretical, as though God views all these bickering Christians as one in spite of themselves. No,

Christ-based unity shows itself in love, in putting up with each other. The classic Christian virtues of humility, gentleness, and patience are evoked here as attendants to the love that unites the community. It is scarcely possible to conceive traditional Christian ethics apart from these gentle virtues. It is important to note that humility and gentleness (it could be translated meekness) are not valued in themselves, but as the accompanying mood to love. Our love, our submission to each other, is not done with bravado or applause, but with humility. There is a quietness to Christian love that is necessary to its character.

The christological grounding of this ethic is established in 4:4–6. The theme of one body, which leads the litany of one Lord, one faith, one baptism, one God, evokes the one-body imagery of 2:16, where Jews and Gentiles become unified and reconciled by Christ into one body. In fact, the two passages mirror one another to a considerable extent. Both use language of peace, unity, and oneness. Both point to Christ and the dynamics between Christ and the community as the key. Note that both passages end with complementary images of the community growing out of the unifying power of the spirit of Christ. It is as though one theological insight, that Christ is one and that all things will be unified in him, is applied in turn, first, to the Jew/Gentile question, and, second, to the general diversity and disagreement in the community. In both cases, the answer to disharmony is the unifying power of the spirit of Christ. Thus the evocative piling up of images of oneness in 4:4–6 has more than an emotional function, although it may have that. It gives the theological logic to the ethic.

The Gifts of Grace

In 4:7 the argument shifts in an interesting way. The section begins with a classic Pauline image: "each of us was given grace according to the measure of Christ's gift." Romans 12:3, 12:6, and 1 Corinthians 12:7 are combined here in order to initiate a discussion of diversity in the community. Paul himself had used this language for the same purpose. Ephesians then offers a quote from Psalm 68:18, which might be better termed a misquote. In Psalm 68, the Lord receives but does not give the gifts. Many suggestions for this error have been offered, from the possibility that the writer has a different text of the psalm to the possibility that he is quoting from a faulty memory. Perhaps it is instructive to note how frequently such misquoting occurred in both Jewish and Christian circles in the ancient world. In any case, Psalm 68 works here only if the Lord is the giver and not the receiver.

The identification of the captives in the first part of the verse is unknown. They may be the cosmic powers who have become subject to Christ. It also may be the case that the author himself has no opinion on their identity, for his purpose is the giving of gifts in the second part of the quote. And yet 4:9–10 elaborates in a curious way upon the idea of ascension. The one who ascended is the one who first descended (some Greek texts even add the word *first*). The significance of this descending and ascending is no surprise: "so that he might fill all things." Just as it is unclear exactly where he ascended, it is unclear where he descended. Some commentators perceive a simple reference to the incarnation; thus, he descended to earth. Others see a reference to Christ's descent into hell, which is described in 1 Peter 3:19. The author seems uninterested in such precision; his point is to underline the universality of Christ's reign.

In any case, Christ gives gifts, and in the giving the great unifier creates a new diversity. This is an important point. It is often argued that Paul, and here Ephesians, uses the body imagery to argue that Christ takes our diverse natural gifts and creates a new unity out of them. It would be as though we bring our talents to the church and, through the power of the Spirit, Christ molds them into the miraculous unity that is the church. That may be a true insight, but that is not the point in Paul nor in Ephesians. Rather, the unified body needs diversity in order to function. Thus Christ apportions diverse gifts to the community. Note what the gifts are; some are apostles, some prophets, evangelists, pastors, teachers (Paul's list in 1 Corinthians 12:28 differs slightly). One does not bring apostleship to the community from outside, as though one could be born with the status; rather, apostleship grows out of the needs of the body, out of the powers of the Spirit. It is the same for all the gifts enumerated here.

The list in Ephesians, in contrast to Paul's list, is confined to persons in leadership roles. The reason for this becomes clear in 4:12; leaders are established by Christ "to equip the saints for the work of ministry, for building up the body of Christ." The ultimate goal is the upbuilding of the entire body, which in turn does the larger ministry of Christ. But leaders have a special role, for they are the foundation of the community (2:20). There is perhaps the faintest beginning here of the growing distinction between ordained clergy and laity. This distinction, which becomes so important in later church polity, emerges even more in the Pastoral Epistles.

At this point, verses 13 and 14 return to the theme of unity. Christ's gift of such leaders enables us to acquire the "unity of the faith and of the knowledge of the Son of God." The unity of faith appears, at this point, to be doctrinal, for 4:14 warns against the dangers of heresy. We must note, however, that the reference to "the measure of the full stature of Christ" points to the mystical core of the Christian life, the miracle of Christ's presence, without which knowledge is not knowledge.

The Body of Christ

The section runs to a wonderful, poetic conclusion in 4:15–16. The body imagery, taken from Paul and developed in 2:16, is here used to depict the miracle of Christian unity and diversity. Readers have long noted the slight shift from the Pauline imagery in which Christ is the whole body. In Ephesians, the community is the body and Christ is the head. This shift fits with the emphasis in Ephesians on the exaltation of Christ. We live out the power of the Christ who is at the right hand of God. This exalted Christ unifies, diversifies, and coordinates the life of the community. Of course, in the rhythm of Ephesians, the community that is thus ordered builds itself up in love. The exaltation of Christ, the unification in Christ, and the life of love are part of the same story. Thus the call to live a life worthy of our calling is grounded in this passage in three things: Christ, knowledge, and love.

The challenge of this passage for us is identical to what it was for first-century Christians. We must take these theological truths to heart. We who are in Christ must seek unity. We must love each other out of the power of the Spirit. It is true that this cannot be done without the divine power that comes in Christ. Belief is not simply belief in an idea but submission to a living Lord. And this Lord wants and demands love and unity. Christ is creating unity at the cosmic level and the human level. This means we must love each other.

There is no map for how love is to be accomplished. The world is too complex for love to take one form. Love requires the creativity of human insight and commitment so that it can find its way into the intricacies of life. Of course, as Ephesians reminds us, no human attempt at love can succeed unless the spirit of Christ guides it.

THE OLD LIFE AND THE NEW
Ephesians 4:17–24

4:17 Now this I affirm and insist on in the Lord: you must no longer live as the Gentiles live, in the futility of their minds. [18] They are darkened in their understanding, alienated from the life of God because of their ignorance and

hardness of heart. [19] They have lost all sensitivity and have abandoned themselves to licentiousness, greedy to practice every kind of impurity. [20] That is not the way you learned Christ! [21] For surely you have heard about him and were taught in him, as truth is in Jesus. [22] You were taught to put away your former way of life, your old self, corrupt and deluded by its lusts, [23] and to be renewed in the spirit of your minds, [24] and to clothe yourselves with the new self, created according to the likeness of God in true righteousness and holiness.

So much of early Christian ethics has the character of turning from the past and turning toward the future. In Gentile communities, this is normally couched as turning from the Gentile way of life to the Christian one. It is no surprise, given the apparent Gentile profile of the audience in Ephesians, that this is the language used here. Paul himself used similar language in 1 Thessalonians 1:9–10. Furthermore, Ephesians has established in 2:11–22 that Gentiles were cut off from the household of God and its blessings. Only as a new creature, as neither Gentile nor Jew, can anyone have access to these blessings.

Whereas 4:1–16 encouraged behavior conducive to unity, here the focus is broader. The overall moral character of the Christian life is described in this passage and those that follow. Whereas love will remain the principle virtue, others will be added. Of course, not only are virtues added, vices are also subtracted.

Putting Off the Old Self

The characterization of the Gentile life given here comes largely from Romans 1:21–24, but the description fits nicely with the general theological views of Ephesians. The precise character of the negatives is important. First, given the importance to the author of correct knowledge of the gospel, the ignorance of Gentiles, which is highlighted here, means they are cut off from salvation. Their minds deceive them, because they do not know the gospel. Ephesians is arguing that for the orthodox Christian knowledge is a source of guidance, comfort, and hope. Knowledge leads to virtue. For the non-Christian or the heretics, their false knowledge is a source of darkness, which leads to vice. Second, the hardness of their heart, their insensitivity, means they cannot love. Third, all this leads to the practice of sexual immorality. We do not have in Ephesians the extended discussion of fornication that we find in Paul, but that is probably because the author simply assumes that fornication is evil. Early Christianity is striking for its strict sexual mores. The only permissible sexual activity was between husband and wife; all else is fornication. And, as Ephesians 5:5 reminds its readers, no fornicator will have a place in the kingdom. This high sexual standard prepares us for the fascinating discussion of the relationship between husband and wife in 5:22–33.

By using these standard Pauline images, the author describes alienation from "the life of God" (4:18) as one of ignorance, hardheartedness, and fornication. These will be balanced by true knowledge of the gospel, love, and sexual fidelity. Thus, whereas 2:11–22 described the theological status of the Gentile alienated from the household of God, 4:17–19 describes the moral state of those who are thus alienated. Consequently, the conclusion given here is that, if your status has changed, your morals must change as well.

This leads to the curious language of 4:20–22: "That is not the way you *learned* Christ! For surely you have heard about him and were *taught* in him, as truth is in Jesus." To "learn Christ" is a curious phrase that is as awkward in the Greek as in English.

We must imagine here some kind of catechetical process that the author can assume his readers have experienced. It is sometimes argued that the combination of liturgical language and catechetical style indicates a baptismal context. Ephesians is imagined as a baptismal homily. This is an interesting and understandable proposal, but we probably cannot be so precise. Catechesis, in any event, occurred in many places besides the circumstances of baptism. The author and his church community have been about the task of teaching. They have taught each other both the cosmic and ethical truths of the gospel. To learn Christ is to learn what virtues belong to the Christian life.

We noted in Colossians that the great mystery of salvation is moral, or at least part of the great mystery is moral. If anything, Ephesians insists even more forcefully that morality and immorality are ultimate questions. Ethics is not incidental to the Christian life, something added on to salvation. If one becomes a citizen with the saints, a member of the household of God, one must live the righteous life. Thus the old life must be put away, the life when one was alienated from God, and the new life, life in the body of Christ, must be put on.

Putting On the New Self

This is not to say that one enters the household of God by first putting on righteousness. The formulations of 4:23–24 are clear about this; righteousness is created by God and is given to us. The readers are to clothe themselves with the new self, which is "created according to the likeness of God in true righteousness and holiness" (4:24). God creates a righteous and holy person who is given to us. Righteousness begins with the creative act of God, not with human efforts or human dreams. On the other hand, this is a human event; we are not talking about non-earthly, nonhistorical, God-confined righteousness. God does not turn us into little gods but into righteous human beings. God creates a righteous and holy person for us. In 4:22 and 4:24 the NRSV translates the Greek *anthropos* as "self." The word means person, human being. Thus we are to put off the old person and put on the new person. In fact, the spirit in 4:23 is probably referring to the human spirit rather than the divine. As we put on the God-created new human self, our human spirits will be continuously renewed.

The theological balance established in this is significant, for it reflects the normal Christian claim. On the one hand, all righteousness must emerge from God's own being. All righteousness is a reflection of God's righteousness. And in one sense God is the ultimate cause of all righteousness and holiness. On the other hand, righteousness involves real humans and real human deeds. It is caught up in the messiness of history and the confusion of human values. It involves good and bad moral behavior. Thus the exhortation to put off the old self and put on the new self created by God must be coupled with mundane imperatives to do this and not do that. The everyday moral imperatives of 4:25–5:2 do not represent a descent from the lofty theology of 4:22–24. Rather, they represent the actuality, the coming-into-being, of that theology. The great cosmic story of salvation is accepted or rejected in choices of whether to lie and steal, whether to be hateful or loving. There is no gospel story without this moral anchor.

RULES FOR THE NEW LIFE
Ephesians 4:25–5:2

4:25 **So then, putting away falsehood, let all of us speak the truth to our neighbors, for we are members of one another. 26 Be angry but do not sin; do not let the sun go down on your anger, 27 and do not make room for the devil. 28 Thieves must give up stealing; rather let them labor and work honestly with their own hands, so as to have something to share with the needy. 29 Let no evil talk come out of your mouths, but only what is useful for building up, as there is need, so that your words may give grace to those who hear. 30 And do not grieve the Holy Spirit of God, with which you were marked with a seal for the day of redemption. 31 Put away from you all**

bitterness and wrath and anger and wrangling and slander, together with all malice, [32] and be kind to one another, tenderhearted, forgiving one another, as God in Christ has forgiven you.

5:1 Therefore be imitators of God, as beloved children, [2] and live in love, as Christ loved us and gave himself up for us, a fragrant offering and sacrifice to God.

Although this passage presents details and specifics of the Christian life, it does not lay out a full ethical program. Instead we find a brief series of imperatives that do little more than suggest the full character of this new life. This is, no doubt, because of the insistence that "love" is the primary and singular characteristic of the Christian life, and that the specifics of how love is actualized are nearly infinite. Thus we should think of 4:32–5:2 as providing an effective conclusion to this section and a summary of the Christian moral life, for in those verses love and forgiveness are again highlighted as the moral key to new life.

This means that we should not attempt to oversystematize or overgeneralize the initial set of imperatives in these verses. These are examples of Christian love, not a full account of it. Nevertheless, most readers have noticed the care with which the examples are chosen. This has not been done haphazardly.

Examples of Love

The exhortations are set up as a series of contrasts between bad and good behavior with a reason given for adopting the good. The language here repeats that of 4:22–24; put off this and put on that. Vice is not overcome through abstention but by replacing vice with virtue. The idea is less, do not do that, and more, quit doing that and start doing this. This pattern of putting off and putting on indicates an essential characteristic of traditional Christian morality. The Christian life is primarily seen through the deeds of the person and not through the spiritual state of the soul. It is not that the latter is of no concern; but it is true that, when the Christian life is described in the New Testament, the most common way is through the moral deeds of the believer. Thus we are not exhorted to remove ourselves from the troubles of the world, as though peace through disconnectedness and self-sufficiency were the goal. Rather, we are exhorted to take on the troubles of the world, of the community, and to create social peace through love. Love, of course, is not a painless emotion. The Greek ideal of tranquillity is not a part of early Christianity. Love is a troublesome enterprise. In fact, as Paul's example showed in 3:1–13, the Christian life is normally connected to suffering.

The first imperative is to put away (or put off) falsehood and speak the truth. Given the importance of knowledge and the dangers of a false gospel, it is fitting that the list begin here. The foundation of the Christian life and of the community is truth, the spoken truth. As we all know, there is no community, there are no constructive relationships, where lies have bred mistrust. Yet it is not the case that truth and truth alone can create community. Love, compassion, and forgiveness are necessary for that.

Nearly all readers have insisted that the apparent imperative "be angry" is not really advising anger. Rather, it is conceding the reality of anger and trying to put a lid on it. Yes, you will get angry, but when you do, "do not let the sun go down on your anger" (4:26). This is commonplace advice in the ancient world; both Gentiles and Jews were worried about destructive passions. However, in Ephesians giving in to anger is connected to letting in the devil. This sense of fighting with the devil obviously anticipates the larger discussion in 6:10–17 of how to fight the devil. The image of the devil in both passages is of an active, evil agent who is looking for opportunities. You can only resist by means of divine weapons. Only the power of God in Christ can resist the devil.

The modern preference for depersonalizing evil is not present in the New Testament. The early Christians shared the common belief of both Jews and Gentiles that all kinds of evil demigods were working in the world. In the New Testament the leader of the demons is called by various names: Beelzebul, Satan, and the devil. But only in Revelation is there a sustained attempt to identify who the devil is and how he is to be recognized. Elsewhere in the New Testament, this evil personage is simply assumed. Outside of the Beelzebul passages in the gospels and the book of Revelation, the most thorough analysis of evil cosmic powers comes in Colossians and Ephesians. Ephesians is largely dependent on Colossians, although Ephesians 6:10–17 will add a few twists.

The advice to thieves strikes most readers as curious. Of course, it is no surprise that ex-thieves were part of the Christian community. It seems that early Christians came more often from low status groups in the ancient world than from high status. But the advice seems so unnecessary. Some readers have speculated that the negative feelings of many Christians toward the Roman world may have led to tolerance of illegal acts. But there is no real evidence for that. Some fringe Gnostic Christians apparently downplayed the importance of morality. But this was rare, and Gnostics were typically more stringent in their morality than were the orthodox. It is more likely that some people needed to be convinced of the value of strict Jewish and Christian ethical standards. The high moral standards expected of early Christians was not what these Christians had been practicing. Thus they had to learn the conservative morality of early

Christianity. Of course, many Gentiles would have brought high moral standards with them into the new community of Christians. For them, this would seem obvious. In some ways, only the radical nature of forgiveness and tolerance separates Christian morality from the best ethical teaching in the ancient world.

It is important, therefore, to note the reason that thieves should work: "so as to have something to share with the needy" (4:28). The needs of the community are what drives Christian ethics. Love is the primary good. Thieves should work because it is the loving thing to do. Again, notice that the argument is not given that hard work is good for the soul, that it creates private virtue. Instead, hard work creates the capacity of the community members to care for one another.

The exhortation to avoid evil talk and pursue words that give grace fits within this same perspective. In language, as in all things, pursue the good of the community. We should recall 2:19–22 and 4:15–16, where the new life is described as a complicated community life, wherein we are all connected to and dependent upon one another, and where our task is to build up not ourselves but the whole body of Christ.

Readers have long wondered what the author means by grieving the Holy Spirit (4:30). More than likely 4:31 is intended to illustrate how Christians can do that. They grieve the Spirit by engaging in vices that harm the unity of the body. Bitterness, wrath, anger, wrangling, slander, these are all aspects of human behavior that violate the peace and harmony of a community. It is again the health of the community that has priority. We have the power to grieve God's Spirit. This Spirit hurts when Christians harm the body of Christ.

Imitation of God

The wonderful summary of Christian ethics in 4:32–5:2 is built upon the notion of people imitating God. As God is loving, as God is forgiving, as God creates community, so should the people of God be and do. People who live in God's household, who are seated at the right hand of God, should behave toward other humans as God behaves toward them. This is probably what it means in Ephesians to be holy, to be a saint (a holy one). All holiness is God's holiness; thus we who are the holy ones of God must show forth some of the being of God. In the New Testament the being of God is not discussed in itself, as it will be in later theology; rather, God's being is displayed in God's deeds. And here we find a delightful account of how God loves.

Thus believers do not become like God in the sense that God's inner being and theirs are alike. Instead, believers imitate God's loving behavior. Thus we are not Godlike in our knowledge, in our sinlessness, in our power, but only in our love. Furthermore, this passage reiterates the constant New Testament refrain about love: It is not so much a feeling, although it does involve the heart; it is deeds of sacrifice for others, the perfect model of which is Jesus dying on the cross for us.

It is also likely that the larger theme of unity is in play here as well. We have noted that it is unity that Jesus' death accomplishes. And the main purpose of love may also be unity, of people with God and with one another. Thus love unifies on the cosmic level and the social, historical level. Just as God's love in Christ has unified the cosmos and has unified Jew and Gentile, so Christ's love working through us will unify the body of Christ. God unifies not by force but by compassion, forgiveness, and grace. Churches find unity not through power and arrogance but through forgiveness, tenderness, and compassion. The ultimate power in the universe, according to Ephesians, is that power at work in Christ to unify all things in him. This means that love is the most potent force in the world, even though it often does not seem to us to be so.

RENOUNCE PAGAN WAYS AND LIVE
AS CHILDREN OF LIGHT
Ephesians 5:3–20

5:3 But fornication and impurity of any kind, or greed, must not even be mentioned among you, as is proper among saints. 4 Entirely out of place is obscene, silly, and vulgar talk; but instead, let there be thanksgiving. 5 Be sure of this, that no fornicator or impure person, or one who is greedy (that is, an idolater), has any inheritance in the kingdom of Christ and of God.

6 Let no one deceive you with empty words, for because of these things the wrath of God comes on those who are disobedient. 7 Therefore do not be associated with them. 8 For once you were darkness, but now in the Lord you are light. Live as children of light—9 for the fruit of the light is found in all that is good and right and true. 10 Try to find out what is pleasing to the Lord. 11 Take no part in the unfruitful works of darkness, but instead expose them. 12 For it is shameful even to mention what such people do secretly; 13 but everything exposed by the light becomes visible, 14 for everything that becomes visible is light. Therefore it says,
"Sleeper, awake! Rise from the dead,
and Christ will shine on you."

[15] Be careful then how you live, not as unwise people but as wise, [16] making the most of the time, because the days are evil. [17] So do not be foolish, but understand what the will of the Lord is. [18] Do not get drunk with wine, for that is debauchery; but be filled with the Spirit, [19] as you sing psalms and hymns and spiritual songs among yourselves, singing and making melody to the Lord in your hearts, [20] giving thanks to God the Father at all times and for everything in the name of our Lord Jesus Christ.

After the magnificent appeal in 4:31–5:2, it is somewhat surprising that the author chooses to rehearse again some of the unpleasant details of the immoral life. But such is the character of most ethical exhortation in early Christian literature; it is rarely systematic and carefully ordered. Instead, it is evocative, repetitive, and frequented by highs and lows. This is true for most moral exhortation; it wants to persuade and energize, not simply to make a logical point. Given this, it is understandable that commentators on Ephesians have been unable to determine a clear ordering principle for chapters 4—6. On the other hand, the theological and ethical themes are consistent, and the exhortation has a clear theological logic.

In these verses the author takes up the metaphor of light and darkness to elucidate the moral dilemma of believers. This was a common metaphor in antiquity in moral discourse, especially in religious moral discourse. The most extensive and closest parallel outside of the New Testament is found in the Dead Sea Scrolls at Qumran. But there is probably no historical connection between Ephesians and Qumran. In any case, the light/darkness motif occurs elsewhere in the New Testament, most notably in the Johannine literature. John uses the light imagery almost identically to Ephesians. The light is God's light, which shines upon us and enlightens us; and then we, with this new insight, become light to others. Darkness refers to the realm of ignorance, vice, and death. Because Ephesians places high value on knowledge and understanding, while at the same time holding to the necessity of a real presence of Christ in the life of the community, the light metaphor is a natural. It enables the author to combine notions of knowledge, virtue, and the power of God. However, as we will see, the metaphor does not work perfectly.

Christian Sexual Ethics

It is no surprise that fornication is the leading vice in this passage. As I noted earlier, early Christianity pursued a rigorous sexual ethic, and it consistently condemned fornication. The Greek *porneia*, translated here as fornication, refers in the New Testament to any copulation that is not between husband and wife. Although most Jewish literature shares this strict ethic and occasionally a Greek or Roman moralist will come close to this, this high standard would have required significant changes in the sexual mores of most Gentiles. But in mainstream Christianity, including both the New Testament and the writings of the early church fathers, and in most Gnostic groups, this high standard is maintained.

Sexual sins were seen as having a unique power. Both the teachings of Jesus and the letters of Paul employ the Jewish reading of Genesis 2:24, wherein sexual activity makes two persons one. The act of copulation was understood by early Christians as having the power to create unity. Thus copulation between husband and wife assisted God's intentions for them. But copulation between others could create a unity contrary to God's intentions. Thus adultery breaks the proper unity between husband and wife, and establishes a unity contrary to the marriage unity. Paul can insist that, when a member of the body of Christ fornicates with a sexually immoral person, the body of Christ itself becomes united to the fornicator (1 Cor. 6:12–20). This distinctive power to create social unity made the sex act something to be treated with special care. The high sexual ethic of early Christianity becomes one of its most distinguishing features. Paul can even summarize the moral life of the Christian as, first, avoiding fornication, and, second, loving one another (1 Thess. 4:1–12). Obviously, the full justification for this sexual ethic is not given in Ephesians. Rather, it is assumed, and this exhortation comes as a reminder.

The Dangers of Vice

"Impurity" and "greed" (5:3, 5) are sometimes seen as indirect references to fornication. It is true that early Christianity could use these terms to designate improper sexual activity and its results. However, there is no reason to assume such a precise limitation of these terms in this passage. The reference to proper and improper language indicates that more than sexuality is being considered here. It is more likely that we are dealing with a typical vice list. Impurity can refer to a whole range of acts contrary to religious law. Greed is a classic Jewish metaphor for idolatry. The reason is obvious. Any*thing* that one desires wholeheartedly becomes one's god and replaces the real God. Thus it is more likely that the vices chosen here are representative not exhaustive. They recall all the vices of the Gentile life.

The warning in 5:5 should be taken at face value. "No fornicator or impure person, or one who is greedy . . . , has any inheritance in the kingdom of Christ and of God." This warning is reinforced in 5:6. God will judge us all according to the morality and immorality of our lives. There is no gospel salvation apart from ethics. The good news and the good life are inseparable.

The argument of Ephesians is not that vice brings with it its own punishment nor that virtue is its own reward. These are potent and influential Stoic ideas, but they are not shared by Ephesians. It is God who makes vice into darkness and virtue into light. It is God's wrath that punishes vice, not the forces of history or the terrors of one's own psychology. Virtue does not place one into the presence of God. Rather, God's wrath makes vice a curse, and God's grace makes virtue both a reality and a blessing.

You Are Light

The simple metaphors of 5:8, "once you were darkness, but now in the Lord you are light," articulate the moral and spiritual dimensions of the new life. You were darkness, you are light; not—you were once in darkness, but now you are in light. This stark metaphor occurs in the same form in the Sermon on the Mount (Matt. 5:14): "You are the light of the world." And the admonition to "live as children of light" (5:8) occurs, somewhat differently, in John 12:36. To be children of light, to be light itself, was language familiar to early Christians. The question is, What does it mean in Ephesians?

The following verses explain. First, the author points to the moral dimension: "the fruit of the light is found in all that is good and right and true" (5:9). The writer is not trying to explain the details of the Christian ethic in these verses, but to evoke images of the Christian moral life in its basic character. There is also a sense here of enlightenment. The gospel is light in that it brings knowledge. Thus the believer should "try to find out what is pleasing to the Lord" (5:10). The light teaches what is proper behavior, and that behavior in turn is a light to others.

The capacity of this light to expose darkness as darkness is introduced as a warning. This warning may represent, in some sense, a vindication for the believers; the evil of nonbelievers will be exposed by the light of judgment. But it seems more to represent a reminder to believers that all deeds of darkness will be exposed. Thus light becomes identified with God's perfect righteousness. When it shines upon you, it produces righteousness in your life. When you sin, this light of righteousness will expose your deeds as darkness.

The little note in 5:14 that "everything that becomes visible is light" has proven awkward for commentators, because it is clearly not true. In fact, when light shines upon dark deeds, it does not turn them into light, but exposes them as darkness. However, the image is not intended to contradict the preceding verses, but to prepare for the call to sleeping believers. Believers who live as children of light become light, for the light of God's righteousness shines from them.

Many commentators have wondered whether the call to the sleeper in 5:14 is not a fragment from early Christian baptismal liturgy. The idea of awaking, rising from the dead, and letting Christ shine upon you fits nicely with early theology of baptism. Furthermore, the phrase "it says" indicates a quote of some kind, even if we do not know what "it" is. The "it" could be scripture, but we cannot find such a quote in extant scripture, including texts not in our Bible. The "it" in Greek could also be a "he" or "she," perhaps God or Christ himself. The origin of this verse remains a mystery even if its function in Ephesians is clear: If you are a child of light, then awaken from darkness and let Christ shine upon you. The christological anchor of all ethics in Ephesians is reiterated here. Truly said, Christ is the real light, even if, in a metaphorical flourish, you who are in Christ are light with him.

The return in 5:15 to the warning to live correctly indicates again that calling someone light is not to declare them light no matter what they do. They do not define the light. The light defines them. Thus, when their deeds are not of the light, they are not of the light either.

Commentators have long wondered over the admonition to make the most of the time, for the days are evil. The Greek word that the NRSV translates as "make the most of" means to "buy" or "buy back." What does it mean to purchase time? And what does "the days are evil" mean? Perhaps the latter reflects early Christian despair over the evil of the created world. But this does not seem to be the worldview of Ephesians. Perhaps it is better to imagine the normal cynicism of all generations toward life. Thus this is proverbial evil, for use in exhortation; it is not a theological statement on the status of time. In any case, the notion that we should purchase or buy back or make the most of time, for the days are evil, fits nicely with the general exhortation in these verses. Time and your life in it will not produce on its own the moral life; you must shake righteous deeds out of moments of your life that do not want them. It is a battle. The great warfare outlined in 6:10–20 is anticipated here. Good things must be pulled with great effort out of a human life that is being attacked by evil powers. The days are evil because there are evil cosmic forces loose in them. Of course, believers, who have seen the light, who have seen the darkness for what it is, who have looked evil in the face and seen it as evil, know that Christ sits above all such powers and will, in time, unite all things. They have seen the end and thus can give thanks to God.

In using the contrast between the wise and foolish life, Ephesians takes up the singular most dominant theme in ancient philosophy. Greek philosophy can be defined, with only slight exaggeration, as an enormous attempt to distinguish the foolish life from the wise one. Ephesians adds nothing to those popular categories. The irony with which Paul himself uses wisdom language in 1 Corinthians is not present here. The wise person knows and does the will of God. No Greek or Jew would disagree. Of course, for the author of Ephesians, the will of God is known in Christ and in the gospel about Christ, and thus the wise person must be a Christian.

The contrast between becoming drunk and being filled with the Spirit recalls the same contrast in the Pentecost story (Acts 2:1–21). It recalls the christological center of the ethical life. It is not the case in Ephesians, nor in Pauline ethics in general, that Christ sets one free to be oneself. We are not set free from the powers of sin so that we can become what we always wanted to be. To be what you want to be is to be controlled by the passions and thus to be under sin. Rather, Christ gives us a choice of whose slave we will be. Will we be slaves of sin or slaves of Christ? There is no third choice. Thus the ethical life can be described as being filled with the Spirit. It is the Spirit which animates and directs our lives.

Ephesians 5:3–20 begins and ends with a reference to language. In some ways, this passage elucidates the distinction made in 4:25 between speaking falsehood and speaking the truth. Falsehood aligns us with the powers of darkness. Against darkness and falsehood we can speak the truth out of the power of the Spirit. Furthermore, the Spirit produces not only the true language of the orthodox gospel but the worship language of songs and thanksgiving. We are encouraged here to speak both to God and to one another in the spiritual language of worship. If the author had precise distinctions in mind among the terms *psalms*, *hymns*, and *spiritual songs*, we cannot be certain what they were. It is likely that psalms refers to Old Testament psalms, and that hymns and spiritual songs refer to early Christian hymns of some kind. But it is difficult to be more specific.

In any case, the basic point is clear enough: Christian language at its core is praise to God. The evocative language of worship gives birth to all Christian discourse. Thus all Christian conversation, whether it be worship, exhortation, proclamation, or teaching, is a species of praise to God. The letter itself serves as a fine example, for it is a poetic praise to God for God's blessings.

THE CHRISTIAN HOUSEHOLD
Ephesians 5:21–6:9

5:21 Be subject to one another out of reverence for Christ.

[22] Wives, be subject to your husbands as you are to the Lord. [23] For the husband is the head of the wife just as Christ is the head of the church, the body of which he is the Savior. [24] Just as the church is subject to Christ, so also wives ought to be, in everything, to their husbands.

[25] Husbands, love your wives, just as Christ loved the church and gave himself up for her, [26] in order to make her holy by cleansing her with the washing of water by the word, [27] so as to present the church to himself in splendor, without a spot or wrinkle or anything of the kind—yes, so that she may be holy and without blemish. [28] In the same way, husbands should love their wives as they do their own bodies. He who loves his wife loves himself. [29] For no one ever hates his own body, but he nourishes and tenderly cares for it, just as Christ does for the church, [30] because we are members of his body. [31] "For this reason a man will leave his father and mother and be joined to his wife, and the two will become one flesh." [32] This is a great mystery, and I am applying it to Christ and the church. [33] Each of you, however, should love his wife as himself, and a wife should respect her husband.

6:1 Children, obey your parents in the Lord, for this is right. [2] "Honor your father and mother"—this is the first commandment with a promise: [3] "so that it may be well with you and you may live long on the earth."

[4] And, fathers, do not provoke your children to anger, but bring them up in the discipline and instruction of the Lord.

[5] Slaves, obey your earthly masters with fear and trembling, in singleness of heart, as you obey Christ; [6] not only while being watched, and in order to please them, but as slaves of Christ, doing the will of God from the heart. [7] Render service with enthusiasm, as to the Lord and not to men and women, [8] knowing that whatever good we do, we will receive the same again from the Lord, whether we are slaves or free.

[9] And, masters, do the same to them. Stop threatening them, for you know that both of you have the same Master in heaven, and with him there is no partiality.

We come at this point to one of the most controversial passages in Ephesians and one of the most difficult for modern Christians. The controversy surrounds less what the passage means, for that seems to be reasonably clear, but more what to do with this passage in modern Christian life. The analysis of family life that is given here, which includes a clear pattern of dominance and submission, does not square with many modern Christians' perception of the ideal Christian family. Many Christians today insist that only some kind of egalitarian model, in which power is equally distributed, can properly inform the modern Christian family. But what we find in Ephesians is not egalitarian. We must admit that Ephesians argues for unequal distribution of authority, even if that authority is exercised in a tender and loving way.

Be Subject to One Another

The passage starts with a rather stunning egalitarian principle. It would be hard to find a principle for social ethics that levels all people more than the opening verse of this passage: "Be subject to one another out of reverence for Christ" (5:21). Most commentators understand this verse as the ethical principle upon which the household rules that follow are built. This is probably true, although the principle is not applied to its full potential.

The phrase "be subject to one another" is so radical that it is difficult to understand. The Greek verb translated as "be subject" is normally used when full authority is given by one person to another and when complete obedience becomes the rule. This does not mean "take account of one another" or "submit to the larger needs of the community." It means "give full authority and obedience to each other." Thus complete submission and vulnerability to the other is the norm. Power is never held by the "I" but is always ceded to the "other." Self-sufficiency, personal autonomy, and ethical independence are hereby excluded. Each person cedes power to whoever is the other. You always have power over me, and I over you. By all accounts, this is a stunning ethical ideal. Of course, it is too radical to be taken in its full implications. Instead, the author uses it to transform and modify the extant social structures of the ancient family. As most readers have noted, in spite of the high ideal of the opening verse, both male dominance and slavery remain intact.

Wives and Husbands

The core of the household rules in Ephesians comes from Colossians 3:18–4:1. The subtlety that the author of Colossians demonstrated in framing his exhortation is mostly lacking in Ephesians. There is less evidence of any nervousness about the role of the submissive partner and the dangers of absolutizing such a one-way power structure. This is apparent in the first line. Whereas Colossians stated, "Wives, be subject to your husbands, as is fitting in the Lord" (3:18), thereby clearly indicating the difference between the risen Lord and the earthly husband, Ephesians declares, "Wives, be subject to your husbands as you are to Lord" (5:22). In fact, Ephesians might well be translated "be subject to your husbands as if to the Lord." The NRSV wants to avoid the implication that a husband could in any way replace the Lord in the life of his wife. But even if the more circumspect translation that the NRSV prefers is correct, the wife is exhorted to be subject to her husband to the same extent as she is subject to the Lord. This is a significant modification of Colossians. And it is crucial for the logic of the passage, for it sets up the proper parallel in order to make the analogy of Christ/church and husband/wife work.

Ephesians 5:22 declares the basic analogy that drives 5:22–33: "For the husband is the head of the wife just as Christ is the head of the church." This analogy works in both directions. The marriage relationship explains certain dynamics in the relationship between Christ and the church, and certain parts of the Christ/church relationship are taken as a model for the marriage relationship. We can assume that the author started with the dynamics of marriage, for the basic genre of the passage is a household code and the author is using Colossians as his starting point. However, the analogy works in both directions. Although wives and husbands are exhorted to behave as the church and Christ, the peculiar unity of marriage explicates, in turn, the unity between Christ and the church.

The exhortation to the wife calls for complete submission. The restatement of the demand of 5:22 in 5:24 shows that the author wants to absolutize the submission of wife to husband. There is no sense here of the wife submitting only as she sees fit or only as it coheres with her faith. No qualifications are given to the demand for the submission of the wife. Balance is achieved only through the exhortation to the husband. Thus the wife falls under the full implication of the initial ethical principle to submit to one another.

The husband, however, is declared the head of the wife and is forcefully consolidated in his traditional position of authority. There is no sharing of power. Just as Christ rules the church, so does the husband rule the wife. But taking on the role of Christ means also taking on the sacrificial love of Christ. This is carefully played out in the concluding phrase of 5:23 and in more detail in the exhortations of 5:25–30. In those verses the author pursues the analogy between the purity of a bride and the purity of the church. However, the logic is twisted a little by the analogy. The paradigm here is Christ's love for the church, not the normal purity of human brides. Christ makes the unclean church pure and holy by dying for it. In the same way, the bride does not come to the marriage pure; rather, the husband makes the bride pure through his love. This is a potent twist to the normal understanding of marriage that this analogy permits. Women are not called upon to come to marriage pure and clean and undefiled, because there is no such purity. Real purity only comes from the love of Christ. Thus a wife can be sanctified only by the love of her husband. She cannot clean her soul or scrub her body or demonstrate her virginity and thereby become pure. She can receive marriage purity only from the love of Christ given by her husband.

The second part of the exhortation to the husband takes up the sexual dimension of human marriage and applies it, by analogy, to the relationship of Christ to the church. These verses are built upon the Jewish and early Christian understanding of Genesis 2:24; by way of copulation, husband and wife become one flesh. We saw in our discussion of Ephesians 5:3 that this notion of the power of sex to make two people one exerted a powerful influence on early Christianity. The strict sexual ethic of early Christians, with the nearly universal prohibition against fornication, goes back to this ancient Jewish understanding of the power of sex. Here, however, we encounter an intriguing innovation; the power of sex to make two persons one clarifies the nature of the unity between Christ and his bride, the church. We must assume that the love command given to the husband in 5:25 is the true analogue, not any sexual activity. The love and sacrifice of Christ for the church creates a unity between them of the same kind as between a loving husband and wife. In this way, the ongoing theme of Ephesians, that all things will be unified in Christ, surfaces once again.

At this point, we can perceive the overall design of these household rules. There is no attempt to overthrow, reconstitute, or even redesign the standard Jewish and Gentile norms for male dominance in marriage. This is simply accepted as fact. On the other hand, the radical principle of mutual subjection is not altogether abandoned. The standard of mutual subjection is injected into this ancient pattern, where it modifies and softens the hard edges of patriarchal marriage norms. It is as though the author held two contrary and incompatible principles, neither of which he could violate. Thus, when he put them together, they were both softened and the results were uneven. On the one hand, there is no attempt here to articulate the basics of a truly egalitarian marriage. By modern standards, the marriage contract articulated here contains injustices in the distribution of power. This must be taken seriously by us. These patriarchal norms are not adequate for us. On the other hand, the radical principle of mutual subjection and the great leveling power of Christian love moderate these ancient injustices. It may be the case that the Christian contribution here is the potential of mutual subjection and love for recreating personal and communal relationships. If that is so, then our task is not to defend or reconstitute the patterns articulated here but to imagine the implications of Christian love for our own relationships. That is no easy task. No matter who you are and what your culture, it is not easy to take on mutual subjection as your primary norm.

Children and Fathers

The commands to children and fathers (not parents) modify Colossians in some interesting ways. The syntax of the command to the children is altered slightly and in such a way that the precise function of "in the Lord" (6:1) becomes unclear. It could mean "Christian" parents, but that seems redundant in the context. It is more likely that this is an inexact reference to Christian duty and thus means "obey your parents since this is fitting for Christian children." Some readers suggest the translation "obey your parents to the extent that it is fitting for a Christian." But this would require a very delicate reading of the Greek and does not really square with the overall mood of the passage.

The quotation of the Fifth Commandment (Exod. 20:12) provides an additional reason for obedience to parents. There is no argument here for the creation of social solidarity or continuity. Nor does the concern seem to be the provision for parents in their old age. Rather, the reason is derived from a divine promise. God will bless you for your obedience. This coincides with the underlying theological logic of Ephesians. We do not love or submit because we can calculate those acts to be prudent and helpful; we love and submit because God's love lives in such deeds and because God acts to bless us when we do.

The gentle reminder to fathers in Colossians that children may "lose heart" is lost in Ephesians. Instead, the author reminds the fathers of the need for instruction and discipline. Such advice fits with the importance of correct knowledge and correct behavior that pervades the letter.

Slaves and Lords

As we noted in our discussion of the household rules in Colossians, the NRSV translates the same Greek word *kyrios* as "Lord" when it refers to God or Christ, but as "master" when it refers to the human lord of a slave. This is perhaps helpful for clarity's sake, but it obscures the predicament of Christian slaves who now have two "Lords." Furthermore, all Christians were wont to call themselves "slaves of Christ" (the NRSV sometimes translates this as "servants," but it is the same Greek word). Thus, how can one person be both a slave of Christ and a slave of an earthly lord?

Having read the author's advice to wives, the solution for slaves is no surprise. Just as wives should obey their husbands to the same extent as they obey their Lord, so should slaves obey their earthly lords "as" they obey Christ. Although this does not say that the earthly lord represents or replaces the heavenly Lord, it does equate the level of obedience. There is no sense here of obeying the earthly lord as long as the commands seem to cohere with the instructions of the heavenly Lord. The Christian ideal of submission seems to predominate here. Christians submit, even to evil persons (Matt. 5:39).

Furthermore, obedience and submission are treated as self-justifying good deeds that will be rewarded by the Lord. Thus God will repay you with heavenly rewards for your obedience to your husband, your father, and your earthly lord. We must admit, however, that few modern Christians would be willing to define submission in itself as a perfect good or as representing the will of God for slaves, children, and wives, no matter what the circumstances. We would want to say that the call for justice is the responsibility of all humans, whether that human is the more powerful or less powerful one in a relationship. Certainly, we would want to say that anyone being treated unjustly by someone with greater power has the Christian moral right to resist that injustice. However, Ephesians does not say this. Whatever dynamics for increased equality and justice exist in this system come from the top down, from the dominant partner. The dominated one submits, for submission is a Christian virtue.

The exhortation to masters contains a warning. They are reminded that every Christian has a Lord and that this Lord shows no partiality. Given what has preceded, this obviously does not mean that in God's eyes there is no such thing as an earthly lord/slave relationship. In a way, God, or at least the Ephesians version of the gospel, has just authenticated and reinforced the social pattern of master and slave. Thus the warning must mean that everyone, no matter what one's earthly status might have been, will be judged by the same standards. When masters are told to "do the same to them" (6:9), they are being told to practice the Christian life of love in dealing with their slaves. They are not being told to obey their slaves.

Questions for Today

The author's willingness to reinforce with Christian approval the patriarchal form of marriage and the dramatic inequalities of slavery is troublesome to modern Christians. Although some Christians, on the basis of this passage and the others like it in the New Testament, want to maintain patriarchy in marriage, almost no one wants a return to slavery. This passage seems to fall short of the Christian ideal. In fact, it fails to realize the potential of its own first principle of mutual submission.

We must remember that there is no such thing as pure Christianity untouched by its surrounding culture. Early Christianity makes no sense apart from its Jewish and Greek and Roman culture. No one, no Christian, has ever stood outside of history. Christian ethics always lives in the moment of history in which it occurs. The author of Ephesians could not imagine life apart from the social structures of the ancient world. How could society exist without marriage, parents, and slavery? The social possibilities available to us were not imaginable in the first century.

Furthermore, there is no attempt in the New Testament to work out a full social ethic. We cannot find a fully articulated program for human social structures. Perhaps it is true that we can find ethical principles from which a social ethic could be built. But that is different. Early Christians, with few exceptions, expressed their Christian values within the context of ancient social structures. They asked, How can we make this social structure more Christian? not, How can we create a Christian society?

For us then, our task is not to recreate the peculiar social structures found in the Bible, but to pursue Christian ethical principles as far as we can. Unfortunately, we have proven ourselves to be just as time-bound, culture-dominated, and self-protecting as the Christians who have gone before us. What is more important is not to say that the author of Ephesians could have done better, although he might well have done so, but to say that we must do better. "Be subject to one another out of reverence for Christ" (5:21).

THE WHOLE ARMOR OF GOD
Ephesians 6:10–20

> 6:10 **Finally, be strong in the Lord and in the strength of his power.** [11] **Put on the whole armor of God, so that you may be able to stand against the wiles of the devil.** [12] **For our struggle is not against enemies of blood and flesh, but against the rulers, against the authorities, against the cosmic powers of this present darkness, against the spiritual forces of evil in the heavenly places.** [13] **Therefore take up the whole armor of God, so that you may be able to withstand on that evil day, and having done everything, to stand firm.** [14] **Stand therefore, and fasten the belt of truth around your waist, and**

put on the breastplate of righteousness. [15] As shoes for your feet put on whatever will make you ready to proclaim the gospel of peace. [16] With all of these, take the shield of faith, with which you will be able to quench all the flaming arrows of the evil one. [17] Take the helmet of salvation, and the sword of the Spirit, which is the word of God.

[18] Pray in the Spirit at all times in every prayer and supplication. To that end keep alert and always persevere in supplication for all the saints. [19] Pray also for me, so that when I speak, a message may be given to me to make known with boldness the mystery of the gospel, [20] for which I am an ambassador in chains. Pray that I may declare it boldly, as I must speak.

The cosmic scale on which the letter began is seen again in this marvelous concluding exhortation. The letter opened by rehearsing the cosmic story of the gospel and closes by placing the single Christian into the center of the cosmic battle. Furthermore, this passage unites the cosmic themes of the opening chapters with the ethical exhortations that follow it. In fact, the passage depends for its meaning on what precedes. Only a reader who has read 1:1–6:9 can appreciate the nuances of 6:10–20.

The Victory of Christ

The first two verses establish the themes. First, "Be strong in the Lord and in the strength of his power" (6:10). The phrase "be strong" does not mean "find your inner strength" but "be strengthened." In fact, the Greek could well be translated as passive. No reader of the rest of Ephesians would doubt at this point that it is God's power that is called upon here. We must recall here the analysis of God's power in 1:19–23 and its application to believers in 2:4–10. It is the power that raised Jesus from the dead, seated him at God's right hand, and put all other powers of the cosmos under his feet. Thus the enumeration of those powers that are conquered in Christ in 1:21 provides the proper understanding of cosmic realities for this exhortation. The reader already knows the fate of those powers named in 6:12 that are attacking the believer.

In this way, when 6:11 exhorts the reader to "put on the whole armor of God, so that you may be able to stand against the wiles of the devil," the reader knows that God, in Christ, has already conquered all the evil powers. The reader is being invited to participate in that victory in his or her life.

The importance of the story of the victory of Christ over the cosmos is reinforced in 6:12. The believer is not struggling against an enemy made of flesh and blood, an enemy a human might reasonably defeat, but against all the superhuman cosmic powers, against which no human can prevail. A persistent Christian doctrine is articulated here. People cannot save themselves. We do not have within us the resources to withstand the evil powers. The wiles of the devil are too strong. Without intervention by God, we will all perish in the darkness. We are not saved by works but by grace.

Therefore, the believer must somehow acquire the power of God that is saving us. This, of course, is the story of Ephesians. Ephesians tells us what that power is and how it connects to us. The account of Christ's cosmic victory and the exhortations that follow place the believer into the household of God where there is righteousness and salvation. All of this is displayed here in the language of warfare.

The Armor of God

The Greek word *panoplia*, translated as "whole armor," refers to both the defensive armor and the offensive weaponry of a soldier. With it the author emphasizes the seriousness of the moral and religious task of every believer. This is warfare, and you must be properly outfitted.

It is fitting that "truth" heads the list of divine powers that are part of the believer's armor. The necessity of truth for the health of the community is described in 4:25–32. The speaking of this truth produces righteousness, which is the second weapon enumerated here. The final proof of both the truth of the gospel and the assurance of salvation lies in the presence of righteousness in the community. The gospel produces righteousness, and righteousness is rewarded with salvation.

It is not altogether clear what "faith" means in 6:16. It meant many things in early Christianity, and it is not clear which meaning Ephesians is using. The Pauline language of 2:8 suggests that "faith" may mean "the reception of the saving and transforming power of God in the hearing and believing of the words of the gospel." But it may also have its more common meanings of "trust" or "belief." Thus the reference here would be to faith as believing and trusting in the truth of the gospel. Whatever the precise referent should be, the mention of faith at this point connects the individual Christian to the truth of the gospel. The gospel must be received as true.

Salvation, of course, represents the ultimate hope and final conclusion of the gospel story. Less certain is the precise meaning of "the sword of the Spirit, which is the word of God" (6:17). The Greek "which is" is a neuter relative pronoun, which most naturally refers back to the neuter noun Spirit. Sword is feminine. However, most commentators have a difficult time explaining how the Spirit itself is the word of God. It is sometimes the case that the Greek neuter relative pronoun can refer to entire phrases and whole sentences. Thus it is grammatically possible for the "which" to refer to the entire phrase "the sword of the Spirit." Given this, the phrase represents a classic Reformed idea: The Spirit is present in the proclamation of the word. In this way, the last phrase returns to the initial phrase. The key to this cosmic warfare is the proclamation of the true gospel.

Most Christian theology, but especially Lutheran and Reformed theology, places tremendous importance on proclamation. Christianity can exist only when and where the gospel is proclaimed. In fact, the Spirit itself enters the believer's life only in conjunction with the hearing and believing of the spoken gospel. Ephesians clearly supports this role for proclamation. However, it is important to note that proclamation is not only the telling of the divine story but exhortation to the righteous life. In Ephesians, the gospel produces righteousness. Faith cannot be disconnected from the ethical life. We may be saved by grace and not works, but there is no such thing as the immoral life of faith. As noted in Ephesians 5:5, no fornicator, no unclean person, has any inheritance in the kingdom of God.

Thus, in order to be faithful to Ephesians, we cannot separate our beliefs from our deeds. The argument of James 1:22–27; 2:14–26 stands: Faith without works is dead, for the very purpose of faith is righteousness. As we have noted throughout our reading of Ephesians, the blessings of God to us in Christ must include the ethical life. To be in God's presence, to partake of salvation, is to partake of God's righteousness. The moral life, as defined in the gospel, is a necessary part of our salvation. Whatever we want to do with this in our own theologies, we should admit that Ephesians insists on righteousness.

The difference in worldviews between Paul and the author of Ephesians emerges in a fascinating way in this passage. In both the letters of Paul and Ephesians, the great cosmic battle between Christ and the evil powers is played out in the soul of the individual believer. The salvation of the individual Christian is a part of the salvation of the cosmos. Paul understands that the future kingdom has begun in Christ and that we partake of that future kingdom as we are in Christ. This tension in cosmic time produces a series of theological tensions that are essential to Paul's thought. The great contrasts of joy and suffering, death and life, appearance and reality, the cross and resurrection, and others derive from the end-time tensions in Paul's thought. In Ephesians, these Pauline tensions are relaxed. It is as though the language of Paul is remembered, but the shift from a temporal to a spatial worldview changes the meaning of the Pauline terms. This is not to say that the author of Ephesians has no sense of time, but that spatial hierarchies and not temporal conflict drive his thought.

The claim in Ephesians 2:6 that we are already seated at God's right hand does not mean that our earthly life is over or that we are not still subject to the attacks of the devil. The assurance that we are already resurrected must mean that the power that placed Jesus at God's right hand and will place us is already available to us. This does not mean that we can ride this power into heaven; it means that we have divine weapons with which we can conquer all the wiles of the devil. Thus it appears that, even if the tension between the future and the present is relaxed somewhat, it has not disappeared altogether. It plays out in our confidence of victory over the devil and not in Pauline end-time tensions.

All of this is reminiscent of Colossians. The author of Colossians seemed greatly concerned to shore up the confidence of his readers. He too emphasized the accomplished nature of our resurrection, reminding his readers that their life (their future?) was hidden above with Christ (Col. 3:3). Thus his readers were admonished to seek the things that are above, not the things below. The author of Ephesians, who shares the spatial perspectives of Colossians, takes over without much modification these spatial categories. He reads the rest of the Pauline letters through the lens of Colossians. Thus the classic Pauline contrasts of faith and works, joy and suffering, death and life, when they are echoed in Ephesians, lack the deep tensions we find in Paul.

In shifting away from the end-time worldview of Paul, Colossians and Ephesians anticipate what mainstream Christianity will do in subsequent centuries. Interest in the coming of the kingdom will never disappear, but most Christian theology will focus upon cosmic hierarchies and not visions of the end of the world.

Pray in the Spirit

This passage concludes with an admonition to prayer. The Spirit, which produced proclamation in 6:17, produces prayer in 6:18. When this passage is combined with 5:18–20, it becomes apparent that the Spirit is the author of all true language in the community. It produces proclamation of the gospel, songs of praise, and prayer. We should note the focus upon language in this passage. The readers are admonished to pray for Paul so that he will speak the gospel.

The request that the readers pray for Paul mirrors Paul's prayer for them in 3:14–19. Furthermore, the readers are advised to pray for all the saints, not just for Paul. The importance of unity, which so dominates this letter, surfaces again in the purpose of prayer. Prayer, like all other Christian moments, should reinforce the unity of the church.

BENEDICTION
Ephesians 6:21–24

> 6:21 So that you also may know how I am and what I am doing, Tychicus will tell you everything. He is a dear brother and a faithful minister in the Lord. [22] I am sending him to you for this very purpose, to let you know how we are, and to encourage your hearts.
> [23] Peace be to the whole community, and love with faith, from God the Father and the Lord Jesus Christ. [24] Grace be with all who have an undying love for our Lord Jesus Christ.

The promise to send Tychicus is typical of Pauline letters. Tychicus is portrayed here probably as the bearer of the letter. We know that Paul normally sent his letters by way of one of his emissaries, such as Timothy or Titus, and that these emissaries normally carried further information. Furthermore, Tychicus has the identical role in Colossians (4:7–9). In both letters, he is to inform the recipients how Paul is doing. Assuming that Ephesians was not a real letter sent by Paul to Ephesus, then we should assume further that this note about Tychicus is copied from Colossians. It has at least two purposes. First, it makes the letter read like a real letter. Pauline letters typically end with these kinds of personal notes. Second, the sending of Tychicus by Paul to comfort the Ephesians models how Christians should care for one another. Thus Paul's concern and care for them expressed in the sending of Tychicus and these greetings coheres nicely with the larger concerns of unity and care for one another that pervade Ephesians. That is to say, such caring for one another fits the mood of the letter.

The benediction evokes classic early Christian themes, which were common throughout early Christianity. Of course, peace, love, faith, and grace have all been mentioned in Ephesians itself. The origin of the benediction is, therefore, uncertain. It may come from the general liturgical life of the larger church and not from the hand of the author. It is used here because it evokes ideas consistent with the letter, rather than being penned to fit. Of course, given the liturgical bent of much of the language of Ephesians, the author would have been quite able to produce a nice liturgical flourish at the end. Whether he did that or used an already existing one, this benediction works well. The focus on peace and love, in particular, recalls the identical focus of the body of the letter. The great theme of unity surfaces one more time.

Of course, a liturgical letter like Ephesians needs a liturgical finish, and Paul himself normally finished with similar benedictions. Paul apparently wanted his own letters to be read in conjunction with worship. Exactly how and at what point is not clear. But the opening prayer and the concluding benediction would make them amenable to such use. On the other hand, we must admit that many ancient letters began and ended in similar ways, and few of them were connected to any worship. In any case, Ephesians is designed in such a way that it would work well in community worship. Many commentators have felt the letter may have been intended for use in baptismal rituals. We probably cannot be that specific, but it does seem to be addressed to the worship life of the community. It is, after all, proclamation, a true articulation of the gospel, and thus would be a proper part of worship. This is the way subsequent Christians have used it.

CONCLUSION

The rich theological imagery of Ephesians opens many avenues for modern readers. In particular, its focus on providential order, its hints of universalism, and its forceful ethics have all influenced subsequent Christian thought. But the primary question this letter raises for me comes from the overall rhetoric of the letter: It is a blessing to God for God's blessings to us. There are many blessings enumerated in the letter, but the key one, the one that organizes all the others, is the conviction that God in Jesus will "fill all in all." This great unification of the diverse and combative forces of the cosmos is mirrored in the unification of humans into one person, one people. Peace is being accomplished. And this vision of peace evokes continual praise and blessing of this victorious God.

All this seems so contrary to the modern theological mood. Instead of unification, we see fragmentation. Instead of people coming together, we sense growing tribalism and antagonisms. Peace is not winning. Peace seems more and more a curious and useless ideal. Power, strength, and resistance fit us better than the submission, humility, and mutual support called for in Ephesians. How can we sing these praises with the author of Ephesians if we cannot see the peace he sees? How can we take on his peaceable ethic if we cannot sing with him?

We do, however, know how to lament. The terrors of life, the absence of God, the evil of our politics and ourselves, these we are well practiced speaking to God. Such laments are proper to the life of faith. The powerful laments in the Bible (in the Psalter, in the prophets, and from Jesus in the garden or over Jerusalem) echo and authorize our own laments. But something is out of balance. In the Psalter, laments are bracketed by praise. All this makes me wonder whether we have lost part of the voice of faith. The praise of God that is proper to us has become muffled.

So what now? Do we praise in spite of the laments in our heart? Is praise a great act of pretense? It is perhaps true that praise based on sight alone will always be hollow. Praise must be based on hope, on faith, on trust in a God who is beyond our understanding. Thus Paul declares in Romans 8:24b–25, "Now hope that is seen is not hope. For who hopes for what is seen? But if we hope for what we do not see, we wait for it with patience." But how do we do that?

Here Ephesians helps us. It asks, "Don't you understand who God is? Don't you believe that God in Jesus Christ has already conquered evil? The spirit in you whispers this truth." Ephesians calls us to remember what we believe. Looking at the evil in the world or in ourselves may lead us to lament, but the gospel in declaring victory leads us to praise.

Now is the time to remember this victory, to let the outrageous claims of the gospel infect our thinking and doing, to hold to these hopes, and to let our voices sing out the wonders of God's victory. Thus, Ephesians leads me to a prayer for the church, the world, and even myself. What is this prayer? The author of Ephesians voices it for me in 3:14–21.

The Pastoral Epistles

Introduction

The overall purpose of the Pastoral Epistles is summed up nicely in 1 Timothy 3:14–15: "I am writing these instructions to you so that . . . you may know how one ought to behave in the household of God." These letters focus upon the details of the Christian ethical life in both its personal and social dimensions. We do not find here, however, a full-blown social ethic for society-at-large, but instructions for how Christians should behave both inside and outside of the church. Thus the letters are exhortation. They argue for a particular version of the moral life.

The context for this exhortation is a church that, in the opinion of the author, has deviated from the apostolic traditions. There is heresy on theological and ethical levels in the church, and the author seeks to redress both. He does this by articulating his version of Christian theology and Christian ethics as the true Pauline version.

These letters, like Colossians and Ephesians, are not written by Paul even though they have Paul's name on them as author. They are unlike Colossians and Ephesians in that they use the pretense of Pauline authorship more aggressively. Whereas Colossians and Ephesians read like careful reworkings of Pauline themes from the Pauline letters, the Pastoral Epistles seem both to deviate more from Pauline ideas and to use Paul's name more aggressively to authenticate some rather non-Pauline ideas. There is more of a sense of deception here. It is important to the author that the readers actually believe that Paul wrote these letters. In fact, the overall argument of the letters is unraveled if Pauline authorship is discounted. How this works should become clear in the comments that follow.

The question then becomes, If Paul did not write these letters, who did? We cannot know the name of the author because he does not give it and no external sources indicate it. What we know about him must come from the letters themselves. It is clear that he considered himself a

Paulinist; he was a potent moralist, committed to a rather sober and quiet form of Christian living. He was in the midst of a deep controversy in his church, which he perceived as touching the nature of salvation itself. He was convinced his opponents were teaching and practicing a form of Christianity that was not Christian and was not leading to salvation. He perceived his church as being in theological and social disarray. He wants order, both social and theological, and he makes his case in the guise of Paul.

Identifying the heresy being fought in these letters has proven to be quite difficult. As was the case with the Colossians' heresy, the problem is not the lack of possibilities but the multitude of them. The heretics are usually identified with an early form of Christian Gnosticism. (Gnostics believed that only people with special spiritual "knowledge" could escape the burdens of the material world and be saved.) The author of the Pastoral Epistles claims that these heretics believe "the resurrection has already taken place" (2 Tim. 2:18). The warning against "what is falsely called knowledge" in 1 Timothy 6:20 sounds, of course, like a Gnostic claim. According to 1 Timothy 4:1–5, these heretics forbid marriage and teach abstention from certain foods. All of this can be seen as typical of Christian Gnosticism. Furthermore, the warning against myths and endless genealogies (1 Tim. 1:4) fits with the kind of cosmic speculation that some Gnostic groups practiced. According to Titus 1:10–16, these heretics either are Jewish or have Jewish tendencies. Thus they do look like some form of early Gnostics with Jewish roots. As we know, there were many such groups. Judaism was quite amenable to Gnostic tendencies.

However, it is not clear how literally these accusations should be taken. Some of the vices of which the opponents are accused appear quite improbable, namely, killing of mothers and fathers, dealing in slavery, and so on (1 Tim. 1:9–10). These accusations appear to function more as a way of attaching obvious evil behavior to these people than describing them accurately. In fact, the overall portrait of these opponents is likely to be quite unbalanced. The author is not giving an unbiased, objective account of them. He is portraying them as heretics on both the theological and ethical level. Therefore, it is probably not advisable to take the author's account of these heretics as fact. As a result, it is quite difficult to identify them with any precision.

Furthermore, the author's problem with these heretics is as much political as theological. They are creating disorder and disharmony in the church. They encourage or permit women to teach men. They prey especially on women, upsetting whole families in the process. And worst of all, they seem to be winning. It is they, not the author and his friends, who are dominant in the church. Thus part of the author's tactic is to insist on proper order: Women should not teach men, and the church should submit to the regular church officers. As we will see, an elaborate political argument is made in the Pastoral Epistles.

These problems and the character of the author's response are typical of church life at the beginning of the second century. The Pastoral Epistles fit nicely into that time period, for they must be later than Ephesians and earlier than Polycarp's letter to the Philippians, which is itself difficult to date but must have been written in the first half of the second century. In any case, most scholars who think Paul did not write these letters would date the Pastoral Epistles between A.D. 95 and A.D. 110, with the later date the more likely. Timothy is described as being in Ephesus, and Titus in Crete. Paul is to be understood as being in prison in Rome. Thus most people would place the origin of the letters either in Rome or Ephesus. Both places would fit, for both are traditional Pauline centers.

The influence of the Pastoral Epistles has been largely on two fronts: church order and Christian ethics. In these letters, the importance placed on bishops, elders, and deacons shaped subsequent discussion about the relationship of clergy and laity. Although the Pastoral Epistles never explain how the offices relate to one another or what the full duties of each office might be, they do place into the hands of these leaders the responsibility for determining what is orthodox and what is not. The leaders are given full authority over the content of church teaching. They determine what is apostolic tradition. Of course, this is not without cost, for they are held to the strict ethical standards of that tradition. All this became crucial in the early church's understanding of what it means to be ordained to church office.

In subsequent Christian discussion about ethics, the Pastoral Epistles, along with some other similar texts, serve as a forceful counterbalance to the rigors of the Sermon on the Mount and the creativeness of Paul. Of course, Paul's attempts to imagine how life in Christ is played out in the mundane affairs of one's life probably laid the foundation for the Pastoral Epistles. Colossians and Ephesians started down this road, but the Pastoral Epistles focus more on the regular affairs of life and offer ethical models within the reasonable reach of most believers. This is not to say that the paradoxical and challenging call to love, suffer, and submit is lacking here, being replaced by a more worldly ethic. In fact, it is quite the opposite. The peculiar Christian fascination with weakness, submission, obedience, and love are not forgotten. Instead, they are remembered, reaffirmed, and then woven into aspects of life in new ways. The life of virtue and love articulated here will have a tremendous impact on Christian ethics.

The Pastoral Epistles have been accused of surrendering the great visions of the kingdom in the teachings of Jesus and the mystical ethics of Paul for mundane, unheroic, bourgeois morality. This is true only in the sense that ordinary Christians with ordinary responsibilities find an ethic that speaks to them. The heroism that emerges is a quiet one, found in the midst of maintaining other duties. Christian virtue is found in the turmoil of ordinary life, not in the pristine order of an otherworldly sect. Christianity is moving into the mainstream of the Greek and Roman world. And the question will always be, What was gained and lost in that transition?

Commentary on 1 Timothy

SALUTATION
1 Timothy 1:1–2

> 1:1 **Paul, an apostle of Christ Jesus by the command of God our Savior and of Christ Jesus our hope,**
> **2 To Timothy, my loyal child in the faith:**
> **Grace, mercy, and peace from God the Father and Christ Jesus our Lord.**

First Timothy begins with a greeting in the traditional Pauline style. Paul is identified in classic terms as an apostle of Christ Jesus. An apostle is a person sent on behalf of another with a specific task, and Paul's task will be detailed in the letter.

First Timothy deviates from the typical Pauline letter in that it is sent to an individual, not a church. Only Philemon parallels the Pastoral Epistles in having a person as recipient. And the letter to Philemon is not addressed just to Philemon, but also to Apphia, Archippus, and the church at Philemon's house. Timothy was one of Paul's inner circle; in fact, he may have been Paul's closest working confidant. This historical intimacy contributes to the setting of the letter. This letter is to be seen as an unguarded, and thus fully articulated, reminder of Paul to his "loyal child in the faith." Here, we are to imagine, Paul could express the full truth of the gospel without any need to couch it for the sensibilities of his opponents or would-be opponents. His other letters were public documents and may have had the guardedness appropriate to that genre. But this letter is "Paul . . . to Timothy."

The greeting contains the triad of grace, mercy, and peace. Of the Pauline letters, only 1 and 2 Timothy include mercy in the greeting. Paul's own letters, as well as Colossians and Ephesians, list grace and peace only. Titus contains the more typical Pauline form. The addition of mercy does

not appear to have special theological significance for the Pastoral Epistles, although mercy is mentioned in 1 Timothy 1:16, 18, and Titus 3:5.
It may be noted that mercy was not a primary category for Paul (grace is
more important), although the word *mercy* does occur four times in Paul's
letters. The presence of this triad probably reflects the author's dependence on the larger church traditions where these terms frequently appear
together, especially in greetings (see also 2 John and Jude).

WARNING AGAINST FALSE TEACHERS
1 Timothy 1:3–11

> 1:3 I urge you, as I did when I was on my way to Macedonia, to remain in
> Ephesus so that you may instruct certain people not to teach any different
> doctrine, 4 and not to occupy themselves with myths and endless genealo-
> gies that promote speculations rather than the divine training that is known
> by faith. 5 But the aim of such instruction is love that comes from a pure
> heart, a good conscience, and sincere faith. 6 Some people have deviated
> from these and turned to meaningless talk, 7 desiring to be teachers of the
> law, without understanding either what they are saying or the things about
> which they make assertions.
>
> 8 Now we know that the law is good, if one uses it legitimately. 9 This
> means understanding that the law is laid down not for the innocent but for
> the lawless and disobedient, for the godless and sinful, for the unholy and
> profane, for those who kill their father or mother, for murderers, 10 forni-
> cators, sodomites, slave traders, liars, perjurers, and whatever else is con-
> trary to the sound teaching 11 that conforms to the glorious gospel of the
> blessed God, which he entrusted to me.

The body of the letter begins without the usual Pauline thanksgiving, but
with a reminder to Timothy of earlier instructions. This reminder sets the
table for the rest of the letter, stating both the basic problem and the author's
solution. The problem is heretics who teach improperly, which results in
vice. The solution is proper teaching by approved teachers of orthodox doctrine, which results in virtue. The battle between heresy and orthodoxy, with
the resultant conflict between vice and virtue, will shape not only this letter
but 2 Timothy and Titus, the other Pastoral Epistles, as well.

Sound Teaching

Timothy is enjoined to instruct "certain people not to teach any different
doctrine" (1:3). Crucial to the argument of the letter is the notion of an
established tradition that can be taught and learned and from which the

church should not deviate. We know, of course, from the New Testament and early Christian literature that the early church had extensive debate and disagreement over the precise shape and content of apostolic tradition. Furthermore, the so-called heretical documents we possess understand themselves as faithful to the apostolic tradition. The question was not whether one should adhere to the tradition of the apostles; everyone agreed on that. The question was, What did the apostles teach?

The author of the Pastoral Epistles offers the perfect solution—letters from Paul to his confidants and co-workers, Timothy and Titus, in which he "reminds" them of the apostolic teaching. Thus the author's opponents can be portrayed as deviating from the teachings of Paul. In actual fact, these "heretics" may have perceived themselves as true Paulinists. In any case, they certainly did not perceive themselves as heretics.

The opponents are accused of devoting themselves to myths and endless genealogies. Titus 1:14 describes these "myths" as Jewish. And 1 Timothy 1:7 claims that these people want "to be teachers of the law." The law was often understood in antiquity as not only being perfectly true, the word of God, but as containing hidden truth. The text was perceived as a riddle, the hidden meaning of which must be teased out. Allegory is often the best method for discovering other truths that are not in the plain sense of the text. In any case, we know of both Jews and Christians who understood the biblical texts as riddles of the cosmic structures and as allegorical accounts of the stories of the gods. Through creative exegesis, these people found marvelous cosmic tales in the mundane language of the Old Testament. This may be the problem here. The accusation of "speculation" fits this scenario.

Whatever the problem was, the author's response is to appeal to ethical truth. The law is not to be the basis for fantastic, cosmic speculation but for moral instruction. These people are perverting the purpose of the text. It is intended to convict vice and promote virtue. But these people who devote so much energy to this moral text actually live immoral lives.

To this misreading of the text, this cosmic speculation, and this immorality, the author counterposes "sound teaching" (1:10), which produces love (1:5). The term *sound teaching* recurs throughout the Pastoral Epistles. The Greek word for sound can mean healthy or reliable or even true as opposed to false. All these nuances seem to be in force in the claims of the Pastoral Epistles. The sound teaching of the letters is reliable; we can trust it and believe it. It is true and orthodox as opposed to the heresies of others, and it produces health or virtue in those who hear and heed it.

The health that this sound teaching produces is described in 1:5 as "love that comes from a pure heart, a good conscience, and sincere faith." Grammatically, "from" refers to heart, conscience, and faith. The three together produce love. It takes proper and honest belief, a good honest heart, and an active, well-instructed conscience to produce the Christian life of love. According to the author, the heretics are lacking in all these areas; thus their lives take on the immorality described in 1:9–10.

The author's initial critique of the teaching of the heretics is that it promotes speculation rather than "the divine training," or the divine plan (*oikonomia tou theou*). This terminology, though frequent in the ancient world, probably comes from Ephesians 1:10 and 3:9. Scholars have speculated whether *oikonomia* means here "God's plan of salvation" or "the education of people by God for salvation." Such a distinction is probably misleading in the case of the Pastoral Epistles. God's plan includes the education of people for salvation. As we will see, teaching and learning form the very core of the church's life. In fact, the church is perceived as much as a school as a cultic community. This is to be expected, for, as we have seen here, there is a conflict between good teaching and bad.

PAUL AS THE EXAMPLE
1 Timothy 1:12–20

1:12 **I am grateful to Christ Jesus our Lord, who has strengthened me, because he judged me faithful and appointed me to his service, [13] even though I was formerly a blasphemer, a persecutor, and a man of violence. But I received mercy because I had acted ignorantly in unbelief, [14] and the grace of our Lord overflowed for me with the faith and love that are in Christ Jesus. [15] The saying is sure and worthy of full acceptance, that Christ Jesus came into the world to save sinners—of whom I am the foremost. [16] But for that very reason I received mercy, so that in me, as the foremost, Jesus Christ might display the utmost patience, making me an example to those who would come to believe in him for eternal life. [17] To the King of the ages, immortal, invisible, the only God, be honor and glory forever and ever. Amen.**

[18] **I am giving you these instructions, Timothy, my child, in accordance with the prophecies made earlier about you, so that by following them you may fight the good fight, [19] having faith and a good conscience. By rejecting conscience, certain persons have suffered shipwreck in the faith; [20] among them are Hymenaeus and Alexander, whom I have turned over to Satan, so that they may learn not to blaspheme.**

After having established the driving issue of the letter as the conflict between good and bad teaching, between virtue and vice, the author uses Paul himself as an example. In his experience as apostle, the ultimate truths of the Christian life can be perceived. Paul's story is told from a peculiar perspective; his life is seen through the lens of the issue that is the focus of this letter. Furthermore, as an apostle, his story illustrates both how God behaves and how people behave.

Moral exhortation in Greek and Roman times often used personal examples. Jews, Greeks, and Christians, when arguing ethics, all looked for personal examples of good and bad behavior. In some ways, this tendency reflects the insight that morality can never be condensed to a series of principles or a list of virtues. The moral life can be understood only in the drama of a real person's life. Thus, to know wisdom one had to find a wise person. Only the life of a wise person can demonstrate what all those wonderful moral principles really mean. Stoics liked to look back to the early founders—Socrates and Zeno. Jews looked back to Moses and Abraham. And Christians in the second century and later would look back to the apostles. The real Christian life can best be seen in the life of a real Christian. We cannot be certain about you and me, but we can be about Paul. We can read Paul's life as a book of Christian truth.

Paul is portrayed here as the prototype of the Christian life. The author actually asserts this very thing: Jesus Christ showed mercy to Paul in order to make him an example (*hypotyposis*) to those who would come to believe (1:16). From Paul's life, true and reliable observations can be drawn. In fact, Christ has organized Paul's life for this very purpose, to provide an example of how God and Christians act. In 1 Timothy 4:12, Timothy himself is urged to make himself an example (*typos*). It is significant that different Greek words are used for Paul and Timothy. Although the NRSV translates both words as "example," it may be better to note the difference in the Greek by translating *hypotyposis* as prototype or paradigm, and *typos* as example.

This account of Paul's life provides the author of 1 Timothy with theological principles that he can use throughout the letter. In Paul, we see the ever-repeating truths of the Christian life. He is the prototype not in the sense that he is a Christian without parallel but rather that he is the Christian with many parallels.

It is important then that Paul is called a blasphemer, a persecutor, and a man of violence, for in this way he duplicates the character and behavior of the author's opponents. In fact, Paul represents all sinners, and God's treatment of Paul shows how God treats all sinners: God has mercy on them.

The Salvation of Sinners

The author introduces at this point (1:15) the first of five so-called faithful sayings (*pistos ho logos*). In this context *pistos* means reliable, believable, and worthy of trust. The NRSV translation of "sure" expresses some of the range of the word. The author uses the phrase "the saying is sure" to point to reliable and believable theological truths. Thus he is claiming that in Paul's reception of mercy, an ultimate, eternal, and ever-repeating truth is displayed: "Christ Jesus came into the world to save sinners."

This theological principle will shape the entire character, tone, and purpose of the letter. Its purpose, or at least one of its purposes, is to save sinners. Thus it wants those sinners to be rebuked, corrected, and even disciplined. But the purpose of that discipline is the rescue of those sinners.

The author wants to create church leadership adequate to this task. The leaders must be orthodox in thought and behavior; their teaching and their lifestyles must cohere with the gospel; and they must be exhorted and encouraged to the task of correcting and saving the heretics.

Paul also illustrates how heretics should be treated. Hymenaeus and Alexander are "turned over to Satan" by Paul (1:20). This probably means not only are they rebuked and corrected but they are dismissed from the community, thrown out into the realm of Satan. But the purpose clause is significant. Paul did this "so that they may learn not to blaspheme" (1:20). Rebuke the heretics so as to save them.

Thus, for all the insistence on orthodoxy, on the rebuke of heretics, on the necessity for strong leadership, and on the adherence to proper hierarchy, the Pastoral Epistles manage a gentle tone. The good fight, which Paul has fought and Timothy is to fight, is not a violent one. Victory in this fight lies in rapprochement between the author and his opponents. God, who is the savior of *all* people (1 Tim. 4:10), wants all people to be saved (1 Tim. 2:4). The author wants to call the heretical back into the fold of orthodoxy.

We cannot precisely identify these heretics. Hymenaeus is mentioned in 2 Timothy 2:17, coupled with Philetus. And Alexander, the coppersmith, is mentioned in 2 Timothy 4:14 as having done Paul great harm. Phygelus and Hermogenes are described as having turned away from Paul in 2 Timothy 1:15. And there is a considerable list of names in 2 Timothy 4:9–22, many of which come from Colossians and Philemon, and some from Acts and Romans.

Naming names gives a lifelike feel to the letters. Paul can be portrayed, in this way, as struggling in the midst of opposition and wavering support. He represents troubled leadership. But naming names may have a further purpose—to discredit some of the author's contemporaries. These names may have had real political and theological connections to persons of the author's own time. However, there is no way to determine what those connections might be.

INSTRUCTIONS CONCERNING PRAYER
1 Timothy 2:1–15

2:1 **First of all, then, I urge that supplications, prayers, intercessions, and thanksgivings be made for everyone, 2 for kings and all who are in high positions, so that we may lead a quiet and peaceable life in all godliness and dignity. 3 This is right and is acceptable in the sight of God our Savior, 4 who desires everyone to be saved and to come to the knowledge of the truth. 5 For**

> **there is one God;**
> **there is also one mediator between God and humankind,**
> **Christ Jesus, himself human,**
> **6 who gave himself a ransom for all**

—this was attested at the right time. 7 For this I was appointed a herald and an apostle (I am telling the truth, I am not lying), a teacher of the Gentiles in faith and truth.

8 I desire, then, that in every place the men should pray, lifting up holy hands without anger or argument; 9 also that the women should dress themselves modestly and decently in suitable clothing, not with their hair braided, or with gold, pearls, or expensive clothes, 10 but with good works, as is proper for women who profess reverence for God. 11 Let a woman learn in silence with full submission. 12 I permit no woman to teach or to have authority over a man; she is to keep silent. 13 For Adam was formed first, then Eve; 14 and Adam was not deceived, but the woman was deceived and became a transgressor. 15 Yet she will be saved through childbearing, provided they continue in faith and love and holiness, with modesty.

God of All People

This exhortation to prayer is not a request for just any kind of prayer but for prayer of a specific kind that engenders a specific kind of behavior. All prayer is made to a God "who desires everyone to be saved and to come to the knowledge of the truth" (2:4). This means that we should pray "without anger or argument" (2:8), not against our enemies or for our own victories. Our God is not to be called upon to intercede in our petty disagreements. This is the God of all people.

This theological conviction is articulated in the brief hymn of 2:5–6a. The origin of this theological piece is unknown. It is traditionally called a hymn because of its liturgical feel. We do not know whether it was sung or from what part of church liturgy it might have come. In any case, its theological purpose is to extol the oneness of God, the oneness of the mediator who gave himself as a ransom for *all*. There are not competing gods out there, with the god of Jesus Christ being the one god who is on your side, to whom you might appeal to be biased in your behalf, who might even damage your enemies. There is only one God, whose basic character is to be savior. Thus your God wants to save every single human being. You and your enemies are no different in that regard. Jesus died for everyone.

This oneness of God reinforces the accommodating tone of the treatment of heretics in 1 Timothy. In this way, the character of God is carefully established at the beginning of the letter, and the rest of the letter becomes an ethical and political meditation upon this character of God. First Timothy insists "The saying is sure and worthy of full acceptance, that Christ Jesus came into the world to save sinners" (1:15). We are then called, as was the author of the Pastoral Epistles, to explore the implications of this. We, like him, must admit at the outset that no one, not even wonderful believers like us, have exclusive claims upon God. Furthermore, our enemies must then be understood as having the same theological status we have; we are all sinners intended for salvation.

The Quiet Life

A second theme emerges in these verses, which is a pervasive one in the Pastoral Epistles—the quiet life. The initial request in 2:1–2 for prayer to be made "for everyone, for kings and all who are in high positions" is "so that we may lead a quiet and peaceable life in all godliness and dignity." The vision of the Christian life is a gentle, moderate one. The harder asceticism of the author's opponents is rejected (see my discussion of 1 Tim. 4:1–5). The tendency in both Colossians and Ephesians to emphasize the quiet, submissive, and moderate character of Christian ethics is emphasized in the Pastoral Epistles. Given the theological convictions that God is savior of all and that the true character of the Christian life is quiet, peaceable, godly, and dignified, it is no surprise that we are to pray for (not against) those in power, who may in fact be persecuting us.

Many readers have felt that the creative tension between church and society that we find in most of the New Testament is somehow lacking in the Pastoral Epistles. These texts seem more at home in the mainstream of ancient society. The sense of being aliens, sojourners, and people of the

end time—which we find in Paul, the gospels, and most of the other letters—has been replaced by a willingness to become good, productive citizens.

Some readers lament this accommodation as a betrayal of the best ideal
of early Christianity. The great visions of the kingdom and the sense of
new reality becomes parodied in normal, moderate lives. Others see this
accommodation as a necessary and even productive stage in the success of
Christianity. Christian ideals had to be taken into the mundane affairs of
life. People had to find ways of being Christian without surrendering all
the other good things and important obligations in life. This is, of course,
an ancient and ongoing discussion. What should the relationship of Christianity be to any culture? The Pastoral Epistles make an important proposal, the details of which will become clear in what follows.

Let Women Be Silent

Equally controversial is the admonition to women in 2:9–15. The initial
comments in 2:9–10 fit nicely with the general theme of pursuing the quiet
life and offer little of great controversy. The call to adorn oneself with good
works could be applied to anyone, for that is the task of all believers. The
problem lies with the call to silence and submission. There is clearly a
problem with the role of women in the author's church. Titus 2:3–5 repeats this call to submission without mentioning the need for silence. And
2 Timothy 3:6–7 indicates that the heretics are improperly influencing
"silly women." There is also a problem with the order of widows.

All this suggests that women are taking leadership positions, that they
are prominent in the teaching activity of the church, and that they are even
teaching men. It is also clear that this behavior violates the author's sense
of order. Here (2:11) women are admonished to learn "with full submission" (*en pasē hypotagē*). The term *hypotagē* is an important one in the Pastoral Epistles. The term is a frequent one in military discussions and indicates the assumption and acceptance of a submissive rank in an
established hierarchy. Bishops are told in 1 Timothy 3:4 to keep their children *en hypotagē* ("submissive"). The verbal form of this word is used to
admonish slaves to obey their masters (Titus 2:9) and all Christians to
obey the secular authorities (Titus 3:1). In fact, the initial description of
the heretics in 1 Timothy 1:9–10 calls them "disobedient" (*anhypotaktoi*).
This seems to be the real problem with women. They are not accused explicitly of teaching incorrectly or incompetently; rather, they are simply
accused of teaching men. Such an act violates the cosmic order.

This order is apparently assumed by the author, as it was by nearly everyone in antiquity. The reference to Adam and Eve is a classic one in Jewish and Christian literature and is used here as it normally was used, as a warning of the seductive power of women. Women are unstable but potent in their misleading of men. Thus they should not teach. Instead, the author insists that "she [the woman] will be saved through childbearing, provided they continue in faith and love and holiness, with modesty" (2:15). Grammatically "they" refers to the children. Thus women are admonished to raise children properly in the faith. In fact, the very salvation of women lies in such successful parenting. It is possible, given a slight grammatical awkwardness, that "they" refers to women. If so, women are being admonished to bear children and to live the moderate life of the good Christian. In any case, women are being confined to domestic roles. They are permitted to teach other women (Titus 2:3–4) and, we must assume, children. But they are not to teach men. Because bishops and elders have primary teaching responsibility for the church, this means that women are excluded from such offices (but see my discussion of 1 Tim. 3:11).

Many modern Christians and many denominations have decided that such a vision of the role of women is not only incorrect but contrary to good Christian theology. Typically they argue that other texts have priority over the Pastoral Epistles and other theological principles are more important than one asserting the cosmic order of male over female. Such sorting and evaluating of theological and ethical principles in biblical texts is, I think, necessary. In fact, in this instance it is hard to find good theological reasons for the submission of women, and it is easy to find the contrary. Personally, I cannot imagine the God of Jesus Christ caring, at the point of ordination, whether someone were male or female. But we should admit that, for whatever reason, the Pastoral Epistles insist on the submission of women to men and the exclusion of women from the most powerful church offices.

The historical exclusion of women from church hierarchies has strong biblical warrant here. It may be that the author is simply reflecting the unconscious bias of his time, a bias that ought not have power over us. We have enough biases of our own. However, it seems to be the case that his opponents did not agree with his vision of the role of women. Some Christians at least were busy elevating the status and power of women. In succeeding generations, these Christians will lose, and the church will become predominantly patriarchal. And the Pastoral Epistles will have played a major role in the defeat of a more elevated and powerful role for women.

QUALIFICATIONS OF BISHOPS AND DEACONS
1 Timothy 3:1–13

3:1 The saying is sure: whoever aspires to the office of bishop desires a noble task. 2 Now a bishop must be above reproach, married only once, temperate, sensible, respectable, hospitable, an apt teacher, 3 not a drunkard, not violent but gentle, not quarrelsome, and not a lover of money. 4 He must manage his own household well, keeping his children submissive and respectful in every way—5 for if someone does not know how to manage his own household, how can he take care of God's church? 6 He must not be a recent convert, or he may be puffed up with conceit and fall into the condemnation of the devil. 7 Moreover, he must be well thought of by outsiders, so that he may not fall into disgrace and the snare of the devil.

8 Deacons likewise must be serious, not double-tongued, not indulging in much wine, not greedy for money; 9 they must hold fast to the mystery of the faith with a clear conscience. 10 And let them first be tested; then, if they prove themselves blameless, let them serve as deacons. 11 Women likewise must be serious, not slanderers, but temperate, faithful in all things. 12 Let deacons be married only once, and let them manage their children and their households well; 13 for those who serve well as deacons gain a good standing for themselves and great boldness in the faith that is in Christ Jesus.

Virtues and Vices

This passage contains the first extensive virtue and vice list and the first set of instructions about church officers. There are virtue and vice lists of various lengths at 1 Timothy 1:9–10; 3:1–7, 8–10, 11–12; 4:12; 6:4–5, 11; 2 Timothy 2:22, 24, 25; 3:2–5, 10; Titus 1:7–8, 10; 2:2–5, 12; 3:3. The frequency of such lists indicates how important virtues and vices were to the author. We have already seen that heretics are known by their vices and that women have been encouraged to adorn themselves with good works. Here, of course, it is church officers who are held to the standards of virtue and vice. As was the norm in early Christianity, the author assumes that Jesus will "judge the living and the dead" (2 Tim. 4:1). Apparently, Jesus will carry out judgment on all Christians, including church officers, based on the two standards of morality and orthodoxy.

Virtue and vice lists occur frequently in Jewish, Greek, and Christian writing in antiquity. It is striking how little these lists differ from one another. Christian lists read much like Stoic and Jewish lists. It is true that this list emphasizes the more gentle and less dramatic of the virtues. There is no sense of the ascetic or antiworldly pleasures virtues practiced by the author's opponents. But it does not seem to be the case that these lists were used to establish identity. They are not a potent way of distinguishing one group from another, except to assert that one group practices virtue and the other vice. Instead, this list draws from the general fund of conservative human values. There is nothing here that any good Roman would not recognize as a virtue.

The Pastoral Epistles have sometimes been accused of surrendering the stringent ethics of the Sermon on the Mount for everyday Greek or Roman morality, and to some extent this is true. However, I do not think the author believes he is surrendering or making any sort of accommodation. Rather, he is calling upon good values as he knows them. The requirement that potential bishops "must be well thought of by outsiders" (3:7) and that they must manage their own households well shows how much this writer is a citizen of his world. He does not share the sectarian mindset of some early Christians, wherein the only good lies within the doors of the church. A bishop must be a good person. Christians, Jews, and Greeks agree on most of what makes a good person. We hold our virtues and vices in common. Thus insiders and outsiders alike should acknowledge the virtuous character of a proper bishop.

What the author does surrender is the patent equation of the church with the good. The good is anchored only in God, and it is found wherever it is found. The church and its leadership are subject to the critique of good virtues. Jesus will judge all people, those in the church and those outside the church, by these very standards.

Even if the author shares his virtues and vices with most other Romans, whether Christian or not, the temperate tone of his ethics is somewhat distinctive. It is not that other New Testament documents or other ancient writers ignored these quiet virtues, but the emphasis upon them, and the lack of emphasis upon the more rigorous virtues, is important. The communal cast to the ethics in Colossians and Ephesians is continued here. However, here the explicit emphasis is less on love and more on gentleness and reasonableness. The radical edge to Christian ethics is certainly dulled in the Pastoral Epistles, for radical behavior upsets the proper balance and dignity of the good life.

In this way, the Pastoral Epistles arm early Christianity with a pattern of morality that it will take into the mainstream of ancient society. We will be known by our modesty, kindness, honesty, reliability; we will not be untrustworthy people. The Pastoral Epistles reject the notion that Christians can live outside of the world in a sacred community, accountable only to each other. Either one is faithful and honest in all one's dealings or one is not.

One of the constant tasks of Christians is to comprehend the relationship of the high ideals of the church with the complexities and demands of secular life. What makes a lawyer a Christian lawyer? What makes a parent a Christian parent? These tasks, which we share with non-Christians, are not extraneous parts of our lives. We are citizens, parents, workers, voters, and we want to be Christian in those moments. The Pastoral Epistles propose that Christians, first of all, will learn and acquire virtues. Then these Christians must take those virtues with them wherever they go. The power of those virtues will shape whatever they do.

Herein lies a classic model for the relationship of the Christian to the non-Christian world. In the church, we reform and mold the soul, and the soul transforms every moment of a person's life. A Christian does not shape a household into a unique Christian shape; rather, the Christian becomes a certain kind of person, and that person behaves with Christian virtues in all relationships and in every moment.

Church Officers

The two leaders mentioned here are bishops and deacons. They are held to very similar ethical standards. The major difference is that the list applied to bishops is more extensive. The list for bishops varies slightly from the one in Titus 1:7–9. Thus we probably should not attempt to find careful distinctions between the ethical requirements for a bishop and those for a deacon. The intent is rather to invoke standard Christian virtues, especially those appropriate for leadership.

The mention of women in 3:11 is a puzzle. As the NRSV notes, the Greek might be rendered as "women," "their [deacons] wives," or even "women deacons." "Women" is the translation with the best grammatical support. But it is difficult to know what such a reference is doing in this passage. The best guess is probably "women deacons." There was no separate word in the New Testament for women deacons. In Romans 16:1, Phoebe is called a deacon with the regular, masculine, Greek word *diakonos*. Thus the passage starts by referring to deacons and then makes a special reference to women deacons. The passage then gives instructions for male deacons to be married only once. This last reference cannot include women deacons, for the Greek reads "husband of one wife." This reading of the passage is admittedly awkward, but it is, I think, the least awkward alternative.

The Pastoral Epistles at different places discuss bishops, elders, deacons, probably deaconesses, and widows. All seem to have official roles of some sort and seem to require some sort of selection and installation. The letters are silent about the specific duties that these groups have. And they do not explain the relationships among them. For instance, we do not know how bishops and elders related to each other or what their relative responsibilities were. This neglect is significant. The author is not trying to design and prescribe a certain form of church order. Rather, he simply assumes an order, which is unknown to us, and attempts to connect those officers to two important things. First, he wants to establish the proper shape of the Pauline teachings and to require the fidelity to those teachings by the officers. Second, he subjects all officers to the high moral standards of that Pauline tradition.

This means that the truth of the gospel governs the adequacy of the church officers. Officers do not define tradition; rather, tradition defines the officers. This is the case for all Christians of all times. We do not define the proper shape of the gospel. It is not as though one can always look at us and see what the true Christian is or what Christ is like. Instead, the gospel creates us into new people. Christ lives in us and shapes us, not into ourselves at our best, but into Christians. We do not define Christ; Christ defines us.

THE PURPOSE OF THE LETTER
1 Timothy 3:14–16

> 3:14 **I hope to come to you soon, but I am writing these instructions to you so that, 15 if I am delayed, you may know how one ought to behave in the household of God, which is the church of the living God, the pillar and bulwark of the truth. 16 Without any doubt, the mystery of our religion is great:**
> **He was revealed in flesh,**
> > **vindicated in spirit,**
> > > **seen by angels,**
> > **proclaimed among Gentiles,**
> > > **believed in throughout the world,**
> > > > **taken up in glory.**

This is an important passage for two reasons. First, the fiction of Pauline authorship and the imagined situation are used in an intriguing way. Second, the author makes use of a curious and elegant christological hymn. In all of this, we learn some interesting new things about the author.

The Authority of Paul

As we noted earlier, the fiction of having Paul write to Timothy, his most trusted confidant, is important for the overall method of the letter. This fiction enables the author to address the heretics and heresies in his church using the voice and authority of Paul. In the fiction of the letter, Paul is writing about his own problems, even though he anticipates future heresies. But it is also the case that "Paul" wants to give specific instructions to Timothy that apply to any and all churches. The instructions here are not specific to one situation or limited to one church. In this way the author creates a conversation between Paul and Timothy that becomes a general exhortation to all churches. Moreover, it is an exhortation with apostolic warrant.

The author creates the fiction with a nice touch. "Paul" imagines a situation when he is absent from the church and wants to leave instructions that can function in his stead. Of course, Paul will never arrive. The author is living in a day of apostolic absence. He reaches back into the past for an apostolic authority and security that his own day lacks. Pauline letters now must take the place of Paul.

We also see here the ethical focus of the letters. The final key is how one behaves. Of course, behavior depends upon a correct understanding of the gospel. We saw this same link between orthodoxy and virtue in Colossians and Ephesians.

The phrase "pillar and bulwark of the truth" when coupled with the term "household of God" (3:15) offers several possible interpretations. The Greek may be rendered as "the house of God . . . the foundation and pillar of truth." This would be a reference to the temple at Jerusalem. Thus the author is comparing the church to the temple, which was a common comparison in the New Testament. The NRSV translation understands the Greek as referring to households, which would certainly square with the other household instructions in the Pastoral Epistles. In either case, in regard to the truth, the church community is given both status and responsibility. Because it has the status of being the source of truth, it has the task of maintaining and promulgating that truth.

The phrase "church of the living God" (3:15) points to the character of God as active. First Timothy 4:10 calls upon "the living God, who is Savior of all people." This probably means that the reference to God as living is a reminder of God's saving activity. Thus the hymn should be read as an account of God's saving activity in Christ.

A Christological Hymn

The hymn in 3:16 is introduced with one of the most loaded religious terms in antiquity, namely, *mystery*. And it seems to possess in this verse its classic meaning. *Mystery* is an account of divine activity that one must learn, understand, and believe if one is to enjoy the benefits of the religion. The hymn gives the mystery—the heretofore unknown account of what God has done in Christ. In this account the secret of the cosmos is unveiled.

The hymn itself is remarkably dense. Every phrase in it has been much debated by scholars, and we cannot chase out all the possibilities here. Almost all readers, however, see an interplay between the fleshly realm and the heavenly, with the two realms mirroring one another. Some readers see a careful chronology of Jesus' life: incarnation, resurrection, ascension, proclamation of the gospel, belief in the gospel, and glorification at the end of time. It is unlikely, however, that "taken up in glory" refers to end-time glorification. It is instead a second reference to the ascension. Thus the hymn might best be understood as follows.

Jesus appeared in the flesh. Because many people see the flesh as contrary to the divine nature, this connection of Jesus with the flesh is problematic. However, the second sentence attempts to overcome this problem. Jesus is "vindicated in spirit" (3:16). This probably refers to the resurrection, which is a sign of God's vindication of Jesus and his ministry. Thus Jesus appears in the fleshly realm, and this appearance is vindicated by God in the spiritual realm, that is, in heaven. In this way, the realm of the flesh itself is given positive value. This will be important in 4:1–5. This appearance and vindication is seen by angels in the spiritual realm, and it is proclaimed and believed in the fleshly realm by humans. Thus both earth and heaven agree to this account of Jesus. Finally, this vindication is reemphasized with the assertion that the ascension included the giving of glory to Jesus.

Read in this way, the hymn becomes a litany to the incarnation. The Johannine assertion that the word became flesh is paralleled here. Furthermore, Jesus' appearance in the flesh, coupled with God's vindication and glorification of him, validates and accentuates our own life in the flesh. Once again, Christology leads to ethics; the story of Jesus shows us how to live this life here.

FALSE ASCETICISM
1 Timothy 4:1–5

4:1 **Now the Spirit expressly says that in later times some will renounce the faith by paying attention to deceitful spirits and teachings of demons,**

2 **through the hypocrisy of liars whose consciences are seared with a hot iron.** 3 **They forbid marriage and demand abstinence from foods, which God created to be received with thanksgiving by those who believe and know the truth.** 4 **For everything created by God is good, and nothing is to be rejected, provided it is received with thanksgiving;** 5 **for it is sanctified by God's word and by prayer.**

This brief affirmation of the goodness of the things of creation builds on the affirmation of the fleshly realm in the hymn of 3:16. It is also the most focused account of the doctrines of the author's opponents. This passage gives weight to the notion that these opponents were Gnostic, for it assumes their antagonism to the world of the flesh.

The critique opens with classic polemical language. First, in the fiction of the letter "Paul" reaches down to the author's day via revelation of the Spirit. The Spirit has revealed to him the heresies that will emerge after his time. The association of these heresies with demons and deceitful spirits is standard, and it illustrates the cosmic horizons of this debate. The reference to the searing of the conscience probably suggests that these persons lack proper moral guidance. From the beginning Christians used the term *conscience* to refer to the part of the person that guides moral choice. We must notice again the connection between heresy and vice. The vices of heresy must be corrected by orthodoxy. Orthodoxy in turn will prove itself in its virtues.

The forbidding of marriage and the abstinence from foods is sometimes associated with the ascetic virtues of Gnostic groups, although the Gnostic communities in the second century do not fit this description any better than many other groups of their time. Even a Jewish community, namely, the Essenes at Qumran, can have tendencies in these directions. Furthermore, ascetic virtues of this sort will earn an important place in mainstream Christianity. Thus we cannot identify precisely the full character of these heretics from these two principles.

But we must note the character of the author's refutation of them. He connects these ascetic principles to a general denial of the world of the flesh. We should recall the affirmation of the world of the flesh in the incarnation hymn in 3:16. Furthermore, classic notions of creation and thanksgiving are advanced here. God created these things (probably both marriage and food) to be received with thanksgiving. The sanctification of these things by "God's word and by prayer" (4:5) probably means that the gospel as given in 3:16 affirms the goodness of the realm of the flesh and that prayers of thanksgiving can transform something ordinary into something sacred.

In all of this an important balance is struck. The great denials of the goodness of the created order in Jewish and Christian circles took the two quite different forms of end-of-the-world theology and Gnosticism. Gnostics emphasized the notion of escape from evil to the good world above. End-time theologians adopted the notion of the advent of a new age in which the evil, created order in which we now live will be destroyed. The Pastoral Epistles admit to neither of these. The goodness of created order is affirmed, and with it the importance and value of life in the flesh is established.

Thus, it is true, as some critics of the Pastoral Epistles assert, that the author adapts Christian thought to the ordinariness of life. This is his intention—to affirm that the virtues and vices of ordinary life are of paramount importance. With this in mind, he will devote much time to seemingly mundane affairs of the community, which are in fact not mundane at all but are the very heart of the Christian life.

This is the so-called bourgeois ethic of the Pastoral Epistles. Christian truth is not found in magnificent theological speculation or in spectacular virtues, but in the quiet morality and order of domestic and ecclesiastic life.

A GOOD MINISTER OF JESUS CHRIST
1 Timothy 4:6–16

4:6 **If you put these instructions before the brothers and sisters, you will be a good servant of Christ Jesus, nourished on the words of the faith and of the sound teaching that you have followed. 7 Have nothing to do with profane myths and old wives' tales. Train yourself in godliness, 8 for, while physical training is of some value, godliness is valuable in every way, holding promise for both the present life and the life to come. 9 The saying is sure and worthy of full acceptance. 10 For to this end we toil and struggle, because we have our hope set on the living God, who is the Savior of all people, especially of those who believe.**

11These are the things you must insist on and teach. 12 Let no one despise your youth, but set the believers an example in speech and conduct, in love, in faith, in purity. 13 Until I arrive, give attention to the public reading of scripture, to exhorting, to teaching. 14 Do not neglect the gift that is in you, which was given to you through prophecy with the laying on of hands by the council of elders. 15 Put these things into practice, devote yourself to them, so that all may see your progress. 16 Pay close attention to yourself and to your teaching; continue in these things, for in doing this you will save both yourself and your hearers.

This exhortation to Timothy about the varied tasks of ministry echoes many of the larger themes of the letter. It also contains an account of the duties of church leaders. But as is the case throughout the Pastoral Epistles, we learn less about the precise assignments of church leaders and more about the character with which those unstated assignments should be carried out. The focus is more ethical and moral than administrative.

Training in Godliness

The exhortation begins with a call to orthodoxy and a reminder of the importance of correct learning and correct teaching. This Pauline teaching must be taught in turn to others. From this we can understand why many readers of the Pastoral Epistles suggest that the author understands the church almost as a school. It is true that the school-like functions of teaching and being taught are essential to the health of the community.

The warning against "profane myths and old wives' tales" (4:7) recalls the polemical context of the letters. The first task of leaders (in fact, of all believers) is to choose which teaching to follow. The fiction of Pauline authorship enters at this point. The author's version of Pauline thought is presented as Paul's own. These are to be understood as Paul's own words.

Teaching and learning are not valued simply for themselves. Their primary value lies in their capacity to produce proper piety: "Train yourself in godliness" (4:7). The word translated here as "godliness" is *eusebeia*, which is the usual word in Greek for the whole range of religious duties. It includes duties to God and to people. The letter itself explains what *eusebeia* is; it is all the virtues and duties that are described therein. And the practice of this godliness is a necessary moment in the process of salvation. It holds the "promise for both the present life and the life to come" (4:8). The God "who is the Savior of all people" (4:10) insists on this godly life. It is fitting that the author adds to the description of God as the savior of all people the addendum "especially of those who believe" (4:10). Believers have been properly outfitted for the godly life; unbelievers have not. Finally, we must note that bodily training is not dismissed altogether. Although it is not clear what the author imagines as "bodily training," he is probably evoking once again his positive evaluation of life in the flesh.

The list of duties that Paul invokes on Timothy in 4:11–16 shows again the importance of both correct teaching and the virtuous life. Timothy must be able to teach and to exhort. And he must show in his own life what the Christian life is: "Set the believers an example in speech and conduct, in love, in faith, in purity" (4:12). The specific duties of Timothy, who probably represents all church leaders, include the public reading of scripture, teaching, and exhorting.

The focus in this is clear. The author is not trying to create or prescribe proper administrative orders. He is promoting the godly life, and his concepts of leadership are subservient to that purpose. For this reason there is no attempt to detail ordination procedures or administrative patterns. In fact, two ordination patterns are mentioned. In 4:14, the council of elders lays on hands. This act of ordination is described as having been prompted by the Spirit. Acts 13:1–3 gives a good parallel. There the Holy Spirit declares that Paul and Barnabas should be set apart for mission. After prayer and fasting "they" lay hands on them. In 2 Timothy 1:6 it is apparently Paul himself who has laid hands on Timothy. There is no attempt in the Pastoral Epistles to work out such divergences in procedure.

Thus the author is not organizing the clergy or trying to distinguish clergy from laity. Rather, he is assuming such distinctions, admitting a variety of procedures and forms of government, and is holding everyone, clergy and laity alike, in whatever form of ecclesiastical government, to the same standards of virtue.

We must note, in conclusion, how all of this is grounded in the character of God. God has inaugurated in Christ a plan of salvation, and God wants all people to be saved thereby. For this to succeed, God needs faithful leaders who will be nourished on the truth and will nourish others with this same truth. The letters detail the doctrinal and ethical truth, and then exhort leadership to take on the tasks of leadership given them: "Do not neglect the gift that is in you" (1 Tim. 4:14); "I remind you to rekindle the gift of God that is within you" (2 Tim. 1:6). If they can do this, then they will save both themselves and their hearers (4:16). Such is the purpose of the letters.

DUTIES IN THE HOUSEHOLD OF GOD
1 Timothy 5:1–6:2a

5:1 **Do not speak harshly to an older man, but speak to him as to a father, to younger men as brothers, 2 to older women as mothers, to younger women as sisters—with absolute purity.**

3 Honor widows who are really widows. 4 If a widow has children or grandchildren, they should first learn their religious duty to their own family and make some repayment to their parents; for this is pleasing in God's sight. 5 The real widow, left alone, has set her hope on God and continues in supplications and prayers night and day; 6 but the widow who lives for pleasure is dead even while she lives. 7 Give these commands as well, so that they

may be above reproach. [8] And whoever does not provide for relatives, and especially for family members, has denied the faith and is worse than an unbeliever.

[9] Let a widow be put on the list if she is not less than sixty years old and has been married only once; [10] she must be well attested for her good works, as one who has brought up children, shown hospitality, washed the saints' feet, helped the afflicted, and devoted herself to doing good in every way. [11] But refuse to put younger widows on the list; for when their sensual desires alienate them from Christ, they want to marry, [12] and so they incur condemnation for having violated their first pledge. [13] Besides that, they learn to be idle, gadding about from house to house; and they are not merely idle, but also gossips and busybodies, saying what they should not say. [14] So I would have younger widows marry, bear children, and manage their households, so as to give the adversary no occasion to revile us. [15] For some have already turned away to follow Satan. [16] If any believing woman has relatives who are really widows, let her assist them; let the church not be burdened, so that it can assist those who are real widows.

[17] Let the elders who rule well be considered worthy of double honor, especially those who labor in preaching and teaching; [18] for the scripture says, "You shall not muzzle an ox while it is treading out the grain," and, "The laborer deserves to be paid." [19] Never accept any accusation against an elder except on the evidence of two or three witnesses. [20] As for those who persist in sin, rebuke them in the presence of all, so that the rest also may stand in fear. [21] In the presence of God and of Christ Jesus and of the elect angels, I warn you to keep these instructions without prejudice, doing nothing on the basis of partiality. [22] Do not ordain anyone hastily, and do not participate in the sins of others; keep yourself pure.

[23] No longer drink only water, but take a little wine for the sake of your stomach and your frequent ailments.

[24] The sins of some people are conspicuous and precede them to judgment, while the sins of others follow them there. [25] So also good works are conspicuous; and even when they are not, they cannot remain hidden.

[6:1] Let all who are under the yoke of slavery regard their masters as worthy of all honor, so that the name of God and the teaching may not be blasphemed. [2] Those who have believing masters must not be disrespectful to them on the ground that they are members of the church; rather they must serve them all the more, since those who benefit by their service are believers and beloved.

The insistence of the Pastoral Epistles that faith must show itself in the moments of everyday life comes to expression in this series of instructions. In all of them, the sense of quiet virtue that pervades the Pastoral Epistles finds expression in rather diverse regulations. Again, although the author is discussing church order, we must note that the author is less concerned with how that order is structured than with the moral character of the people involved. Virtue is the key.

The initial directive not to speak harshly to older persons and to speak with purity to women is an ancient commonplace. This request could have been spoken by nearly anyone in antiquity. Thus the author is simply repeating a common and widely accepted value. What is important is that he applies this value to Timothy, who here represents those in authority. Authority does not give one permission to forgo common civility and respect for others. In fact, the author would say that it is particularly necessary for those in leadership to show respect for others, for they must be models of proper Christian behavior.

The Status of Widows

The discussion of widows is the most lengthy and focused discussion of any issue in the Pastoral Epistles. When dealing with elders, deacons, and bishops, the author assumes that they are properly organized. He does not detail election procedures or duties, but only the requirements of character. But with widows the issue seems less resolved. He is perhaps breaking some new ground on the administrative level.

We know from later debates in Christian literature that the order of widows becomes both important and controversial. The order of widows becomes a method through which Christian women could have independence from men. The ancient world was not kind to unattached women, unless those women were wealthy. Women, whether Jew or Greek, typically had to find a male relative or husband in order to have regular social and economic status. There were exceptions, but they seem to be confined to the upper classes.

The churches with which the Pastoral Epistles are concerned apparently had established an official order wherein unattached women could be enrolled. The larger church community offered the necessary economic support to those in the order, and the duties and rights of the order provided the needed social status.

In later years this order came under criticism because of the presence of young women in the membership. A third-century collection of non-biblical stories of Paul, *The Acts of Paul and Thecla*, gives a fascinating account of how the young and beautiful Thecla escapes an unwanted marriage through the protection of wealthy Christian women and through the taking of a vow to Christ. This escape is seen by her non-Christian husband-to-be and her own parents as a violation of her cultural duties. Paul himself, according to the story, refuses to baptize her. Only other women will protect her.

In order to understand the discussion in 1 Timothy it is helpful to imagine similar problems. It appears that the order of widows is growing too fast; it is becoming a financial burden on the church; and young widows are causing problems. From the language of 5:12 it is apparent that enrollment in the order entailed a vow of fidelity to Christ, perhaps a marriage vow. Christ becomes the male to whom they are attached. There is no mention here of problems with potential husbands feeling deserted. Rather, the young widows themselves want to marry and thus violate their marriage pledge to Christ. Whether the order was creating problems with the non-Christian world is not clear.

The author offers the following solution. First, the original family of the widows is responsible for them. A special injunction is given to wealthy women to support widows among their relatives. However, if there is no other option, the church will provide.

The author must be making a distinction between widows and enrolled widows. The requirement that a widow be at least sixty before being enrolled would mean that a fifty-year-old "real" widow would be left unprotected. It is best to imagine two issues. One involves financial support; the other the enrollment in the order. Only "real" widows, those who are "left alone" and are sixty years old, can be enrolled. Once enrolled they cannot revoke their pledge to Christ, and they must take on pastoral duties. "Real" widows who are younger are entitled to financial support, but they should not take the pledge to Christ that enrollment requires.

The warning against younger widows being enrolled because they become gossips and busybodies suggests that "enrolled" widows had visitation responsibilities. In the same way, it seems likely from 5:10 that the order also took on other service duties. From 5:5 it seems that the order also had prayer duties of a community kind. The conviction that monks do the praying that others do not have time to do is perhaps anticipated here. Their aloneness gives them time to do the praying the community needs done.

In all of this, the author displays his conviction that the household is the basic social unit. Women must belong to a household, and the first option should always be their traditional household units. The church should be the household of last resort. Yet it is important that the church is considered a potential household. As the author thinks of the church as household, the traditional household hierarchies invade the church. We have seen that pattern in both Colossians and Ephesians, and it continues here. The household in antiquity was patriarchal. Thus the more that household norms influence the church's thinking about itself, the more patriarchal its administrative patterns become.

Finally, we must note that widows are held to much the same ethical standards as all other church leaders. Given the ethical vision of the author, this is, of course, to be expected. All officers must be examples of the Christian life. Enrolled widows must show how all widows should live.

Duties and Rights of Elders

The instructions about elders concern recompense and discipline. The NSRV translates *timē* as "honor" in the text (5:17) and "compensation" in the notes. But given the scriptures that follow and the concern for church finances that the widows issue evoked, "compensation" is probably better. The notion that elders could be convicted and rebuked by the community shows how thoroughly the author is subjecting everyone in the community to his high ethical standards. Virtue is the key, and leaders have the greater responsibility here. They must, in fact, be "above reproach" (1 Tim. 3:2) and "blameless" (Titus 1:6, 7). The image here is of a community that disciplines itself. Leaders guide and discipline the community, and the community disciplines the leaders in turn.

The Obedience of Slaves

The appeal to slaves echoes Colossians 3:22–25 and Ephesians 6:5–8, but adds its own emphases. The concern about the gospel being blasphemed recurs in the appeal to slaves in Titus 2:10. Disobedient slaves would suggest to the Roman world that Christianity was a subversive religion. This was, of course, exactly what the Romans frequently thought. After all, the Romans had crucified the founder. Disobedient slaves bring disrepute and even danger to the whole community.

Furthermore, the author insists that, when masters are members of the community, slaves should obey them even more. In this, we detect the dangers in the social leveling that often occurred in Christian communities. The author does not explicitly censor such leveling, but he does not really support it. In fact, the household norms, which he favors, include strict hierarchies. Of course, everyone is equal in God's sight, and everyone will be judged by the same standards.

In this passage we can see the great accomplishment of the Pastoral

Epistles. No matter who the person or what the circumstance, the moral questions are the ultimate ones. Do you live the life of virtue or not? How virtue is expressed will be somewhat different depending on who you are and what your duties are. But, on the last day, all such distinctions will disappear, and the question of virtue and vice will remain. For the author of the Pastoral Epistles, as for the authors of Colossians and Ephesians, ethical questions are the ultimate ones.

FALSE TEACHING AND THE GOOD FIGHT OF FAITH
Timothy 6:2b–21

6:2b **Teach and urge these duties. [3] Whoever teaches otherwise and does not agree with the sound words of our Lord Jesus Christ and the teaching that is in accordance with godliness, [4] is conceited, understanding nothing, and has a morbid craving for controversy and for disputes about words. From these come envy, dissension, slander, base suspicions, [5] and wrangling among those who are depraved in mind and bereft of the truth, imagining that godliness is a means of gain. [6] Of course, there is great gain in godliness combined with contentment; [7] for we brought nothing into the world, so that we can take nothing out of it; [8] but if we have food and clothing, we will be content with these. [9] But those who want to be rich fall into temptation and are trapped by many senseless and harmful desires that plunge people into ruin and destruction. [10] For the love of money is a root of all kinds of evil, and in their eagerness to be rich some have wandered away from the faith and pierced themselves with many pains.**

[11] But as for you, man of God, shun all this; pursue righteousness, godliness, faith, love, endurance, gentleness. [12] Fight the good fight of the faith; take hold of the eternal life, to which you were called and for which you made the good confession in the presence of many witnesses. [13] In the presence of God, who gives life to all things, and of Christ Jesus, who in his testimony before Pontius Pilate made the good confession, I charge you [14] to keep the commandment without spot or blame until the manifestation of our Lord Jesus Christ, [15] which he will bring about at the right time—he who is the blessed and only Sovereign, the King of kings and Lord of lords. [16] It is he alone who has immortality and dwells in unapproachable light, whom no one has ever seen or can see; to him be honor and eternal dominion. Amen.

[17] As for those who in the present age are rich, command them not to be haughty, or to set their hopes on the uncertainty of riches, but rather on God who richly provides us with everything for our enjoyment. [18] They are to do good, to be rich in good works, generous, and ready to share, [19] thus

storing up for themselves the treasure of a good foundation for the future, so that they may take hold of the life that really is life.

[20] Timothy, guard what has been entrusted to you. Avoid the profane chatter and contradictions of what is falsely called knowledge; [21] by professing it some have missed the mark as regards the faith.

Grace be with you.

The False Rewards of Godliness

These verses form a fitting conclusion to 1 Timothy, for they summarize the author's understanding of the ethical life. The ancient world had sophisticated discussions of the power of human desire and the vices that result from that desire. The author's analysis of the problem of desire and wealth in 6:3–10 sounds like many other such analyses by his contemporaries. Everyone, including our author, admitted that desire, the passions, leads to vice and evil. The debate concerned how passion could be controlled and how virtues could be acquired. And our author will give his own, rather unique, answers.

The author signals his unique vision in 6:3, wherein he identifies his vice-filled opponents as those who do not agree with and do not teach "the sound words of our Lord Jesus Christ." Those sound words have been articulated in the letter as orthodox, Pauline tradition. This means that proper gospel tradition is the fundamental solution to virtue and vice. As we have seen throughout the letter, the holding of heterodox opinions leads to a life of vice. Of course, the holding of the sound, orthodox teachings leads to virtue.

The author describes these heterodox teachers in classic terms; they are overrun by their desires. This is the ultimate evil in Greek thought, to be governed by the passions rather than reason. The twist here is that orthodox tradition, rather than reason, is the alternative to passion.

In 6:6–8, the author gives his second twist to this classic discussion. Any Stoic would recommend contentment with simple food and clothing. One way to control desires is to be satisfied with less. The author, who believes in the goodness of creation and the enjoyment of food and drink (recall 1 Tim. 4:1–5), also believes in moderation. The call to moderation is traditional and nearly universal in Greek thought. More distinctive is the contrast the author makes between this life and the future life. Herein emerges the author's Christian perspective. In fact, this focus upon the life to come becomes the driving image of 1 Timothy 6. This is where one's desire should be addressed. Desire the good things of the next life. Implied in this is the traditional Christian argument that the future life is more significant that the present life. Of course, we should remember that this same author is insisting over against his opponents on the goodness of creation and our life in it. In all of this, he is pursuing a balance between enjoyment of this life and desire for the life to come.

The problem of the rich fits naturally with the larger problem of desire. Desire comes from wanting things in or of the world; it comes from making a claim upon the many good things in life. Rich people, more than anyone else, are vulnerable to the domination of these desires. They can have so much. Their desires become attached to the things of the world. They become driven by desire, "pierced . . . with many pains" (6:10). For many Greeks and early Christians, this is the ultimate death, to be eaten up by one's own passions.

The True Rewards of Godliness

The remedy, as we have seen, is twofold: to hold to orthodoxy and to attach one's desires to eternal life. Both of these emerge in the exhortation in 6:11–16. These verses are filled with key and often-repeated images from the Pastoral Epistles. The list of virtues—righteousness, godliness, faith, love, endurance, gentleness—recalls the quiet, communal tone of the ethics of the Pastoral Epistles. The call to "fight the good fight of faith" (6:12) reiterates the general mood and purpose of the letter—to exhort the faithful, orthodox, and virtuous life.

The author grounds the call to make the good confession (i.e., to hold to orthodoxy) and to pursue eternal life in the story of Jesus. Jesus himself made the confession and thereby becomes connected to the saving activity of God. As God acted in Jesus, so will God act for us. Thus the exhortation to the orthodox, virtuous life is thereby connected to a theological promise—a promise that God will reward faithful behavior in this life with eternal rewards. In this way, the praise to God that concludes these verses serves as a statement of God's capacity to reward. God possesses the eternal blessedness and will bestow gifts of heaven on faithful Christians.

Christian ethics has traditionally been constructed in this way. The faithful Christian life with its virtues is not self-justifying. Its value lies in great part in God's response to it. God will, in the next life, reward the virtues and faithful deeds of this life. The Christian life is always built on some such promise. Thus Christian ethics depends on the truths of the larger Christian story. They do not stand on their own. The story of salvation gives them meaning and credibility. Furthermore, as we have seen, a Christian must partake of the larger resources of the church in order to acquire these virtues. We need the power of baptism and the instructions of the tradition in order to realize the virtuous life.

The specific promise is punctuated in 6:14 by the admonition "to keep the commandment without spot or blame until the manifestation of our Lord Jesus Christ" (6:14). The promise is hereby connected with a warning: We shall be judged.

The christological framework of the Pastoral Epistles can at this point be grasped. Jesus works by means of two appearances. At the first, Jesus revealed the truths about himself and gave to the church the resources for the righteous life (e.g., 1 Tim. 3:16). At the second appearance, Jesus will judge persons accordingly. Jesus does not seem to function by way of mystical presence in the community, as he does in Paul or in Colossians and Ephesians. The piety of the Pastoral Epistles is not mystical in the same way. The Spirit may be present, but Jesus is perceived as absent. Jesus has been here and will return, but he is not here now.

It is important for us to remember how many different perceptions of Jesus the church experiences. Christians differ from one another in their experience of the divine. The Pastoral Epistles are written by a sober, non-mystical, and gentle believer. The mystical flights of John or the deep meditations on suffering of Paul are lacking here. Yet, this sober theology has a rightful place in our tradition. The Bible authenticates many different experiences of God. This is perhaps one of the reasons Christians have different favorite texts.

The final admonition to the rich can be understood as the conclusion to the discussion of desire and its dangers. The Pastoral Epistles and early Christians in general may have been suspicious of wealth, but they do not forbid it outright. The author's advice to the rich becomes identical to his advice to anyone: Avoid desire for the things of the world; instead, desire the gifts of the future life, showing that desire in good deeds. This is the classic Christian response to the question of wealth: Store up your wealth in heaven and not in the transient goods of this world. For the author of the Pastoral Epistles, such wealth is acquired through fidelity to the apostolic traditions and practice of the good Christian virtues.

Guarding the Tradition

The final instructions to Timothy and the concluding benediction continue the mood of summary that began in 6:2b. First, "guard what has been entrusted to you" (6:20a). This guarding of tradition is precisely what the letter wants to accomplish. We have seen that the guarding of this tradition is a creative process. The author and those who heed his admonition must rearticulate the tradition in the new moment. This is always both a conservative and innovative act.

On the other side, the author warns against the heretics, coining the classic phrase that will be used by the orthodox against all Gnostics: "Avoid the profane chatter and contradictions of what is falsely called knowledge" (6:20b). The reference to contradictions is sometimes seen as a reference to Marcion's own compilations of "contradictions" or, as it is sometimes translated, "antitheses." (Marcion was an influential Christian Gnostic.) However, there is little evidence that the opponents referred to in the Pastoral Epistles were practicing Marcion-style antitheses, which consisted of detailing the contradictions between the Old and New Testaments, the law versus the gospel. In the Pastoral Epistles, "contradictions" probably means something like "illogical propositions."

In any case, this concluding exhortation rehearses a key project of the letter—distinguishing orthodoxy from heresy. As we have seen, this distinguishing includes both theology and ethics.

In all of this, the author's deep reliance on tradition is clear. Tradition, properly learned and properly practiced, gives life. The modern back-to-the-Bible movement seems, at first glance, to have it right. The health of modern churches lies in remembering the language and visions of our tradition. But we must also remember that such remembering is a creative act. The many faces of tradition must be sorted, reordered, and reconfigured. It takes the living Spirit to understand the past.

CONCLUSION

Of the many marvels of 1 Timothy, the one I would like to recall at this point is the author's universal perception of God. In 1 Timothy God is described as "God our savior who desires everyone to be saved." And key to the author's perception of God is the truth that "there is one God." Even Christ in 1 Timothy "gave himself as a ransom for all." A classic Christian image is hereby outlined: One God over all the people of the world.

On the one hand, this image of God sits at the very heart of what most Christians would want to say about God. How can God not be the God of all people? Every human being is a child of God. We all say this one way or another. On the other hand, this universal vision of God raises puzzling questions about the particularities involved in faith in Jesus. Why

Jesus? Why not just God? Why listen to Christian tradition and not to all other religious traditions? If God is the God of all, God must have been nourishing and guiding others, these others who are not Christians. Who are we, the Jesus people, to think we have the only truth? Don't we need to surrender either this vision of God caring equally for everyone or our vision of Jesus as the way?

What strikes me about 1 Timothy is the author's refusal to surrender either side of this dilemma. He thinks them both at the same time. Jesus is the only key, the only final judge. And God is God of all. This seems to me to be the most powerful and disturbing option. To escape this tension is to surrender something essential to the Christian life. We are to hold fast to our traditions; we are to proclaim the Lordship of Jesus Christ; we are to perceive God through the lens of Jesus. And the God we see through this particular lens is the God of all people, who holds all people with the same hand.

Commentary on 2 Timothy

SALUTATION
2 Timothy 1:1–2

> 1:1 **Paul, an apostle of Christ Jesus by the will of God, for the sake of the promise of life that is in Christ Jesus,**
> **2 To Timothy, my beloved child:**
> **Grace, mercy, and peace from God the Father and Christ Jesus our Lord.**

Second Timothy is the most personal and emotional of the Pastoral Epistles. It, like 1 Timothy, is ostensibly a personal exchange between Paul and his trusted confidant, Timothy. In fact, it, like 1 Timothy, is a public document written to the larger audience of Pauline churches. Many of the themes encountered in 1 Timothy are reiterated here. The concern for tradition, the refutation of heretics, the appeal to Paul as a model, the insistence on virtues, and a Christology based on two appearances all recur here with slight nuances. The most notable absence is the reduced concern for church offices. This letter will focus on the themes of suffering and death to an extent not anticipated in 1 Timothy.

The salutation is nearly identical to the one in 1 Timothy. The slight differences do not signal any detectable thematic divergences between the letters. The author is simply selecting from the rich fund of theological images that animate his writings. Nevertheless, a reminder of the "promise of life that is in Christ Jesus" (1:1) fits with the themes of suffering and death in the letter. Of course, the denotation of Paul as "an apostle of Christ Jesus by the will of God" is necessary for the theology and argument of the letter. The call to return to tradition works best when the author's version of that tradition is presented as Paul's own.

THANKSGIVING AND ENCOURAGEMENT
2 Timothy 1:3–18

1:3 I am grateful to God—whom I worship with a clear conscience, as my ancestors did—when I remember you constantly in my prayers night and day. 4 Recalling your tears, I long to see you so that I may be filled with joy. 5 I am reminded of your sincere faith, a faith that lived first in your grandmother Lois and your mother Eunice and now, I am sure, lives in you. 6 For this reason I remind you to rekindle the gift of God that is within you through the laying on of my hands; 7 for God did not give us a spirit of cowardice, but rather a spirit of power and of love and of self-discipline.

8 Do not be ashamed, then, of the testimony about our Lord or of me his prisoner, but join with me in suffering for the gospel, relying on the power of God, 9 who saved us and called us with a holy calling, not according to our works but according to his own purpose and grace. This grace was given to us in Christ Jesus before the ages began, 10 but it has now been revealed through the appearing of our Savior Christ Jesus, who abolished death and brought life and immortality to light through the gospel. 11 For this gospel I was appointed a herald and an apostle and a teacher, 12 and for this reason I suffer as I do. But I am not ashamed, for I know the one in whom I have put my trust, and I am sure that he is able to guard until that day what I have entrusted to him. 13 Hold to the standard of sound teaching that you have heard from me, in the faith and love that are in Christ Jesus. 14 Guard the good treasure entrusted to you, with the help of the Holy Spirit living in us.

15 You are aware that all who are in Asia have turned away from me, including Phygelus and Hermogenes. 16 May the Lord grant mercy to the household of Onesiphorus, because he often refreshed me and was not ashamed of my chain; 17 when he arrived in Rome, he eagerly searched for me and found me 18—may the Lord grant that he will find mercy from the Lord on that day! And you know very well how much service he rendered in Ephesus.

First Timothy, 2 Timothy, and Titus, for the most part, share theological perspectives and theological language. Almost all readers of the letters detect a common viewpoint. However, each letter has its own emphasis. Second Timothy is the most striking in its distinctiveness. In tone, 2 Timothy is the most personal of the three. Paul, in anticipation of his own death, is sharing intimate and poignant thoughts with his most trusted confidant. Furthermore, this imagined setting of Paul on the eve of his execution gives occasion for a careful meditation on suffering and death. We will see these themes woven throughout the text.

The Faith of Our Parents

Pauline letters normally begin with a prayer or a literary reference to prayer. Second Timothy 1:3–7 is not a prayer in itself but an exhortation grounded upon prayer. The reference to prayer is not only traditional but provides the proper tone to the personal exhortations that follow.

The references to Paul's ancestors and Timothy's mother and grandmother have occasioned much speculation. We are told in Acts 16:1 that Timothy was the "son of a Jewish woman who was a believer; but his father was a Greek." The reference to his mother could also be translated more simply as a "faithful Jewish woman." It is not clear in Acts whether this meant his mother was a Jew or a Jewish Christian. She may have been a Jew who married a Gentile and then converted to Christianity. We have no information on his grandmother. The reference to the good worship by Paul's own ancestors suggests that the author of 2 Timothy is not distinguishing in this passage between the faith of a Jew and that of a Christian. This means that the faith that dwelt in Lois and Eunice could have been good Jewish faith in God.

The ultimate point for the author is the faith environment that the family creates. We should recall the importance of the household for the author. Stable households are necessary to the Christian life. Church officers must be successful at teaching and maintaining the faith in their homes. One of the greatest sins of the author's opponents is that they upset households. This letter was written in a time when the home was becoming central to the Christian life. Modern concern with the religious character of the family is anticipated here. Families must teach and practice the Christian life. We learn from our parents, and we pass it on to our children. The maintenance of tradition, which is so important for the author, must be practiced not only in the church but also in the home.

The Laying On of Hands

The exhortation in 1:6 seems to recall either an ordination event or a dedication to a special task. Laying on of hands does not necessarily indicate ordination to an established office. There has been much speculation as to why 2 Timothy 1:6 indicates that Paul laid hands on Timothy, whereas 1 Timothy 4:14 states that it was the council of elders. Of course, Paul could have participated in a general ordination service in which he, the apostle, and the elders all laid on hands. It is more likely that the author of the Pastoral Epistles is not recalling an actual event, but is stylizing the rite of laying on hands to fit different contexts. First Timothy is working on identifying and enrolling proper leadership in the church. Second Timothy is focusing on the personal relationship between Paul and Timothy. In any case, the point of the reference here is to call for Timothy to "rekindle the gift of God that is within you" (1:6).

This call to rekindle the *charisma* ("the gift of God") introduces a major theme of the letter. Paul is portrayed in 2 Timothy as an abandoned (or nearly abandoned) church leader who remains faithful to the tasks given him. Timothy is encouraged to rekindle his call to leadership even though people are turning away from him. Thus, 2 Timothy is a call to all orthodox church leaders to be faithful to the true gospel even if people are following heresy.

Timothy is first of all reminded that the Spirit he was given was not a "spirit of cowardice, but rather a spirit of power and of love and of self-discipline" (1:7). The description of the Spirit as a spirit that enables the ethical life fits, of course, with the overall theology of the letter. The danger of cowardice comes, as we will see, from the problem of suffering and the scandal of the crucifixion. Thus the call to rekindle the gift of God leads to a call not to be ashamed "of the testimony about our Lord or of me his prisoner" (1:8).

The Problem of Suffering

Herein lies the first aspect of the problem of suffering that will dominate this letter. The story of Jesus is an embarrassment. To have the Lord of the church be crucified, to have the eternal judge of heaven and earth die on a cross, is a scandal. As Paul declares in 1 Corinthians, the cross is foolishness. It does not fit with the Roman sense of the power of a ruler.

It is no coincidence that the author identifies the Spirit as a spirit of power. Of course, in the paradoxes of the gospel, this is power to face and admit to suffering. Thus Paul asks that Timothy not be ashamed of the suffering of Jesus or of Paul himself. The logical conclusion is that certain members of the author's church were somehow circumventing the story of the crucifixion and denying the essential role of suffering in the Christian life. In a variety of ways, the author will insist on suffering as a proper and even necessary part of faithfulness to the gospel.

The Suffering of the Church Leader

The fact that Paul's capacity for enduring suffering is anchored (1:8–11) in both the power of God and the promises of the gospel is crucial to the theology of the letter. "Paul" is asking Timothy and, through Timothy, all church leaders, to take on the suffering that comes with the gospel. This suffering can be endured only through the empowerment of the Spirit and through the promise of reward. The theological content of the grace that has come in Jesus Christ is that Jesus has "abolished death and brought life and immortality to light" (1:10). We can endure the suffering and death that faithful leadership produces because God is present in that suffering and because God will reward us. Given this theological conviction, the author will enjoin suffering on his readers. Paul will model the proper response to suffering and death, and he will appeal to his readers to accept it in their lives.

This theological promise is in turn anchored in an assurance of God's capacity to preserve Paul's *parathēkē*. The NRSV gives two possible translations for the Greek "my *parathēkē*," suggesting either "what I have entrusted to him" or "what has been entrusted to me" (1:12). The former would suggest that Paul has been accruing credit in heaven. The latter would refer to the apostolic tradition with which Paul has been entrusted and which he is in turn entrusting to Timothy. The latter fits better, in my opinion, with the theology of the Pastoral Epistles. The author is calling upon God to preserve within the life of the church the true apostolic version of the gospel, the version that remembers the truth of the crucifixion and accepts Christian suffering. This also fits with the constant mention of shame. Neither Timothy nor Paul should be ashamed of the gospel. This reading also fits better with the concluding admonition to Timothy to "guard the good *parathēkē*" (1:14, NRSV: "the good treasure entrusted to you"). Furthermore, as we have seen in 1 Timothy, the author is concerned with establishing and preserving the true tradition.

Thus the argument runs something like this. Both the crucifixion of Jesus and the sufferings that frequent the Christian life are embarrassments to some people. Nevertheless, they are essential aspects of the gospel story and the Christian life. They are connected with the promise of reward in heaven, from the God who abolished death and manifested eternal life. Despite the shame some people have over this gospel, this is indeed the true gospel. The author is convinced that God will always find loyal church leaders who will hold to this gospel and teach it to others. The tradition, with all its embarrassments, is secure, because God will secure it.

The passage concludes with an illustration of faithless and faithful reactions to the sufferings of the gospel. Phygelus and Hermogenes are otherwise unknown, as is Onesiphorus. There has been much speculation about their relationship to Paul or to the author. Most readers think that

Phygelus and Hermogenes were either historical enemies of Paul or infamous heretics who are here being associated with Paul. The same kind of guesses are applied to Onesiphorus; either he was an actual friend of the historical Paul or a figure known to the author's community who is here associated with Paul. Whatever the actual truth, they all function in 2 Timothy as examples of faithless and faithful reactions to the imprisonment of Paul. One can either flee the scandal of the cross and its suffering, or one can embrace them. These reactions are here portrayed in personal terms. Do we remain attached and loyal to those who suffer for the gospel, or do we become ashamed of them and turn away?

A GOOD SOLDIER OF CHRIST JESUS
2 Timothy 2:1–13

> 2:1 **You then, my child, be strong in the grace that is in Christ Jesus;** [2] **and what you have heard from me through many witnesses entrust to faithful people who will be able to teach others as well.** [3] **Share in suffering like a good soldier of Christ Jesus.** [4] **No one serving in the army gets entangled in everyday affairs; the soldier's aim is to please the enlisting officer.** [5] **And in the case of an athlete, no one is crowned without competing according to the rules.** [6] **It is the farmer who does the work who ought to have the first share of the crops.** [7] **Think over what I say, for the Lord will give you understanding in all things.**
>
> [8] **Remember Jesus Christ, raised from the dead, a descendant of David— that is my gospel,** [9] **for which I suffer hardship, even to the point of being chained like a criminal. But the word of God is not chained.** [10] **Therefore I endure everything for the sake of the elect, so that they may also obtain the salvation that is in Christ Jesus, with eternal glory.** [11] **The saying is sure:**
> **If we have died with him, we will also live with him;**
> [12]   **if we endure, we will also reign with him;**
> **if we deny him, he will also deny us;**
> [13]   **if we are faithless, he remains faithful—**
> **for he cannot deny himself.**

This passage repeats the themes of the first chapter, putting them in the form of a direct exhortation to Timothy that is grounded in the example of Paul's behavior and in the promises that are in Christ. Thus the description of Paul's behavior will demonstrate how faithful persons respond to the gospel and its suffering. Paul's behavior, along with that of everyone who suffers, is anchored in the gospel story, which is a story of death and resurrection. The theological argument is a classic Christian one:

Christians endure suffering and death because, just as Jesus passed through suffering and death into life, so shall we.

The call to "be strong in the grace that is in Christ Jesus" (2:1) repeats the call in 1:6 to "rekindle the gift of God that is within you." The commandment to entrust (here we have the verbal form of *parathēkē*) to faithful people what you have heard echoes 1:14. This insistence that the tradition be entrusted to faithful people was a constant theme of 1 Timothy and is a key idea in the Pastoral Epistles. The author declares that tradition must be cared for through the offices of the church. Leaders must not only hold to the correct Pauline gospel, but they must be able to teach others (2 Tim. 2:2), others who are also reliable people. If there is any job that we know for certain belongs to church office in the Pastoral Epistles, it is this task of maintaining tradition. In fact, the necessity for an ecclesiastical structure comes from the importance the author places upon apostolic tradition. Without reliable and accessible tradition, it is very difficult, in the author's opinion, to manage the Christian life. Thus the church must find persons able to monitor and maintain the ancient apostolic teachings.

The bold call to "share in suffering like a good soldier of Christ Jesus" (2:3) evokes the theological controversy that seems to underlie this letter. The call in 1 Timothy 1:7 not to be ashamed of suffering is simplified here into a direct call to suffer. This call will be reinforced by Paul's own claims about his apostleship in 2:8–10. He suffers and endures imprisonment both for the gospel of Christ and for the elect. Of course, this is the task of an apostle—to become dedicated both to the gospel and to the hearers of the gospel.

A Hymn of Christ

Paul's story and the general call to suffering are anchored in the christological hymn in 2:11–13. It is the hymn that gives the rules mentioned in 2:5. The series of analogies in 2:4–6 point to the Christology in 2:11–13, but we do not need to press these analogies too far. Their purpose here is to demonstrate that there are rules that must be followed. The true rules of the cosmos, the rules of the Christian life, are found in the story of Christ. This is the basic Christian claim. We see God through the lens of Jesus Christ. Thus the gospel of Christ manifests the real truth of the world. The final reality is the Christ reality. Here the story of Christ points especially to the problem of suffering and death.

The christological hymn in 2:11–13 is introduced with the now-familiar "the saying is sure." As we have seen elsewhere, the author uses this phrase to introduce doctrine that he considers to be completely reliable. The hymn that follows articulates an ultimate truth. In fact, the author adds the brief note at the end of the hymn that "he [Jesus] cannot deny himself" (2:13). The revelation of God's character in the story of Jesus is not a one-time, peculiar, never-to-be-repeated event. If anything, the Jesus story is the opposite, for it is the revelation of God's true character. Thus the theological truths of the Jesus story, of the gospel, will be forever repeated. The story of Jesus outlines the ultimate forces and patterns of the cosmos because this story manifests the true character of God.

Almost all readers of 2:11–13 detect liturgical patterns in the syntax of the hymn. The most likely conclusion is that this hymn has been hammered into liturgical shape in the worship life of the church. Thus the author would be quoting a hymn his readers are likely to know. It is possible, of course, that the author is simply imitating liturgical style and that he wrote these verses himself.

Whatever the origin, the hymn has a crucial function in the letter. Here we find the christological truth of Christian suffering and death. It is striking how well the hymn addresses the theological theme of the letter. It is a hymnic meditation on suffering and death, just as the letter is a theological exhortation to Christians not to be ashamed of the suffering and death of Jesus and to admit suffering in their own lives.

"If we have died with him, we will also live with him" (2:11). Herein is the basic claim of the Christian gospel. The story of Jesus' death and resurrection is our story as well. It is our story, if we are connected with Jesus, if we die "with" him. There are many proposals in Christian theology for how we become and remain connected with Jesus' death. The author may be assuming Paul's own sense of mystical connection by way of baptism (compare Rom. 6:3–5), but there is little direct evidence for it. What is clear is that the hymn itself details how this connection is maintained. We must endure the suffering that the gospel brings upon us. We must confess our faith in the true Jesus story, the version that includes suffering and death, for, if we deny Jesus, Jesus will deny us. In this way, the hymn expresses the constant theme of the letter to take on the suffering of the gospel.

The final line of the hymn is not as clear as the others. The question is whether the affirmed faithfulness of Jesus is a threat or a promise. The disorder of our faithlessness is addressed throughout this letter and, in fact, throughout the Pastoral Epistles. It is clear what our faithlessness looks like. Jesus' response of faithfulness to our faithlessness must mean that, at a minimum, the truths of the gospel stand even if we deny them. This theological fact is both good news and bad, depending on how judgment falls on someone.

This passage works with a classic Christian truth. There is no resurrection without crucifixion; there is no crown without the cross. For all Christians this means there is no joy, no genuine hope, apart from suffering. We must die in order to live. Christians have meditated upon the puzzling truths of all this for two thousand years. What it means from moment to moment, for life to life, will be quite different. We have drawn many diverse and profound insights from this truth. And this study cannot rehearse them here. Of course, 2 Timothy itself, along with 2 Corinthians, Mark, John, and Revelation, is one of the most important meditations on this theme in the canon.

REBUKING OF HERESY
2 Timothy 2:14–26

2:14 **Remind them of this, and warn them before God that they are to avoid wrangling over words, which does no good but only ruins those who are listening. [15] Do your best to present yourself to God as one approved by him, a worker who has no need to be ashamed, rightly explaining the word of truth. [16] Avoid profane chatter, for it will lead people into more and more impiety, [17] and their talk will spread like gangrene. Among them are Hymenaeus and Philetus, [18] who have swerved from the truth by claiming that the resurrection has already taken place. They are upsetting the faith of some. [19] But God's firm foundation stands, bearing this inscription: "The Lord knows those who are his," and, "Let everyone who calls on the name of the Lord turn away from wickedness."**

[20] In a large house there are utensils not only of gold and silver but also of wood and clay, some for special use, some for ordinary. [21] All who cleanse themselves of the things I have mentioned will become special utensils, dedicated and useful to the owner of the house, ready for every good work. [22] Shun youthful passions and pursue righteousness, faith, love, and peace, along with those who call on the Lord from a pure heart. [23] Have nothing to do with stupid and senseless controversies; you know that they breed quarrels. [24] And the Lord's servant must not be quarrelsome but kindly to everyone, an apt teacher, patient, [25] correcting opponents with gentleness. God may perhaps grant that they will repent and come to know the truth, [26] and that they may escape from the snare of the devil, having been held captive by him to do his will.

This is one of the many passages in the Pastoral Epistles that address the problem of heretics. As we have seen, this letter has addressed the problem of heresy by insisting on the suffering and death aspect of the gospel. The author demands the clear articulation of the truth of the gospel and the rebuke and correction of heresy. Thus far, we might assume that heretics should be treated brusquely and even highhandedly. This passage contends otherwise.

The key theme of this passage is that Timothy and the church leadership must not become entangled in fights and controversy. The concluding verses (2:23–26) sum up the argument nicely. "Have nothing to do with stupid and senseless controversies" for they "breed quarrels" (2:23). In fact, a servant of the Lord who wants to rebuke heretics, which is a duty of a church leader, must do so with gentleness. The qualities that are exhorted in verses 24–25 seemed designed to forestall any fights and bitterness that doctrinal disagreement can cause. The Greek word translated in verse 24 as "patient" means, more literally, "putting up with evil." The reason for this gentleness in the rebuke of heretics is given in verses 25–26: God may, perhaps through your rebuke, move them to repentance. The author will note in Titus 3:3 that "we ourselves were once foolish, disobedient." We should recall the notion from 1 Timothy 2:4 that God wants all people to be saved.

Herein lies the key to understanding heresy and heretics. We are to remember the enormous danger of their doctrines. These doctrines must be refuted. But we must not fight with the people themselves, for God wants and is working to save them. The universalistic and tolerant tone of the Pastoral Epistles is evidenced here.

This exhortation to gentleness is not an attempt to downplay the danger of heresy. The image in 2:17 evokes the horror of heresy as potently as any in the New Testament. The NRSV translation "their talk will spread like gangrene" softens the Greek a bit. A more literal translation would read "their talk will feed like gangrene." Heresy is a vivid danger that must be overcome with the firm foundation of God's word.

The statement in 2:18 that these heretics are "claiming that the resurrection has already taken place" has occasioned much speculation. There is a textual variant here with good support that would read "a resurrection has already taken place." Both textual readings suggest the kind of enthusiasm that later Gnostics held. The first reading, which is the more likely, indicates that these heretics had spiritualized the resurrection. Their idea may be that the resurrection really happens whenever we receive the spirit of God. From that moment on, the believer is connected with God in an unbreakable way. This leads naturally to a denial of death. We pass through death but do not ourselves die as long as we are already connected with God's spirit. The resurrection has already happened. This rendition of the heretics explains the author's focus on death and suffering as necessary pieces of the gospel. This kind of spiritualism would deny both.

We should notice how important good Christian virtues are in this passage. The virtues and vices connected to the servant of God who engages heresy are typical of the virtues and vices enjoined throughout the Pastoral Epistles. This means that the virtuous behavior required of a rebuker of heretics is important not only because such treatment might lead to repentance, but also because this is how a faithful person always behaves. Good Christians are to be gentle, kind, and patient no matter what the circumstances. The virtues we acquire in the Christian life are carried with us everywhere. We are not to be angry, bitter, and pugnacious one moment, and kind and gentle the next. The author is insisting that we cannot let heretics overthrow our faith; we cannot let them call forth vices that deny the person God calls us to be. This is the danger of heretics; they knock over faith, upset good households, and feed like gangrene on the church. We meet their ideas with truthful rebuke and their persons with the quiet, loving virtues of a good Christian. This is the author's ultimate proposal for how the church handles the heretics in our midst. It is advice the church has often ignored.

GODLESSNESS IN THE LAST DAYS
2 Timothy 3:1–9

> 3:1 **You must understand this, that in the last days distressing times will come. ² For people will be lovers of themselves, lovers of money, boasters, arrogant, abusive, disobedient to their parents, ungrateful, unholy, ³ inhuman, implacable, slanderers, profligates, brutes, haters of good, ⁴ treacherous, reckless, swollen with conceit, lovers of pleasure rather than lovers of God, ⁵ holding to the outward form of godliness but denying its power. Avoid them! ⁶ For among them are those who make their way into households and captivate silly women, overwhelmed by their sins and swayed by all kinds of desires, ⁷ who are always being instructed and can never arrive at a knowledge of the truth. ⁸ As Jannes and Jambres opposed Moses, so these people, of corrupt mind and counterfeit faith, also oppose the truth. ⁹ But they will not make much progress, because, as in the case of those two men, their folly will become plain to everyone.**

Of the many passages in the Pastoral Epistles that address heretics and their beliefs and practices, this passage is the most extensive. It does not, however, yield many specifics about the author's opponents. The problem is that accusations made against them are the stock accusations typically made in antiquity against immoral enemies. All the vices enumerated in verses 2–5 are the usual vices in such attacks. The claim that women in particular are susceptible, along with the hints of sexual impropriety, is also typical. Thus it becomes difficult to determine where the author is employing the normal rhetoric of his times and where the specific accusation fits the crime.

However, when these accusations are compared with the ongoing charges against these heretics throughout the Pastoral Epistles, a fairly consistent portrait emerges. Although the vices cited here cannot be taken as fully accurate, they are not nonsense. The quiet, communal virtues so important to our author do not appear to have been equally important to his opponents. They apparently were pursuing more rigorous personal virtues. They were ascetic and perhaps even self-centered. Thus the sense of being anti-communal, which this passage conveys, may not be entirely unfair. The author's opponents may well have focused upon individual spiritual accomplishments rather than upon the order and peacefulness of the larger community. Furthermore, this attribution of vices to heretics is at the heart of the author's theology. The true gospel leads to the life of virtue; heresy leads to vice. As Jesus said, "You will know them by their fruits" (Matt. 7:20).

In the same way, women may have been quite active in the movement. We should recall at this point the discussion about the order of widows in 1 Timothy 5:3–6:2. The proper behavior and role of women in early Christianity was much debated. It is unfortunate that we do not have the direct voices of early Christian women in the canon or in second-century patristic literature. We do not know what they would say. These women probably did not hold to the kind of hierarchy envisioned in the Pastoral Epistles wherein male officers have primary authority and wherein the role of women is severely curtailed. It is clear, in any case, that the author sees them as out-of-order and as being engaged in heretical speculation.

Finally, these opponents fall under the threat and promise of judgment. This vision of judgment as uncovering and displaying all evils, sins, and heresies is commonplace and important in early Christianity. And it is a key idea in the Pastoral Epistles. The ultimate truth of the author's version of the gospel is grounded in both the apostolic credentials of Paul and the bright lights of judgment day. Truth may look foolish now, and falsehood may look wise, but both will be shown for what they are when the day of the Lord comes. The reference to Jannes and Jambres comes from Exodus 8:18–19, although the specific names are not in the Bible. They come from later Jewish texts.

This rather aggressive and severe reproof of the heretics serves as a balance to the tenderness of 2 Timothy 2:14–26. Of course, the harshness of this account must be balanced by the loving tones of 2 Timothy 2:14–26. The author wants two things in regard to heresy. First, heresy and its people must be severely and honestly corrected by the truths of the gospel. Second, all reproof must be done with the hope of repentance. Reproof must be gentle and loving; it must not engender conflict.

PAUL AS THE EXAMPLE
2 Timothy 3:10–4:8

3:10 **Now you have observed my teaching, my conduct, my aim in life, my faith, my patience, my love, my steadfastness, ¹¹ my persecutions and suffering the things that happened to me in Antioch, Iconium, and Lystra. What persecutions I endured! Yet the Lord rescued me from all of them. ¹² Indeed, all who want to live a godly life in Christ Jesus will be persecuted. ¹³ But wicked people and impostors will go from bad to worse, deceiving others and being deceived. ¹⁴ But as for you, continue in what you have learned and firmly believed, knowing from whom you learned it, ¹⁵ and how from childhood you have known the sacred writings that are able to instruct you for salvation through faith in Christ Jesus. ¹⁶ All scripture is inspired by God and is useful for teaching, for reproof, for correction, and for training in righteousness, ¹⁷ so that everyone who belongs to God may be proficient, equipped for every good work.**

4:1 In the presence of God and of Christ Jesus, who is to judge the living and the dead, and in view of his appearing and his kingdom, I solemnly urge you: ² proclaim the message; be persistent whether the time is favorable or unfavorable; convince, rebuke, and encourage, with the utmost patience in teaching. ³ For the time is coming when people will not put up with sound doctrine, but having itching ears, they will accumulate for themselves teachers to suit their own desires, ⁴ and will turn away from listening to the truth and wander away to myths. ⁵ As for you, always be sober, endure suffering, do the work of an evangelist, carry out your ministry fully.

⁶ As for me, I am already being poured out as a libation, and the time of my departure has come. ⁷ I have fought the good fight, I have finished the race, I have kept the faith. ⁸ From now on there is reserved for me the crown of righteousness, which the Lord, the righteous judge, will give me on that day, and not only to me but also to all who have longed for his appearing.

This passage is one of the most important and effective in the Pastoral Epistles. The personal tone, the evocative imagery, and the general passion of the theology have made this a favorite passage of readers of the Pastoral Epistles. In fact, it is often this passage in particular to which defenders of Pauline authorship point. It is argued that it feels too genuine not to have come from Paul himself. I do not think that is true, but it is certainly true that this passage is effectively and warmly drawn.

The passage is also important because it articulates with such clarity and force the central ideas of the Pastoral Epistles. It is a marvelous summary of the theology of the letters, couched as a meditation by Paul on his own ministry. And it pulls together the various literary and thematic lines of 2 Timothy, gathering them into a precise and inviting Pauline portrait. It is at this point that we see the author at his best.

The strong denunciations of the heretics in 3:1–9, especially the harsh catalog of vices, is immediately balanced by the pleasant imagery of the catalog of virtues that is applied to Paul. In effect, the author says, "You have seen the horrors of heresy; now recall the wonders of the good Christian life." Readers have long been struck by the thoroughness of the list applied to Paul. Paul's life has been studied by Timothy. In Paul, Timothy and others can see the Christian life as it is supposed to be.

The crucial role of apostolic authority surfaces once again. For a church uncertain about doctrine and about the proper shape of the Christian life, the life and teachings of Paul serve as an anchor. It is fitting then that the list starts with "my teaching, my conduct" (3:10). The portraits of Paul in the Pastoral Epistles are decisive to the argument of the letters. We need not only doctrines; we need examples.

Given the themes of 2 Timothy, it is appropriate that the list concludes with references to persecutions and sufferings. The persecutions in Antioch, Iconium, and Lystra are detailed in Acts 13:50; 14:5–6, 19. It is curious that according to Acts, Paul had not yet even met Timothy. Of course, the author of the Pastoral Epistles is not trying to sort out such historical anomalies; he is drawing the relationship for theological and pedagogical purposes.

We can see once again the literary function of all the portraits of Paul, Timothy, Titus, and others (both good and bad) in the Pastoral Epistles. They are examples to be used in learning and practicing the Christian life. Thus we do not get full biographies of anyone, but only portraits useful to the theology and ethics of the author. In any case, suffering and persecution are understood in the Pastoral Epistles, as they are in Paul, Mark, Revelation, and elsewhere in the New Testament, as regular, inevitable, and even necessary parts of the Christian life. Simply put, a good Christian will suffer and will be persecuted.

The sectarian mindset of early Christianity is unmistakable in all this. Christians understood themselves as having become separate from the powers and values of the world around them. It is not, of course, that early Christians did not share many of their values with non-Christians. It is an undeniable historical fact that they did. In fact, the Pastoral Epistles seem to want to appeal to outsiders by claiming that the virtues (at least some of them) to which these outsiders had always aspired can be realized in the Christian church. Nevertheless, the theme of opposition is persistent and important. In spite of shared values, Christians felt themselves alienated from the world around them.

The detailing of the authority of scripture in 3:15–17 has become a crucial passage for Christian understanding of the inspiration of scripture. Despite this role, it is quite difficult to determine precisely what this passage is claiming. The NRSV notes two translation options for 3:16: "All scripture is inspired by God and is useful for teaching" or "Every scripture inspired by God is also useful for teaching." The Greek is ambiguous at this point. This is probably because the author is not attempting a precise analysis of the inspiration of scripture; rather, he is focusing upon the essential pedagogical value of scripture, the inspiration of which he assumes. The conclusion in 3:17 fits this reading. The purpose of all this is "that everyone who belongs to God may be proficient, equipped for every good work." A major purpose of the Pastoral Epistles, as we have seen, is the equipping of the saints for good deeds. Here, the author simply notes in passing that inspired scripture is a necessary element of that equipping.

In the midst of the Pauline reminiscences of 3:10–17 and 4:6–9, the author inserts a direct exhortation to Timothy. The image of people having itching ears so that they follow whatever teachers will scratch them has long struck readers as being particularly fitting and effective. Furthermore, this image captures the author's ongoing frustration with the unreliability of church members of his day. They do not want the truth; they just want their itches scratched. People have always been this way, even in Paul's day, as the subsequent description in 4:16–18 demonstrates.

All of this comes to an emotional peak in Paul's joyful acceptance of death in 4:6–8. Paul is drawn as the perfect church leader who is to be imitated. He is faithful to the orthodox gospel, even though it brings persecution and death. He is faithful to the gospel, even though his own churches turn away from him to have their ears scratched with more pleasant teaching. The theological and moral lesson is obvious; all church leaders must imitate Paul's fidelity to truth despite the costs that ensue.

As subsequent ages have learned, there is both great strength and subtle danger in an appeal to orthodox tradition. It takes a wise and Spirit-directed church to discern the spirits properly. New teaching can be dangerous, but it can also manifest great truths. Tradition itself, as important as it is to the identity of the church, can sometimes sanction non-Christian behavior on the grounds of habit. Old sins should not be confused with good tradition. Thus the debate that animates the Pastoral Epistles has not gone away: What is sound tradition, and what is not?

PERSONAL INSTRUCTIONS AND BENEDICTION
2 Timothy 4:9–22

4:9 **Do your best to come to me soon,** [10] **for Demas, in love with this present world, has deserted me and gone to Thessalonica; Crescens has gone to Galatia, Titus to Dalmatia.** [11] **Only Luke is with me. Get Mark and bring him with you, for he is useful in my ministry.** [12] **I have sent Tychicus to Ephesus.** [13] **When you come, bring the cloak that I left with Carpus at Troas, also the books, and above all the parchments.** [14] **Alexander the coppersmith did me great harm; the Lord will pay him back for his deeds.** [15] **You also must beware of him, for he strongly opposed our message.**

[16] **At my first defense no one came to my support, but all deserted me. May it not be counted against them!** [17] **But the Lord stood by me and gave me strength, so that through me the message might be fully proclaimed and all the Gentiles might hear it. So I was rescued from the lion's mouth.** [18] **The Lord will rescue me from every evil attack and save me for his heavenly kingdom. To him be the glory forever and ever. Amen.**

[19] **Greet Prisca and Aquila, and the household of Onesiphorus.** [20] **Erastus remained in Corinth; Trophimus I left ill in Miletus.** [21] **Do your best to come before winter. Eubulus sends greetings to you, as do Pudens and Linus and Claudia and all the brothers and sisters.**

[22] **The Lord be with your spirit. Grace be with you.**

The personal notes and greetings that conclude the letter serve a variety of purposes for the author. Paul's troubles, his abandonment by once-loyal followers, his mistreatment by enemies, his fidelity to his apostolic tasks, and his persistent confidence find illustration in these concluding remarks. The greetings from one community to another and the travel from one church to another depict the various Christian churches as maintaining unity despite the geographical difficulties. These Pauline churches, through letters and emissaries, manage to care for one another. And of course, these very personal remarks give an aura of genuineness to the letter. Real Christian letters often have such personal exchanges, and thus these verses make the letter read like a real Pauline letter.

Even if it is the case, which I think it is, that the author has fabricated this setting, it is not the case that he simply made up all these details. Many of these names are found in Colossians, Philemon, Acts, and the genuine Pauline letters. We cannot, of course, chase down all these details in a study of this length. But it does seem that the author is working with Pauline tradition that he understands to be genuine. This is not to say, of course, that his tradition was perfectly accurate. Certainly, such personal details in Colossians and Acts must be treated carefully.

Demas is mentioned in Philemon 24 and Colossians 4:14, although the association with Thessalonica and his desertion are unique to this text. Crescens is not mentioned elsewhere in the New Testament. Titus, of course, is well known. In Titus 3:12, Titus is summoned to join Paul in Nicopolis, to spend the winter with him. Nicopolis is a common city name in the Roman world, but the most likely one is in Dalmatia, which is just to the north and east of Greece. Tychicus is a key figure in Colossians, and Mark and Luke both appear in Philemon and Colossians. The designation of Alexander as "the coppersmith" makes it uncertain whether this is the Alexander mentioned in 1 Timothy 1:20 or Acts 19:33, but I think the best guess is that the author is thinking of only one Alexander. Prisca (Priscilla) and Aquila appear in Acts 18:1–3, 1 Corinthians 16:19, and Romans 16:3. According to Acts 18:19, Paul leaves them in Ephesus. Onesiphorus we have seen in 2 Timothy 1:16–17. Erastus in Acts 19:22 accompanies Timothy to Macedonia on Paul's orders. He also sends greetings from Corinth in Romans 16:23. Trophimus is mentioned as a companion of Paul in Acts 20:4 and 21:29, where he is named "the Ephesian." Eubulus, Pudens, Linus, and Claudia are otherwise unknown.

Scholars have not been able to reconstruct a historical situation that works for all these personal details. It is probably the case that the author is working with disparate traditions of different quality, and he does not rework them all into one historical viewpoint. The general setting given for 2 Timothy is that Paul is writing from Rome, during his final imprisonment, to Timothy who is in Ephesus. But, as many readers have pointed out, many of these details work better if Paul is still in Caesarea. All of this cannot be pursued here, and these questions are in some sense extraneous to the argument of the letter. These notes have a purpose other than the accurate reconstruction of all the historical details of a moment in Paul's life. These notes are here for the theological and ethical edification of the readers.

The request that Timothy bring Paul's cloak, the books, and "above all" the parchments has caused many readers to insist that such a realistic detail is beyond the scope of a pseudepigraphical letter. We know now that this is not true; pseudepigraphical letters frequently use such mundane and seemingly extraneous details. It is also unclear whether the correct translation is "books, and above all the parchments" (4:13) or "books, namely, the parchments." From the context, it is difficult to determine whether these are supposed to be already completed books or parchments that Paul could use for letter writing. In any case, the role of literature and writing in Paul's life and thus in the lives of his communities is hereby emphasized.

The author gathers the themes of persecution, abandonment, and faithfulness into a wonderful summary in 4:16–19. Paul was abandoned by all his companions. Only the Lord remained. Here lies the theological anchor of the letter. God saves the person who is faithful in the midst of suffering. In the terrors and doubts of persecution we see God as God truly is. God is our savior. The letter wants to steel us for faithfulness; it asks, Can you trust in God alone?

The concluding benediction is quite brief and echoes the typical Pauline benediction.

CONCLUSION

Readers of 2 Timothy have long been struck by the prominence and approval given to suffering in the Christian life. In 2 Timothy suffering becomes almost the principal sign of a Christian. And suffering is at least one of the things that connects the believer with Christ. Perhaps the imagery is focused best in 2 Timothy 2:11: "If we have died with him, we will also live with him." Second Timothy can be read effectively as a meditation on the cross.

Nothing is more difficult to think about in the Christian tradition than the cross and the approval of suffering it evokes. And nothing distinguishes Christian thought from other religious traditions more than this fascination with death and suffering. For the Christian, in death is life. To my mind there is no more astonishing sentence in Christian theology. Especially when we recognize that in 2 Timothy and other Christian texts this death is occurring now, in every moment of the Christian life. Death must mark the life of the Christian.

What are we saying? In truth, I do not think we can understand our own words here. Death is not something that can be understood, for in death we are not. We cannot think from inside it. Our thoughts cannot pierce it. And yet we are called here to meditate on it, and not only to meditate on it, but to live out of it.

Let me make two brief comments. First, there is witness here to a shattering that not only frequents the Christian life but animates it. There is an undoing of the self that activates our lives. And this undoing reaches from our social selves, with its many obligations and promises, to the deepest unknowns of our psyches. To be a Christian is not simply to become more of what we already are; to be a Christian is to die and be reborn. Second, theologians have long commented that the cross marks the border of all Christian theology. The reality of the cross, of death, of suffering connected with death, cannot be fathomed. The cross cannot produce tame propositions in our theology. The cross marks the unknown. And thus here we are in God's hands. Only God can see into death; only God can be in death. Thus, we cannot explain the proper function of suffering; we can only live it in faith.

Commentary on Titus

SALUTATION
Titus 1:1–4

> 1:1 **Paul, a servant of God and an apostle of Jesus Christ, for the sake of the faith of God's elect and the knowledge of the truth that is in accordance with godliness, 2 in the hope of eternal life that God, who never lies, promised before the ages began—3 in due time he revealed his word through the proclamation with which I have been entrusted by the command of God our Savior,**
> 4 **To Titus, my loyal child in the faith we share:**
> **Grace and peace from God the Father and Christ Jesus our Savior.**

Although Titus is the shortest of the three Pastoral letters, it is packed with theological language. It is, therefore, fitting that the salutation in Titus should contain the most developed theological imagery of the three salutations. Although there will be little in the theological and ethical imagery that we have not seen in 1 and 2 Timothy, much of this language will be used in striking ways. We will find passages that quite effectively summarize what are otherwise scattered theological themes in 1 and 2 Timothy. Titus will compress much of this language into clear and compact arguments.

Titus was one of Paul's co-workers, although he does not seem to have had the status of Timothy or Silvanus. We hear of him first in Galatians 2:1–3. Paul states that he and Barnabas took Titus from Antioch to Jerusalem and that he was not compelled to be circumcised, even though he was a Greek. Titus is also the main emissary from Paul to Corinth during the conflicts recorded in 2 Corinthians (2 Cor. 2:13; 7:6, 13, 14; 8:6, 16, 23; 12:18). In 2 Timothy 4:10 we hear that he has gone to Dalmatia. In none of this is there any connection between Titus and Crete. Of course, not even Paul himself is directly connected to Crete, except that on his sea voyage to Rome Paul's captors discuss wintering in Crete, but decide unadvisedly to continue (Acts 27:7–15). The designation of Titus in 1:4 as "my loyal child" or, as it might better be translated, "my genuine child" indicates that the author thought Titus was converted by Paul. This may be an accurate tradition, but there is no way to tell for certain.

The theological imagery of verses 1–3 is typical of the Pastoral Epistles. The primary themes of 1 and 2 Timothy are repeated here. The looseness and imprecision of the Greek syntax is not completely apparent in the English of the NRSV. The passage reads as an evocative collection of images. And the relationships among these images cannot be precisely diagrammed. That is not to say that the theological images collected are not crucial to the author's theology. We know, by this point, that they are. The terms *faith, truth, godliness, promise, hope, eternal life*, along with the notion that these truths are now revealed in the gospel, are the key concepts in the author's theology. In this salutation, which has a liturgical feel, the author simply evokes and reminds the reader of more careful theological arguments in 1 and 2 Timothy and later in Titus.

PAUL IN CRETE
Titus 1:5–16

1:5 I left you behind in Crete for this reason, so that you should put in order what remained to be done, and should appoint elders in every town, as I directed you: 6 someone who is blameless, married only once, whose children are believers, not accused of debauchery and not rebellious. 7 For a bishop, as God's steward, must be blameless; he must not be arrogant or quick-tempered or addicted to wine or violent or greedy for gain; 8 but he must be hospitable, a lover of goodness, prudent, upright, devout, and self-controlled. 9 He must have a firm grasp of the word that is trustworthy in accordance with the teaching, so that he may be able both to preach with sound doctrine and to refute those who contradict it.

10 There are also many rebellious people, idle talkers and deceivers, especially those of the circumcision; 11 they must be silenced, since they are upsetting whole families by teaching for sordid gain what it is not right to teach. 12 It was one of them, their very own prophet, who said,

"Cretans are always liars,
vicious brutes, lazy gluttons."

13 That testimony is true. For this reason rebuke them sharply, so that they may become sound in the faith, 14 not paying attention to Jewish myths or to commandments of those who reject the truth. 15 To the pure all things are pure, but to the corrupt and unbelieving nothing is pure. Their very

minds and consciences are corrupted. [16] They profess to know God, but they deny him by their actions. They are detestable, disobedient, unfit for any good work.

Much of this initial exhortation to Titus echoes similar passages in 1 and 2 Timothy. Both Timothy and Titus are depicted as carrying out Paul's orders in his absence and as empowering others to continue the work of leadership. In this way, these letters use Paul's apostolic credentials to authenticate the powers and responsibilities of duly selected church officers. Timothy and Titus provide illustration for how good leaders should behave, whereas the heretics serve as negative models. Here Titus is depicted as carefully selecting and installing church leaders who are both worthy and competent for the task. The political result of all this is that the Pastoral Epistles insist that the church should submit to its officers and not to unofficial, wandering preachers. The official order in the church and the home must be maintained.

The Standards of Leadership

The key criteria for leadership, in this passage and throughout the Pastoral Epistles, are orthodoxy and the virtuous life. There is nothing new here. The author does not explain the relationship or difference between elders and bishops. Many scholars suggest that these offices rarely occurred in the same community; churches either had a group of elders or a single bishop. If that is true, the author is attempting to apply the categories of orthodoxy and virtue to church leadership no matter what the form. He is seeking as large an audience as possible and does not care which pattern is used.

Furthermore, we do not know from the Pastoral Epistles themselves how the author is using the terms *elder* and *bishop*. The word in Greek for bishop is a common word that simply means an overseer. It may not have the monarchical connotations in the Pastoral Epistles that it will acquire in later times. Although the term *elder* seems to come out of the Jewish synagogue, it is not clear what the role of an elder might have been in these churches.

The author articulates his understanding of right teaching and right teachers in verse 9. This is as succinct a formulation as we find in the Pastoral Epistles. A leader must have a firm grasp of the correct, not the incorrect, teaching. And he must be able then to instruct others in that teaching and refute the heretics. This is, of course, the project of the Pastoral Epistles themselves: to articulate the true gospel, to teach it to others so that they can teach others in turn, and to refute the heretics. The letters themselves model this leadership behavior.

The Danger of Heresy

The account of the heretics in 1:10–16 is also in the typical language of the Pastoral Epistles. As we have noted earlier, it is difficult to tell which of the accusations in the Pastoral Epistles reflect actual misbehavior of the heretics and which are part of the stock rhetoric of philosophical refutation. It is likely that the heretics are upsetting families, because we find this specific accusation also given in 2 Timothy 3:6 and because the author of the Pastoral Epistles seems so concerned about social disorder involving women. The image of their unfitness for good works echoes the positive reference to the good works of the faithful (2 Tim. 2:21; 3:17; Titus 3:1). But behind all of these accusations lies the author's conviction that bad theology leads to bad ethics. Heretics lead a life of vice, just as orthodox and faithful believers lead the life of virtue.

The connection of the heretics to faulty Jewish ideas is unique to Titus. However, the notion of myths occurs in 1 Timothy 1:4; 4:7; and 2 Timothy 4:4. Whether we are talking about Gnostic-style myths about the gods of the cosmos or about Jewish heterodox legends cannot be decided. Whatever the case, these heretics are involved in speculation (1 Tim. 1:4) that is taking them outside the proper orb of apostolic tradition. The author insists instead that Paul's tradition, at least as it is configured in these letters, forms both the theological anchor and the limits of proper theology. We should not go beyond the range of the tradition that precedes us. The conservative nature of these letters surfaces here in the strongest way. But, as we noted before, proper loyalty to tradition is both an act of remembrance and an act of re-creation. Tradition must be constantly reconfigured in order to be honest to itself.

The connections of these heresies to the island of Crete is impossible to confirm. The Cretan poet who calls the Cretans liars is identified as Epimenides by Clement of Alexander, Jerome, and Augustine. However, calling Cretans liars also occurs in a hymn to Zeus by Callimachus. In any case, the author is calling the Cretans' own traditions against them.

Finally, the notion that to the pure all things are pure is an important concept in antiquity and in the theology of the Pastoral Epistles. The language of purity is, of course, cultic language. It refers to the cleanness and uncleanness related to temples, to the holiness of gods and goddesses.

Here we can see the persistent Christian notion that the heart of the worship life is ethics. True cleanliness and true uncleanliness are based on morality and immorality. Thus the ultimate categories of the Christian life are moral ones. We have seen throughout the Pastoral Epistles how much the author holds to this idea. Good Christians will be seen in their virtues: "You will know them by their fruits" (Matt. 7:20).

EXHORTATIONS TO MEN, WOMEN, AND SLAVES
Titus 2:1–15

2:1 **But as for you, teach what is consistent with sound doctrine. ² Tell the older men to be temperate, serious, prudent, and sound in faith, in love, and in endurance.**

³ Likewise, tell the older women to be reverent in behavior, not to be slanderers or slaves to drink; they are to teach what is good, ⁴ so that they may encourage the young women to love their husbands, to love their children, ⁵ to be self-controlled, chaste, good managers of the household, kind, being submissive to their husbands, so that the word of God may not be discredited.

⁶ Likewise, urge the younger men to be self-controlled. ⁷ Show yourself in all respects a model of good works, and in your teaching show integrity, gravity, ⁸ and sound speech that cannot be censured; then any opponent will be put to shame, having nothing evil to say of us.

⁹ Tell slaves to be submissive to their masters and to give satisfaction in every respect; they are not to talk back, ¹⁰ not to pilfer, but to show complete and perfect fidelity, so that in everything they may be an ornament to the doctrine of God our Savior.

¹¹ For the grace of God has appeared, bringing salvation to all, ¹² training us to renounce impiety and worldly passions, and in the present age to live lives that are self-controlled, upright, and godly, ¹³ while we wait for the blessed hope and the manifestation of the glory of our great God and Savior, Jesus Christ. ¹⁴ He it is who gave himself for us that he might redeem us from all iniquity and purify for himself a people of his own who are zealous for good deeds.

¹⁵ Declare these things; exhort and reprove with all authority. Let no one look down on you.

The Virtuous Life

This passage echoes several other passages in the Pastoral Epistles. It is striking that the virtues applied here to persons who do not appear to be church officers are nearly identical to the virtues required of officers (see 1 Tim. 3:1–13; Titus 1:5–10). The pattern outlined here is the one consistently given in the Pastoral Epistles. First, one must "teach what is consistent with sound doctrine" (2:1). This sound doctrine must be taught in turn to others (2:3, 7). And this sound doctrine must produce the Christian virtues, which enable the teacher to become a model of the Christian life. It is significant that every member of the community is subject to the same standards and same tasks. We must learn good doctrine and teach it to others, so that we all can acquire the virtuous life. Virtue is a community enterprise.

The author of the Pastoral Epistles is trying to create communities, at home and at the church, where the virtuous life becomes possible. This desire explains his ardent concern for order. Communities, both the household and the church, need reliable and predictable chains of authority. But the fundamental concern is not with order but with proper doctrine. It is only the truths of the gospel that can produce virtue. This means that we must teach the truths of the gospel to each other with both our words and our lives.

However, this human effort in and of itself will not be sufficient. As Christians have always insisted, it is really only God who can author the virtuous life. Thus the references to the power of God's grace in 2:11–14 and cleansing of the Holy Spirit at baptism in 3:4–7 are essential to the author's understanding of how all this works, for it is only through the divine powers that come in the gospel that new life, the life of virtue, is possible. This linkage between the power of the gospel and exhortations to the Christian life is fundamental. The paradox of insisting both that God creates the ethical life in us and that we must put on this God-created life is an invariable tenet of Christian thought. As Titus 2:14 puts it, "He it is [Jesus] who gave himself for us that he might redeem us from all iniquity and purify for himself a people of his own who are zealous for good deeds."

This combination of theological truths and ethical exhortations leads to the sense of mundaneness that many readers of the Pastoral Epistles detect. These letters have occasionally been downgraded and slighted because they do not have the theological profundities of Paul or John, nor the ethical complexities of Jesus himself. But the essential insight of the author of the Pastoral Epistles comes at this precise point. The marvels of God's deeds in Jesus Christ come to life in the mundane details of our lives. The Christian truths must be lived out in the messiness and confusions of our relationships to each other, both in the home and the church. Most of our moments are captured in the mundane and ordinary, and yet the author of the Pastoral Epistles insists that all such moments must be directed by the marvels of the gospel.

Readers have long noticed that the author focuses upon the need for Christians to act submissive in their relationships. He sees no evil in the submission to authority. It is true that these authorities must be selected carefully; they must measure up to the standards in these letters. But proper authorities deserve obedience. As we know, history has found both good and bad in such behavior. Perhaps the author's insistence upon morality and ethics as the highest criteria can serve as a safeguard. If the pattern of dominance and submission does not produce the virtuous life in all persons involved, then the pattern must be broken. The submission of one human to another, although necessary to social order, is always complex and problematic. In any case, this passage, like the Pastoral Epistles themselves, insists that the powers of God must issue in the virtuous life: "For the grace of God has appeared, bringing salvation to all, training us to renounce impiety and worldly passions, and in the present age to live lives that are self-controlled, upright, and godly" (2:11–12).

The Outsider

The concern for what outsiders might say has often struck readers as curious. The Pastoral Epistles are an internal document, written by one Christian to other Christians; no outsiders are imagined as readers. Nevertheless, the opinion of outsiders is given importance. Older women are advised to teach younger women to love their husbands, to love their children, to be good household managers, and to be submissive to their husbands, all so that "the word of God may not be discredited" (2:5). This is reminiscent of the instructions in 1 Timothy 5:14 that young widows should "marry, bear children, and manage their households, so as to give the adversary no occasion to revile us." Younger men are encouraged to virtue so that "any opponent will be put to shame, having nothing evil to say of us" (2:8). Slaves are instructed to submit to their masters "so that in everything they may be an ornament to the doctrine of God our Savior" (2:10). In 1 Timothy 6:1, slaves are admonished to honor their masters "so that the name of God and the teaching may not be blasphemed." And in 1 Timothy 3:7, the author insists that a bishop "must be well thought of by outsiders."

All these passages show a high regard for the opinion of outsiders. The instructions to women and slaves suggest the presence of a frequent problem for early Christians; namely, membership in a Christian community often created problems for women and slaves in their households. We have discussed this earlier in this study. Here the solution given is that both women and slaves should submit fully and energetically to the authority structures in their households. There is no mention here of the theological problems of giving allegiance and obedience to non-Christian structures. The concern seems to be over the social safety of the church. We must not give outsiders grounds for attack against us. Thus we must submit to the social structures in the world around us, not because they are good and proper structures but because failure to do so will endanger the community.

On the other hand, the Pastoral Epistles lack the sectarian feel of other Christian documents. The virtues admonished here would have been recognizable to non-Christians. These Christians seem to have their feet in both the church and the world, and they see neither as perfectly good or evil. The church has heresy and vice; the world knows virtue and maintains good order. The task of the Christian is to maintain the good and overcome evil wherever they are found.

Furthermore, the author of the Pastoral Epistles sees submission as a good in itself. The power of the cross as a primary symbol in Christian thought is apparent here. The Christian victory over the world is indirect; it is found through submission and failure. The cross must precede the resurrection.

EXHORTATIONS TO ALL BELIEVERS AND BENEDICTION
Titus 3:1-15

3:1 **Remind them to be subject to rulers and authorities, to be obedient, to be ready for every good work, [2] to speak evil of no one, to avoid quarreling, to be gentle, and to show every courtesy to everyone. [3] For we ourselves were once foolish, disobedient, led astray, slaves to various passions and pleasures, passing our days in malice and envy, despicable, hating one another. [4] But when the goodness and loving kindness of God our Savior appeared, [5] he saved us, not because of any works of righteousness that we had done, but according to his mercy, through the water of rebirth and renewal by the Holy Spirit. [6] This Spirit he poured out on us richly through Jesus Christ our Savior, [7] so that, having been justified by his grace, we might become heirs according to the hope of eternal life. [8] The saying is sure.**

I desire that you insist on these things, so that those who have come to believe in God may be careful to devote themselves to good works; these things are excellent and profitable to everyone. [9] But avoid stupid contro-

versies, genealogies, dissensions, and quarrels about the law, for they are unprofitable and worthless. [10] After a first and second admonition, have nothing more to do with anyone who causes divisions, [11] since you know that such a person is perverted and sinful, being self-condemned.

[12] When I send Artemas to you, or Tychicus, do your best to come to me at Nicopolis, for I have decided to spend the winter there. [13] Make every effort to send Zenas the lawyer and Apollos on their way, and see that they lack nothing. [14] And let people learn to devote themselves to good works in order to meet urgent needs, so that they may not be unproductive.

[15] All who are with me send greetings to you. Greet those who love us in the faith.

Grace be with all of you.

The exhortation to specific groups gives way to a general exhortation to all readers. This passage focuses upon the community's relationship to outsiders and the proper treatment of heretics and their controversies. The latter is, of course, a persistent theme of the Pastoral Epistles; and the former, although less prominent, surfaces from time to time in the Pastoral Epistles and is one of the key themes of the preceding passage. Furthermore, both chapters 2 and 3 of Titus ground their exhortations in theological assurances. We noted the importance of the interdependence of ethical exhortations and theological propositions in the preceding discussion.

A Moral Reminder

Here the opening request that believers should "be subject to rulers and authorities" (3:1) echoes the similar command in 1 Timothy 2:1. This command, when coupled with the call to obedience and gentleness, reflects the author's belief in submission as the Christian ideal. This ideal of the Christian life as gentleness and submissiveness is then grounded in one of the most important theological passages in the Pastoral Epistles.

This passage establishes the crucial role of the Spirit and its linkage with baptism. There is no ethical life, no moral regeneration, apart from the Spirit. As we have noted previously, although the Pastoral Epistles are couched largely as moral exhortations and although they insist over and over again that we must flee the vices and practice the virtues in order to obtain salvation, it is also the case that humans do not possess the capacity to do this on their own. As this passage notes, we can escape our passions and the hatefulness of the life of passion only through the power of God.

Note how the list of vices touches upon so many of the themes of the Pastoral Epistles. We were disobedient, but now we can obey the proper authorities. We were led astray, but now we can follow the sound doctrines of the gospel and heresies. We gave into passions and pleasures instead of self-control and prudence. We received and gave hate instead of love.

Most scholars want to connect 3:3–7 to early Christian baptismal liturgy. In fact, many of those scholars think that 2:11–14 and 3:3–7 together form the core of the baptismal liturgy in the author's tradition. Thus chapters 2 and 3 are moral exhortations grounded in a baptismal liturgy that would have been quite familiar to the author's initial audience. It is impossible to demonstrate with much certainty historical claims such as this, but there is nothing inherently improbable about it. This could well be pieces of liturgy that the author uses for its familiarity and authority.

Whether these verses come from the liturgy or the hand of the author, they are important to the theology of the author. The terminology is traditional Pauline, although some of it is used in non-Pauline ways. And it is all woven into the author's own theological logic. The mercy and lovingkindness of God appeared in Christ. When we are baptized, God pours the Holy Spirit upon us through Christ. This gives us the life of righteousness and opens up to us eternal life.

The Tension between Mercy and Justice

This is not to deny that the life of virtue is necessary for salvation. We must not disconnect these theological assurances from the exhortations that surround them. Rather, it is God's mercy and God's power that enable the virtuous life. It takes God's gifts in Christ, together with human zealousness for good works, to produce virtue. God will in the end be a righteous God. God will reward virtue and punish vice. Thus the key to salvation is not God's compassion on judgment day, but God's divine gifts in Christ now.

This is an old Christian argument: What is the relationship between God's love and mercy and God's righteousness and justice? Paul himself insists that God's mercy does not cancel out God's righteousness. God will not pretend you are righteous if you are not. God will not forget. And God will have justice and righteousness. When God created us, God created us to be a certain kind of people, to be righteous and just. God will not deny these intentions for us. Thus God must make us righteous. In

Paul, this is done through the christological miracles of justification and sanctification. In the Pastoral Epistles, this is done through the power of the Spirit, which enables us to take on the truths of the gospel. We must, of course, have the correct gospel. Otherwise, we may stumble into heresy and the life of vice. Reliable apostolic teachings, taken on with the powers of the Spirit, produce virtue and, in turn, salvation. God's mercy is now in the gifts of the gospel, both its truths and its regeneration in the Spirit.

The final exhortation is a fitting one for the letter to Titus. It is for peace in the community. Of course, peace cannot be attained at the price of heresy. We must hold to the truth as gently, honestly, forcefully, and peacefully as possible. Heretics must be reproved, but controversy must be avoided. This is the persistent and unwavering treatment of heresy and heretics in the Pastoral Epistles. And this passage reiterates these themes quite effectively. We can imagine, of course, that keeping this balance was quite difficult, for it certainly is for us today. How do we balance love and acceptance with righteousness of the truths of the gospel? Our gospel is often critical of us and painful to hear. We cannot quench the fire of the gospel because of our desire to be gentle. To the credit of the Pastoral Epistles, the tension between the harsh judgments of orthodoxy and the tolerance of Christian love is maintained throughout. Reprove one another, but do it with gentleness and humility. Do it in order to save one another, for God wants all people to be saved.

Final Greetings

Artemas and Zenas the lawyer are mentioned in the concluding greetings and nowhere else in the New Testament. Tychicus we have seen in Colossians, Ephesians, and 2 Timothy (and probably in Acts 20:4 as well). There were at least seven cities in the Roman world named Nicopolis, but most scholars think the author is referring to the one on the western coast of northern Greece. Whether Titus or Paul had any historical connections to the city is unknown. The person called Apollos may be the evangelist named in Acts and 1 Corinthians, but Apollos is a common name.

All these greetings serve the depiction of the Pauline entourage as busy and as caring for one another. These greetings add a look of genuineness to the letter, and they present these persons as paradigms of good Christian caring.

Pauline letters often refer to the main theme or one of the main themes in the concluding passage. In different ways this occurs in both 1 and 2 Timothy. In a parallel fashion 3:14 recalls a main theme of Titus; devote yourself to good works. This final request serves as a reminder of the over-all purpose and genre of the Pastoral Epistles. They are exhortations. They are calling believers in Jesus Christ to the righteous life that God has made possible in Christ. Your personal realization of virtue is the mode through which God wants to save you. Learn the truths of the gospel, and take on the life of virtue that the Spirit empowers within you.

CONCLUSION

Titus highlights what is perhaps the core motif of the Pastoral Epistles, namely, the life of virtue. We have seen how the author returns to the standards of virtue again and again in these letters. Virtues are for him the organizing center of life. In fact, to be a Christian means to live out the virtues.

Modern Christians may view this confidence in the power of virtues as almost quaint. Our lives are so beset by competing values and complex ethical questions that it seems inconsequential whether one is properly virtuous or not. Being honest, hardworking, temperate, chaste, and so forth may be admirable, but such quiet virtues are probably irrelevant to the major tasks of life, which involve accomplishing something out there in the world. You and I would rarely summarize the Christian life as the pursuit of virtue.

And I wonder what we have lost. I think of how the author, who is caught in a battle for the life of his church with enemies he regards as deadly to the health of his community, insists on being just as gentle and honest with them as with his friends. He will always be himself, a self that is shaped by the quiet virtues enumerated here.

When I think of the bitter battles troubling the church today and of the vicious and vitriolic tone of the debate, I know that the quiet virtues of the Pastoral Epistles would be a blessing to us. Perhaps we can never know who is right or wrong about many social issues, but we can know honesty, gentleness, and modesty. We can treat each other well. The author of the Pastoral Epistles would enjoin us to be kind to one another, even to our enemies, no matter what.

So we are back to the ancient command from Jesus himself to love our enemies. The author of the Pastoral Epistles has heard that command better than we.

The Question of Authorship

Colossians

The question of the authorship of Colossians is not resolved. In fact, we probably do not possess the historical data or the critical tools to reach a clean decision on who the author was. As was mentioned in the Introduction to this volume, it is my opinion and it is the perspective of this study that Colossians was not written by Paul. But the data are not clear, and the arguments for and against Pauline authorship are not conclusive. Furthermore, the authority and power of Colossians remain unaffected by the question of who wrote it. Its position in the canon is secure, and its theological and ethical arguments are potent no matter who the author was. The church did not canonize the mind of Paul but certain texts proven to have authority.

As far as we know, Pauline authorship of Colossians had been assumed by everyone until the early nineteenth century, when historical examination of the Bible with its critical questions accelerated. Prior to the rise of historical methods, there were no reasons to question Pauline authorship. After all, Colossians says it is by Paul, it sounds like Paul, and it contains many classic Pauline ideas. Thus it was not until recent times that any questions emerged.

However, in the beginning of the nineteenth century, certain German scholars perceived what they thought were discrepancies between Colossians and the other Pauline letters. There has been an ongoing attempt since then to analyze the similarities and dissimilarities between Colossians and other Pauline letters. Originally, there was a tendency among English-speaking scholars to defend Pauline authorship, but that seems to be less and less the case. Presently, scholars are simply divided.

There are five arguments most frequently made against Pauline authorship. First, scholars have noticed a whole range of syntactical and grammatical deviations. This extends from the way sentences are put together to the use of conjunctions and prepositions. These scholars believe that although much of the terminology is Pauline, the grammatical structures in which these terms occur are different from those of Paul. This can be difficult to notice in English translations because these shifts have to do with peculiarities in the Greek. But even in the NRSV most readers will note more appositions and loose modifications than in other Pauline letters.

Second, scholars note that, although the letter has many Pauline terms and phrases, they are actually used in non-Pauline ways. Such key terms as "faith," "the body of Christ," "minister" (*diakonos*), "Spirit," "mystery" and "baptism," although perhaps Pauline in origin, are not employed in the usual way of Paul. These deviations, they argue, are better explained as being the result of someone reading Paul and deriving new meanings from Pauline terms, than it is for Paul to change his usage of key terms.

Third, the larger arguments in Colossians are constructed differently from a typical argument by Paul himself. This is as clear in the English as in the Greek. Paul's tendency to argue by way of strong paradoxes, sudden shifts in imagery, and hard theological and ethical edges is lacking here. In Colossians, we find the building up of appositions, frequent repetitions, and a certain fragility to theological structures. Here again, it is argued that this is best explained not by imagining Paul in a new mood or unique situation but as the result of a different hand.

The fourth argument comes from a detection of literary dependence of Colossians on Philemon and Philippians. In this case, scholars believe they see evidence of someone using Pauline letters as literary sources. Paul himself, they argue, would be more likely to use his memory. It is certainly the case that Paul reworks earlier material. We see him in Romans changing both his analysis of the law from what it was in Galatians and the precise shape of his exhortations for the strong to bear the burdens of the weak from what it was in 1 Corinthians. These kinds of things are what we would expect. We would not expect the use of his own letters as literary sources.

The fifth argument has been the most compelling. Here scholars argue that a fundamental shift in theological and ethical outlook has occurred. Although we may note some Pauline terms and Pauline ideas, we are no longer in the Pauline theological universe. The author of Colossians perceives Christian reality in a fundamentally different way. Several shifts, such scholars argue, are striking and not reasonable to attribute to Paul himself. Paul's view of the world, in which end-time events drive the ethic and theology, is now surrendered. Paul imagined the Spirit and its gifts to be end-time realities existing in our midst; he insisted on the incomplete nature of Christian ethics and salvation; he argued that believers presently partake of the cross and not the resurrection; and he saw the inevitable subjection of the cosmic powers to Jesus as still in the future. In Colossians all this has changed. Here we have entered what is primarily a spatial universe, where salvation is complete (at least from God's point of view). Paul's view of how God relates to creation has changed.

Along with this move away from end-of-the-world perspectives, other things have changed as well. For instance, apostles are perceived differently and with a different role. The manner in which Christology and ethics are connected has changed. There is an un-Pauline focus upon the cosmic Christ. The church, the Spirit, knowledge, and the content of the mystery are, according to these scholars, all treated differently. Furthermore, when all these theological shifts are added up, we are, it is argued, no longer within reasonable deviations of one person's writing. Paul could not have moved this far on so many fundamental issues. Thus, it is not reasonable to conclude that Paul could have written Colossians.

When all these arguments are combined, many scholars think a convincing case against Pauline authorship has been made. And, in fact, I am one of them. But it must be admitted than none of these arguments constitute compelling proof. Many scholars, looking at the same data and tracing the same arguments, conclude that Paul probably wrote the letter. Their case is much more simple. The letter sounds like Paul, contains concepts typical of Paul, and says it is by Paul. Furthermore, all of the so-called deviations can either be refuted or explained. For example, the so-called fundamental theological shifts can be explained because Paul is writing in a situation strikingly different from what we normally find. The church at Colossae is a church he does not know and from which he needs nothing. And there is at Colossae a unique heresy that compelled Paul to change both his mood and the focus of theology. But, in fact, nothing fundamental has changed. Paul emphasizes in Colossians the present nature of salvation in ways we have not seen from him before. This is what he needs to do to combat a heresy where the power of Christ over the cosmic powers is doubted. This is, in fact, what we would expect Paul to do. There is nothing here more problematic than the considerable differences we find among Galatians, 1 Corinthians, and 1 Thessalonians, for example. The problems have been overrated. There are finally, they argue, no compelling reasons to deny that Paul wrote it.

Several mediating positions between these two points of view have been offered. Some scholars have wondered whether Paul might have changed secretaries or whether he gave his secretary unusual freedom over the composition. We know Paul normally dictated his letters to a secretary, but the exact role of his secretaries is unknown. Others have wondered whether Timothy, who is co-sender of the letter, or another member of Paul's entourage might have composed it.

However, I think the most successful conclusion is that neither Paul nor a member of his entourage wrote Colossians. Rather, it was written after Paul's death by someone profoundly affected by Paul. Whether he knew Paul or only his letters or both is not clear to me. But whatever the case, he is giving us in Colossians the first written commentary on Paul's theology. In so doing, he produces a magnificent and profound letter.

This decision will affect to a limited degree how we interpret the letter. The letter says the same thing no matter who wrote it. Thus most of what we note here about what the letter says and means for us would be the same if we thought Paul wrote it. I would like to believe that this study can be helpful to people no matter what their conclusion may be as to authorship.

Because we are operating on the assumption that Paul did not write the letter, we cannot use our knowledge of Paul and his ideas to explain difficulties in Colossians. Paul's letters can explain where the author's ideas originated, but they should not be used to explain what the author really meant. We will have to approach Colossians as a self-contained work. For instance, Colossians mentions the Spirit only one time (1:8), and it is not clear exactly what the passage means. Furthermore, the phrase "your love in the Spirit" sounds Pauline. Nevertheless, we should not use our knowledge of Paul's understanding of the Spirit in order to fill in the content of Colossians 1:8, for we cannot be certain that, even if the author of Colossians wants to be Pauline here, he is interpreting Paul exactly as we do. We must remember that, given our assumptions of authorship, Colossians is interpreting Paul; Paul is not interpreting it.

EPHESIANS

The question of the authorship of Ephesians involves the authorship of Colossians. Few people who doubt the Pauline authorship of Colossians would not also doubt that of Ephesians, because, for the most part, the arguments against Pauline authorship of Colossians are even more convincing for Ephesians. In fact, many readers of the letters hold Pauline authorship for Colossians and non-Pauline for Ephesians. Yet, it must be said, other readers maintain Pauline authorship of both.

Nevertheless, this study takes the position that Paul wrote neither. The same kind of stylistic and linguistic problems we discovered in Colossians occur in Ephesians. The Greek syntax is unlike that of the genuine Pauline letters. Ephesians is composed largely of extremely long, loosely connected sentences. Ephesians 1:3–14; 1:15–23; 2:1–10; and 3:1–9 are all single sentences in the Greek. (The NRSV breaks each of these into smaller sentences.) The author is also fond of loose and unclear connections by way of the genitive case (which is much like the English "of "). And he also uses the dative case with the preposition *en* in order to connect single words to larger sentences. It is, of course, true that Paul himself uses all these constructions (as any writer of Greek would), but not to the extent we find in Ephesians. It is the judgment of many readers, and is my judgment, that this is not Paul's style.

Most readers notice that traditional Pauline terms are used in Ephesians in un-Pauline ways. The usual list includes such key terms as "mystery," "church," "plan" (*oikonomia*), "fullness," and even the verb "to save." Furthermore, the classic Pauline phrase "in Christ," is not used the way Paul has used it. This suggests a writer who has read Paul and incorporated Paul's language, but is using it in a new way.

A curious problem concerning authorship arises from Ephesians 1:15; 3:2–3; and 4:21, where it is implied that this church does not know Paul personally. This is, of course, impossible for Ephesus. According to Acts 19:10, Paul resided in Ephesus for at least two years. However, we are not certain whether this letter was originally addressed to Ephesus. Our three oldest Greek manuscripts of Ephesians—P^{46}, Sinaiticus, and Vaticanus— do not contain the designation "in Ephesus" in Ephesians 1:1. Defenders of Pauline authorship can appeal to this textual problem; it was by Paul, but not to Ephesus, or perhaps only to one group of believers in Ephesus, but not to the whole church. In any case, most readers admit, if the letter was originally addressed to Ephesus, then it was not by Paul.

However, as is the case with Colossians, the most persuasive evidence against Pauline authorship is also the most subjective. Many readers detect theological shifts in Ephesians from the other Pauline letters. Some of these concern specific issues. For instance, whereas the "church" in Paul refers to the local congregation, in Ephesians it refers to the cosmic, universal church. Whereas Paul describes Christ and only Christ as the one foundation of the church (1 Cor. 3:30), Ephesians refers to the apostles and prophets as the foundation and Jesus as the cornerstone. In fact, the whole treatment of Paul's apostolic credentials has shifted to a view typical of later times. The apostles have assumed canonical status, and apostleship is no longer simply one, albeit the most important, of the spiritual gifts. The treatment of marriage in Ephesians and especially the notion of the church as the bride of church strike many readers as unPauline.

But the more fundamental issue involves the shift away from Paul's end-time view of the world. Nearly every reader of Ephesians perceives a striking scarcity of the typical Pauline references to the second coming and the great day of the Lord. Defenders of Pauline authorship explain this shortage as an interesting coincidence. Paul's emphasis in Ephesians (and Colossians) on the present-day cosmic status of Christ may mean only that he is not focusing on the second coming, not that he has abandoned it. And they note that future judgment is mentioned constantly (e.g., Eph. 1:10–12, 14; 5:5, 13; 6:9, 13). However, I think the problem is more difficult than that.

There is a fundamental shift in Paul's worldview as seen in his genuine letters to what we find in Ephesians. My reading of Paul is that he is a theologian from beginning to end who is driven by visions of the coming of the kingdom. Each and every one of his letters is driven by the notion of the turning of the ages and the end-time gift of the Spirit. Paul cannot be Paul without this end-time tension. When we read Ephesians, we do not discover that Pauline tension. We have shifted to another view of the world. This is not Paul.

In fact, the view of the world we do discover is that of Colossians. In Colossians and Ephesians we encounter the concept of the cosmic, enthroned Christ, who rules the universe through his body, the church. As was noted in the section on Colossians, we have shifted from a temporal focus to a hierarchical one. Both letters are concerned with ordering the cosmic powers—in particular, to subject them to Christ. This view of reality will become a classic and essential Christian one, but it is not Paul's.

The simplest conclusion is that Paul did not write Ephesians.

THE PASTORAL EPISTLES

The arguments against Pauline authorship of the Pastoral Epistles follow the same lines as those of Colossians and Ephesians. If anything, all the arguments against Pauline authorship are more persuasive regarding the Pastoral Epistles. The linguistic, grammatical, and stylistic deviations from the Pauline letters are pronounced, and they are quite noticeable in the English of the NRSV. The style and language of the Pastoral Epistles would be unusual for Paul.

However, the most important argument is the theological one, as it was with Colossians and Ephesians. The theology of these letters is distinctly different from Paul's. Whereas Colossians and Ephesians shifted from Paul largely through their focus on cosmic hierarchies, the Pastoral Epistles avoid such cosmic speculation. Instead, the author of the Pastoral Epistles promotes an epiphany Christology wherein Christ's work occurs in two distinct appearances: his original appearance in the flesh and his future return as judge. The shape and function of this Christology is quite different from Paul's, although it intersects and overlaps with many Pauline ideas. And the author's concern for hierarchy is not with the relative rank of the cosmic powers, but with proper order within the church. He wants to establish who can teach whom. Furthermore, Paul's sense of ethics as end-time behavior, Christ living in the believer, has nearly disappeared. Ethics becomes what it will become in mainline early Christianity; it is the task of all believers. It must be taught, learned, and practiced. All people will be judged by Jesus for their virtues and vices. This is classic Christian ethical thinking, but it is different from that of Paul.

Defenders of Pauline authorship, for the most part, do not disagree with this assessment of the theology of these letters. Almost all readers perceive a striking theological shift from the Pauline letters. Instead, they argue that these shifts fall within the reasonable range of Paul and his ministry. It is argued that Pauline authorship explains, of course, the many similarities and echoes of other Pauline letters (especially Ephesians) and that changed circumstances have required a new theological arsenal from Paul. They note (correctly, I might add) that the Pauline letters have considerable variety in their theological language. They note that differences between Galatians and 1 Corinthians are no fewer than the differences between the Pastoral Epistles and the Pauline letters.

With this in mind, these scholars look for a setting within Paul's ministry that explains both the problems indicated in the letters and Paul's reaction. This is not all that easy to do. Paul's imprisonment and his account of his activities do not square with any known moment in his ministry. Thus most defenders of Pauline authorship posit a second Roman imprisonment. They imagine that Paul was released from his first Roman imprisonment, that he traveled to Spain as he intended, that he returned to the east where he had the contacts imagined in these letters, that he was arrested again, and that he is in prison in Rome for the second time at the writing of the letters. This is not all fantasy, because some early church traditions agree with this account of Paul's life.

The theological shifts must be attributed to certain real shifts in Paul's thinking. The dangers of heresy dealt with in the Pastoral Epistles do not seem to warrant the degree of change that occurs here. Thus it must be argued that Paul has calmed down. The constant and wearying dangers of heresy have convinced Paul of the need for hard and fast traditions. The persistent disorder and bickering in his churches have convinced Paul that reliance on the Spirit and its gifts for ordering the church is insufficient. Paul is now admitting the need for real church offices with real authority. Paul in his maturity changes his mind about church order.

As with Colossians and Ephesians, numerous mediating positions have been suggested. The author is not Paul but one of his entourage writing with Paul's authority. Paul has a new secretary to whom he gives unusual freedom of composition. Of course, these theories are hard to square with the personal tone of the letters. These are letters written to persons not churches, and they contain numerous personal moments. It is hard to imagine Paul having one of his entourage do this for him, like a business-man having his secretary write a personal letter to his son. Finally, it has been suggested that the personal notes in the letters are fragments from genuine Pauline letters that a later editor incorporated into non-Pauline letters.

In my opinion, none of that works very well. Pauline authorship produces too many problems and requires a strained reading of the text. The simplest and most satisfactory solution is that the letters were not written by Paul.

For Further Reading

Colossians

Houlden, J. L. *Paul's Letters from Prison (Philippians, Colossians, Philemon, and Ephesians)*. Pelican New Testament Commentaries. Harmondsworth, Middlesex: Penguin, 1970.

Lincoln, Andrew T., and A.J.M. Wedderburn. *The Theology of the Later Pauline Letters*. New Testament Theology. Cambridge: Cambridge University Press, 1993.

Martin, Ralph P. *Colossians and Philemon*. New Century Bible Commentary. London: Oliphants, 1974.

Martin, Ralph P. *Ephesians, Colossians, and Philemon*. Interpretation. Louisville, Ky. : Westminster/John Knox Press, 1992.

Pokorný, P. *Colossians: A Commentary*. Siegfried Schatzmann, trans. Peabody, Mass.: Hendrickson, 1991.

Schweizer, Eduard. *The Letter to the Colossians: A Commentary*. Andrew Chester, trans. London: SPCK, 1982.

Ephesians

Allan, John A. *The Epistle to the Ephesians*. Torch Bible Commentary. London: SCM Press, 1959.

Brown, Raymond, E. *The Churches the Apostles Left Behind*. New York: Paulist Press, 1984.

Houlden, J. L. *Paul's Letters from Prison (Philippians, Colossians, Philemon, and Ephesians)*. Pelican New Testament Commentaries. Harmondsworth, Middlesex: Penguin, 1970.

Lincoln, Andrew T., and A.J.M. Wedderburn. *The Theology of the Later Pauline Letters*. New Testament Theology. Cambridge: Cambridge University Press, 1993.

Lincoln, Andrew T. *Ephesians.* Word Biblical Commentary, Vol. 42. Dallas: Word, 1990.

Martin, Ralph P. *Ephesians, Colossians, and Philemon.* Interpretation. Louisville, Ky.: Westminster/John Knox Press, 1992.

Mitton, Charles Leslie. *Ephesians.* New Century Bible Commentary. London: Oliphants, 1976.

The Pastorial Epistles

Barrett, C. K. *The Pastoral Epistles in the New English Bible.* New Clarendon Bible. Oxford: Clarendon Press, 1963.

Hanson, Anthony T. *The Pastoral Epistles.* New Century Bible Commentary. Grand Rapids, Mich.: William B. Eerdmans Publishing Co., 1982.

Houlden, J. L. *The Pastoral Epistles: I and II Timothy, Titus.* Pelican New Testament Commentaries. Harmondsworth, Middlesex: Penguin, 1976.

Karris, Robert J. *The Pastoral Epistles.* New Testament Message, Vol. 17. Wilmington, Del.: Michael Glazier, 1979.

Kelly, J.N.D. *A Commentary on the Pastoral Epistles: I Timothy, II Timothy, Titus.* Black's New Testament Commentaries. London: Adam & Charles Black, 1963.

Scott, Ernest F. *The Pastoral Epistles.* Moffatt New Testament Commentary. London: Hodder & Stoughton, 1936.

Young, Frances. *The Theology of the Pastoral Letters.* New Testament Theology. Cambridge: Cambridge University Press, 1994.

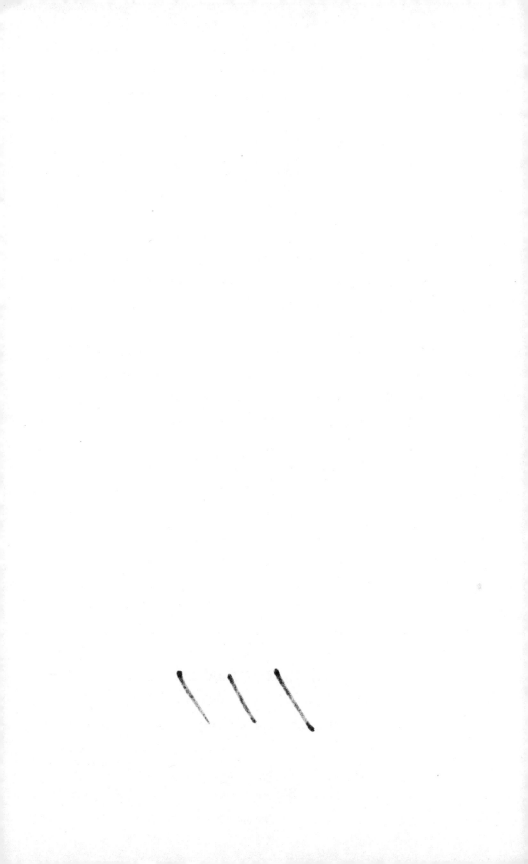

Printed in the United States
1241900005B/73-84